Shameless

Shameless

Sexual Dissidence in American Culture

Arlene Stein

NEW YORK UNIVERSITY PRESS

New York and London

NEW YORK UNIVERSITY PRESS
New York and London
www.nyupress.org

© 2006 by New York University
All rights reserved

Library of Congress Cataloging-in-Publication Data
Stein, Arlene.
Shameless : sexual dissidence in American culture / Arlene Stein.
   p.   cm.
Includes bibliographical references and index.
ISBN-13: 978-0-8147-4027-9 (cloth : alk. paper)
ISBN-10: 0-8147-4027-8 (cloth : alk. paper)
ISBN-13: 978-0-8147-4028-6 (pbk. : alk. paper)
ISBN-10: 0-8147-4028-6 (pbk. : alk. paper)
   1. Lesbianism—United States. 2. Religious right—United States.
3. Modernist-fundamentalist controversy.   I. Title.
HQ75.6.U5S74 2006
306.76'630973—dc22   2005036206

New York University Press books are printed on acid-free paper,
and their binding materials are chosen for strength and durability.

Manufactured in the United States of America

c 10 9 8 7 6 5 4 3 2 1
p 10 9 8 7 6 5 4 3 2 1

For Nancy

Contents

Acknowledgments   ix

Introduction   1

PART I   Up from Shame   17

1   Shapes of Desire   24

2   The Year of the Lustful Lesbian   39

3   Rock against Romance   59

4   Crossover Dreams: Lesbianism and Popular Music   71

5   Sisters and Queers: The Decentering of
     Lesbian Feminism   84

PART II   Shamed Again   103

6   Revenge of the Shamed: The Christian Right's
     Emotional Culture War   111

7   Whose Memories? Whose Victimhood?   129

8   Make Room for Daddy: Anxious Masculinity and
     Emergent Homophobias   151

     Epilogue   174

     Notes   179
     Index   201
     About the Author   213

Acknowledgments

This volume collects an array of my writings, and there are
many people who helped these essays see the light of day—too many
for me to thank here. I'll mention a few whom I have yet to acknowledge: Christine Williams and Dana Britton, for their suggestions on
"Make Room for Daddy"; Mary Bly, Cynthia Eller, and Elizabeth
Leake, my writing gal pals, for reading the introduction and giving me
helpful comments on it; Julie Dorf, Judy Gerson, Sabine Hark, Travis
Kong, Lisa Kramer, Chet Meeks, Jodi O'Brien, Ruth O'Brien, Jenni
Olson, Wendy Oberlander, Ken Plummer, and Judy Stacey for helpful
conversations and good cheer. The Social Science Research Council
made it possible for me to spend two years researching and writing
about conservative sexual politics; Gail and Birdie Hoezle were indis-
pensable guides on that journey. I am also grateful to my students at
Rutgers University, and to my colleagues in the Department of Sociology, and in Women's and Gender Studies. King-to Yeung provided
expert computer assistance. The artists who appear in these pages gen-
erously gave me permission to reprint their work, and a number of
friends shared photos and other materials. Salwa Jabado helped wrestle
the manuscript into a book. Ilene Kalish at NYU Press supported this
project from the start and provided invaluable editorial suggestions; her
reputation as editor extraordinaire is well deserved. And I thank members of my family: David Evan, Debbie Nadolney, Barbara Solomon,
Nancy Solomon, and Lewis Solomon-Stein, for being there for me.

Introduction

In a recurring dream, I arrive at a cavernous university auditorium barely in time to teach a class, having overslept. I enter the room out of breath, apologetic, and as I begin my lecture, I realize that in my haste I've forgotten to get dressed, and I'm standing in front of a crowd completely naked, overcome with shame and embarrassment. The dream ends, and I awaken flushed with high anxiety and deep relief. Thank goodness, I think to myself, it's only a dream. Of course, this is a fairly common dream, and one need not be a psychoanalyst to figure out its meaning. Imagine the ultimate shame of being unclothed, vulnerable, my power diminished by exposure. I don't remember very many of my dreams, but I seem to remember this one each time I have it, a testament of its power to unsettle me and reveal my inner demons.

Shame is a powerful emotion. It leads individuals to feel vulnerable, victimized, rejected. Since it tends to hide, shame forces its sufferers to hide as well, for fear that they might be found out. It's no surprise that my anxiety dream reveals my naked body for all to see: shame often arises in relation to bodies and desires. Having the wrong desires, having desires at all, or failing to express one's desires in the proper ways can at times seem dangerous, and sometimes even life threatening. Shame can gnaw at the soul, making us smaller, turning us inward, diminishing our potential for love, creativity, and connection, even limiting our very humanity.

American culture is a curious mix of the shameless and the shamers, a seemingly endless parade of Pamela Andersons and Jerry Falwells strutting their stuff and wagging their fingers. Sometimes the shameless and the shamers are the same people. We know full well from the myriad sex scandals involving religious leaders, and from reports that moral conservatives are some of the most avid watchers of less than morally virtuous television shows, that public and private lives are often at odds —what one says is often very different from what one does. "Many

Who Voted for Values Still Like Their Television Sin," reported the *New York Times* days after the 2004 presidential election, suggesting that the electorate's supposed closer embrace of traditional cultural values is at odds with their television choices, which veer toward "murder, mayhem, and sexual transgression."[1] Collectively, Americans are an unwieldy, contradictory bunch, constantly on the move, our persuasions and commitments shaped as much by the exigencies of the marketplace as the content of our convictions. In this din, it is often hard to get a handle on what exactly we believe in, if anything at all.

This may be particularly true of sexuality. In the United States, as feminist scholars Janet Jacobsen and Ann Pellegrini note, "sex is the site of often contradictory moral worries." It is simultaneously seen as a private concern outside of the realm of politics and public life, while it is also "invested with amazing and paradoxical powers." Sexual behavior is often seen as the basis of family life, and indeed of our sense of nationhood, and at the same time thought to be "so powerful that it threatens to dissolve family ties and thereby unravel the nation itself."[2] It is no wonder, then, that a group of enterprising political activists has been able to convince many Americans that sexual liberalization has produced a moral crisis of threatening proportions.

Three decades ago, feminist and gay/lesbian activists placed sexual issues on the public agenda, making compelling arguments for the political nature of personal relationships, and the importance of democratizing intimate life. They raised questions about the compulsory nature of heterosexuality as an institution, and criticized the "double standard" of sexuality that prioritized male needs and saw women as subservient to them. They urged us to cast off shame, proclaiming that sexuality is a positive form of self-expression rather than something to be shunned, hidden from sight. They helped to liberalize sexual attitudes and loosen prohibitions on sexually explicit material, premarital sexuality, and homosexuality. Thanks in part to their efforts, today women and men are no longer considered wholly different beings when it comes to the expression of intimate desires, and the chasm separating the heterosexual and homosexual worlds has narrowed. For better and for worse, commercial imperatives stepped in to complete the trend, making sexual expression a much more visible part of our popular culture—in television, movies, magazines, and the like—than just a few decades ago.

But a funny thing happened on the way to the sexual revolution: just as we were coming to enjoy the fruits of liberalization, conservatives were organizing within congregations and local communities to over-turn the expanding sense of possibility many of us took for granted. They mobilized to bring back sexual shame, arguing for abstinence-only sex education, limitations on abortion, and prohibitions of gay/lesbian civil rights. They warned that Americans had abandoned questions of virtue, were no longer concerned with raising children who knew how to be good, and were creating a society in which questions of "charac-ter" were neglected in favor of individual self-fulfillment and short-term pleasures. They lamented that our capacity for shame seems diminished. "SHAME," blares the cover of *Newsweek*. The subtitle tells the story: "Intolerance has gotten a bad rap in recent years, but there should be a way to condemn behavior that's socially destructive."[3] Some propo-nents of shame urge us to place restrictions on personal life and inti-mate expression, suggesting that homosexuality, consensual sexual ac-tivity among teenagers, and nonprocreative sexual expression in general are socially destructive.

This volume considers how progressive social movements have tried to sever the link between sexuality and shame, and how conservatives, in contrast, use shame as a weapon against liberalization. These essays are informed by my experiences living in San Francisco in the 1980s and Oregon in the 1990s, and by debates about American sexual poli-tics circulating in activist and intellectual circles across the nation. In San Francisco, which has long incubated a lively mix of radical sexual ideas, I witnessed the rise of HIV, the emergence of queer politics, and debates about feminist sexuality and self-expression. When I moved from San Francisco to Oregon in the early 1990s, I stepped foot onto Ground Zero in the culture wars, a state that was reeling from a series of divisive electoral campaigns about whether or not to prohibit gays and lesbians from receiving legal protections against housing and job discrimination, which set the stage for a national battle for same-sex marriage. Those who thought the liberalization of sexual attitudes was here to stay, myself included, have been taken aback by the extraordi-nary ascendance of conservative sexual moralizing in this most sexual-ized of societies.

The essays collected in the first half of this volume, "Up from Shame," address the ways gay Americans, particularly lesbians, forged new identities, subcultures, and ways of being on the heels of the sexual and feminist revolutions, reinventing themselves and challenging others to accommodate their desires and to recognize their humanity. These essays document a time of expanding possibilities and extraordinary cultural and intellectual ferment, when American culture was openly reckoning with previously forbidden secrets. They also speak to some of the internal disputes that emerged within gay and lesbian communities around the problems entailed in building a collective identity on something as elusive as desire. All told, the first part of this book captures a moment in which many people were empowered to make changes that allowed many of them to live happier and more fulfilled lives.

The second half of the book, "Shamed Again," written during the past few years, shows how conservatives have used shame to try to rein in sexual expression and dissent. Having learned from feminists that politics is and should be about more than economics, the right has used this insight to great success, mobilizing individuals to protect "family values" and defend "morality," embracing a highly selective and exceedingly narrow notion of what family values are, and what morality means. Activist parents claim that they should be able to control what their kids do and don't know, that girls should be protected from early sexual activity, and that same-sex relationships deserve condemnation —not recognition. They have transformed such beliefs into policy in school districts throughout the nation, in the form of abstinence-only sex education programs, restrictions on their teenagers' rights to privacy, and prohibitions against gay/lesbian civil rights.

The idea that sexual restriction (of abortion, premarital sex, sexually explicit materials, to name but a few examples) is repressive and that the lifting of such restrictions is a generally progressive development is not terribly fashionable today in some circles. It is certainly not in favor on the right, among those who view the sexual revolution, the rise of feminism, and the "permissive society" as the root cause of many of our troubles today. But even many feminists question whether lifting restraints upon sexual expression has really benefited women and girls. In the 1980s, some of these women began to speak out against the sexualization of our culture, especially the rise of pornography and other explicit representations of sexuality, and the general relaxation of sexual rules. They asserted that we had discarded the double standard—"good girls don't"—and replaced it with a pleasure imperative, "good girls do." Such divisions came to a head in what came to be known as the feminist "sex debates," a series of pitched battles around pornography, prostitution, and sadomasochism. Though the battles have since died down, many women—and men—remain somewhat ambivalent about the legacy of the sexual revolution.

One need not be a dyed-in-the-wool conservative to balk at the hypersexualization and commercialization of our culture and lament that many young women have a difficult time saying no. When Karin Martin, a sociologist, interviewed working-class and middle-class girls and boys in the early 1990s, she found that sex is often disappointing for girls, who remain conflicted about their femininity and their own sexuality. Sex and romance are the organizing principles in many teenage girls' lives, and often girls actually have sex in order to find love. Boys, on the other hand, report more positive experiences: sex makes them feel grown up, masculine, bonded with other men, and sexually powerful. For teenage girls, "first and early experiences of sex usually result in feeling confused, unsure of themselves and their bodies."[4] No wonder some young women have looked to the abstinence movement and "virginity pledges" for relief.

While the old sexual double standard may have exaggerated the differences between men and women, say some, at least it allowed women to refuse the sexual advances of men. Today, that may be less possible: teen sexuality, for example, is increasingly visible in the pages of girls' fashion magazines, and on billboards advertising the latest girl pop star decked out in décolletage and come-hither looks. As one of my savvy undergraduates lamented recently: "When driving through Manhattan last week, it was virtually impossible to ignore the many titillating billboards showcased all over the city. Erotically dressed mannequins are displayed in the windows of all stores. Sex is everywhere." Turn on the television, and one can see endless discussions of people's intimate lives: tabloid talk shows feature discussions of sexual topics, and the private lives of public figures dominate the news, blurring the distinction between what is public and what is private.[5]

While recognizing some of the negative consequences of the sexualization of our culture, I continue to believe that sexual restriction is more dangerous than its opposite: liberalization. For I remember the days, not so long ago, when uttering the word "lesbian" was absolutely taboo, even among those of us who called ourselves feminists, and when there were only two types of girls: sluts and virgins. Comprehensive sex education, and more intelligent, open public discussions of sexuality in general, has helped to counter the commonplace assumptions that sex is magical, romantic, and that girls can only value themselves if boys value them—that their value resides chiefly in their bodies. Greater access to sexual knowledge has given many people the capacity to make reasonable decisions based on what they want rather than what they think they should want, and has meant that many young people today who find themselves attracted to members of the same sex are less likely to imagine that they are alone in their affections, and to experience the shame of that imagining. This is no small accomplishment.

A Brief History of (Sexual) Shame

Shame is a judgment against the self, a feeling that one is bad, defective, incompetent, inadequate, weak, unlovable, or disgusting. Shame is different from guilt. Guilt, like shame, is rooted in negative judgment, but it is limited to a particular act. Guilt arises from a thought or an act that goes against a moral code of values. A guilty person can express remorse, make amends, ask forgiveness, or receive punishment. Shame, in contrast, arises from the failure to live up to an internal ideal image of oneself, the self one is "supposed to be." It is more elemental, reflecting upon one's total being. Shame arises from seeing one's self negatively from the imagined point of view of others. It leads one to feel awkward, self-conscious, apologetic, embarrassed, and even ridiculous, degraded, and humiliated in the eyes of others. These threats can be major offenses, or trivial ones: they may actually have occurred, or they can be imagined or anticipated, as in my dream of forgetting to dress in the morning. And shame, as my dream also suggests, is often linked to fears of bodily exposure, literal or actual. During wartime, as we have been reminded of all too clearly of late, it is not uncommon for conquering armies to humiliate their captives by stripping them and exposing their naked bodies for all to see.

We all carry around with us a certain degree of shame, some of which we certainly need in order to live with and alongside others. Other than a few libertines, few of us would be happy living in a society where others parade around naked on a daily basis. Clearly there are healthy forms of shame, which enhance a person's capacity to be modest, to exercise discretion, and to be respectful of social standards, of the boundaries of others, of one's need for privacy, and even one's connection to others.[6] But when people actively promulgate shame in order to control others, especially when the consequence is that some are driven to think of themselves as permanently and totally flawed human beings, we have to question their motives, and we have to guard against shame's corrosive effects.

Most people will agree that the association of sexuality and shame is religious in origin. From its earliest beginnings, Christianity spoke of the separation of body and soul and suggested that if spiritual perfection were to be attained, the tendencies of the flesh must be eradicated. The body was, in early Christians' interpretation of the fall from grace, "antagonistic to spiritual development," writes sociologist Gail Hawkes in a history of sexuality in the West. "Conceived in its mildest form as a weakness and in its most extreme as active evil," bodily desires were considered unruly, negative, and disruptive.[7] Early Christians therefore took it upon themselves to order desire, drawing distinctions between "good" sex (marital, procreative) and "bad" sex (pleasure lacking a higher purpose beyond individual gratification). In other words, religion transformed sex and desire into a moral problem.

As this religiously based morality met the modern world, individuals were expected to internalize new rules and expectations and control their bodies, thoughts, and behavior, lest they drift into shamefulness. In the early modern period in Europe, new social rules—what sociologist Norbert Elias describes as the modern "civilizing process"—cropped up to shape behavior in an increasingly complex world, driving shame underground. Examining a nineteenth-century advice book, Elias describes how mothers are told to answer the sexual questions their daughters ask by telling them of the wonders of the spirit, and how the "Lord gives the mother her child." They are cautioned to "occupy [their] daughters' thoughts so incessantly with the good and beautiful that they are left no time" to ponder sexual questions. If a mother does her job well, her "truly well brought-up girl . . . will from then on feel shame at hearing things of this kind spoken of." Sexuality was enclosed within the nuclear family, "submerged in shame and embarrassment," lest the "spiritual purity" of children, especially girls, be compromised. What this suggests, according to social psychologist Thomas Scheff, is that modern individuals are not only supposed to be ashamed of our unclean thoughts, we are supposed to be ashamed of being ashamed.[8]

While Victorians set into motion a series of modern codes and sensibilities about proper behavior, contrary to the stereotype, they did not ban talk of sex. In fact, they talked endlessly about it and its corrupting influence, and they designed elaborate medical and scientific procedures for rooting out "improper" behaviors and desires. Some eight thousand prostitutes plied their trade in London in the mid-nineteenth century, and in Leeds, a medium-sized industrial town in the north, there were two churches, thirty-nine chapels, four hundred fifty-one taverns, and ninety-eight brothels. Yet the newly rich, insecure middle class insisted upon an outward respectability and conformity: hence, the desire of Oscar Wilde's Jack Worthing to keep up appearances for the sake of his ward, "little" Cecily, whom he kept hidden in his country house like some princess in a fairy tale. Victorians elevated women as domestic goddesses who embodied purity and faithfulness, who civilized unwieldy male passions. They opposed the debauchery of traditional aristocratic behavior, the sordid and squalid ways of the poor, and the homosexuals, prostitutes, and unapologetically sexual women who failed to keep their desires hidden. Paradoxically, they set into motion a virtual explosion of talk about sex.

Middle-class Victorians saw themselves as the very essence of civilization, and believed their rational and restrained culture had a good deal to teach the rest of the world. On both sides of the Atlantic, moral reformers inspired by these views unleashed a series of campaigns targeting sexually active adolescent girls, producers and consumers of prurient novels, and "fallen women" and lascivious men whom they considered to be threats to middle-class respectability and propriety. Anyone, they suggested, could practice self-restraint and personal responsibility; anyone could develop good character by keeping their impulses and desires under wraps. The rest deserved social disapproval.

If Victorians perfected shaming as a strategy to keep people in line, they also gave birth to some of shame's greatest critics. Writing at the turn of the twentieth century, Sigmund Freud tied shame to sexual repression, which he believed made modern civilization possible but also generated a variety of individual pathologies, along with "modern nervousness" and despair. While mature adults, he believed, must repress their shameful desires, we all carry residues of shameful feelings around with us nonetheless, feelings we try desperately to hide from view. Though Freud believed that sexual repression was unavoidable, others took a more radical approach, and in Germany there were stirrings of a nascent movement against sexual shame led by Magnus Hirschfeld, an early sexologist and activist for homosexual rights. Hirschfeld distressed conservatives because he challenged the Christian view that premarital sex was by definition a sin. Instead, he promoted an ethics of consent, emphasizing that the key moral issue was that there be no coercion in sexual encounters. So threatening was Hirschfeld's project that the Nazis burned his books and banished him, driving sexual dissidence underground. A movement founded on uniformity, discipline, and unadulterated power could not suffer sexual and other forms of diversity, nor those who would claim pleasure for its own sake.

During the post–World War II era in the United States and Europe, domesticity reigned supreme and sexual dissidence lived underground. Nineteen-fifties America was an era of "father knows best" ideals, when political dissidents were hunted down and homosexuals hounded from their jobs. Lively queer subcultures thrived in a few cities, but most people who harbored "unnatural" desires—or any unconventional desires for that matter—did so in private, living double lives. But it was at this time that Alfred Kinsey, who grew up with exceedingly Victorian parents, blew the lid off shame, revealing in his voluminous surveys that the private sexual practices of ordinary Americans frequently diverged from the norm of marital, reproductive heterosexuality. Kinsey collected more than 20,000 sexual histories and found that masturbation was nearly universally practiced, that two in five males had had homosexual experiences, and that women actually experienced sexual desires. For the vast majority of Americans, such subjects were not the stuff of polite conversations. In uncovering the enormous gap between public norms and private practices, Kinsey helped to fuel the widespread conviction that American culture, at least when it comes to sexuality, is shot through with hypocrisy. The dissemination of Kinsey's reports helped to fuel a wave of dissidence among those who refused to live double lives, keeping their desires under wraps.

If shame typically leads to secrets and hiding, how appropriate then that a series of social movements, beginning in the late 1960s, would focus on speaking publicly about unspeakable things, explicitly in order to loosen shame's grip. The feminist movement, the New Left, and the gay/lesbian movement each proclaimed the importance of liberating the individual from the shackles of repression. If Victorianism meant knowing one's place and respecting the norms and hierarchies of one's station, sixties radicals were the preeminent anti-Victorians, dedicated to freeing the individual from social constraints and contesting notions of respectability. "If it feels good, do it," was the battle cry of the sexual revolution, which saw the loosening of moral strictures and the valuing of pleasure itself as the key to personal fulfillment and social progress.

On its heels, the gay and lesbian liberation movements urged those who had ever harbored same-sex desires to come out of the closet and declare their sexual identifications proudly and publicly, to counter the shame and secrecy associated with homosexuality in our culture. Feminists similarly began to discuss painful relationships, sexual abuse, and experiences of powerlessness that were before kept private, speaking for the first time about taboo subjects and mobilizing a public expression of feelings against a culture of shame. But in an important way these shifts were already underway as economic necessity drew more and more women into the paid labor force, and a media revolution eroded rural autonomy and meant that cultural isolation was a thing of the past. Greater numbers of middle-class women entered marriage with sexual information and expertise, and with increased economic power, the gulf between husbands and wives narrowed. The contraceptive revolution diminished the anxiety about unwanted pregnancies that gave sex such different implications for males and females. The disengagement of sexuality from polarized gender definitions weakened certain barriers to sexual expression in marriage and diminished the culture of shame in ways that were particularly significant for women, girls, and sexual minorities. As these profound inequalities of power seemed to fade away, intimate life was profoundly democratized, and sexual arrangements came increasingly to be seen as subject to choice and change.

In the late 1980s, while I was writing my first book, a study of women's sexual identities, I encountered a number of women who had married in the years before feminism and gay liberation. They had been so captivated by feminist ideas, and the possibility of making a life outside of heterosexual marriage, that they promptly left their husbands and declared themselves to be lesbians. What this suggests is that knowledge can be unsettling, for it necessarily challenges established ways of doing things. As sociologist Anthony Giddens has suggested, at this moment in time our existence as individuals is largely "contingent," a project to be improvised rather than a blueprint to follow. In other words, at the turn of the millennium, many, if not most aspects of our lives are up for grabs, in large part because we have more access to knowledge about how other people live than ever before.

The self, Giddens writes, has become a "reflexive project": we talk about "finding ourselves," "healing ourselves," "constructing identities" and so forth. Never before have our selves been so subject to choice and change. The prevalence of divorce, for example, has irrevocably changed the meaning of marriage. It is nearly impossible to enter into a marriage today and not be aware of the tenuousness of that institution. Thanks to a new self-scrutiny and self-understanding and the increasing capacity of women to leave bad marriages, the old "till death do us part" script may be in its waning days. Increasingly, relationships are entered into for their own sake, for what can be derived by each person from a sustained association with another, and continued only if they deliver sufficient satisfactions for each individual. Same-sex intimacies, existing as they do outside of recognized legal and symbolic structures, one might argue, have always taken this form. Increasingly, it seems, heterosexual relationships do as well, as marriages have come to offer fewer of the guarantees—or shackles—of the past.

The Tyranny of Choice

While many of us welcome this reflexivity and the freedoms it offers, the very possibility of individual choice troubles others. They look around at the instability of many of the traditions and structures they once held dear and find this fluidity deeply threatening, *unsettling*. The democratization of personal life and the freedoms it makes possible are not a good thing, they warn. They lament that the old "marital bargain" that tied men to the family and obligated women to persevere "through thick and thin" has been severed, and that couples have few incentives to make their marriages work. Adding insult to injury, they say, gays and lesbians are seeking access to an institution that they have been instrumental in helping to destroy. For them, homosexuality is of a piece with a host of other offenses: easy access to abortion and contraception (and the separation between sex and procreation implied by that), the escalation of sexually explicit content on TV, the ready accessibility of pornography and "sexual perversity" on the Internet, and the "defining down" of deviance of every kind—all of which constitute the "social pathology of our time," according to conservative critic Gertrude Himmelfarb, writing in 1998 in the not-ironically named journal, *The Public Interest*. Things were much better before tradition, self-restraint, and respectability gave way to "anything goes," they say.

Such arguments against the "permissive society" have long been conservatives' stock in trade. Recently, I heard an advocate for abstinence make this case before a group of college students. She began her talk by speaking of the 1960s: "It was a dangerous time," she said, "a time of excess, or if-it-feels-good-do-it attitudes, when sex became meaningless and disease ran rampant." For social conservatives, that decade which ushered in the sexual revolution and gave us the sexualized society was a watershed era, the moment when American society was challenged at its core, when restraint and tradition gave way to reckless abandon. In the lost and lamented *before,* marriages tamed male desire, and gays stayed in the closet; in the disastrous and terrifying *now,* men leave their wives for other men, women leave their husbands for other women, and marriage has little meaning. *Before* we all had a sense of place and a respect for the greater good of everyone; *now* we have a corrosive society, a society out of bounds, where confusion and vice reign supreme.

Conservatives argue for the "remoralization" of society and the reassertion of traditional values against what they see as a rising tide of cultural anarchy. If 1960s America is their modern counterpart to the biblical Sodom and Gomorrah, Victorian England is their Eden, when upstanding men and women knew their place—and the rest were shamed into recognizing theirs or reformed accordingly. Reasserting traditional norms, they rail against sexual excesses on college campuses, low rates of marriage among the poor, and the decline of modesty. Sexual repression is the answer, they claim. They protest when an elementary school teacher reveals that she's a lesbian, charging that she's flaunting her sexual desires in front of impressionable kids, and they support the "don't ask, don't tell" policy insuring that military personnel keep their private lives private. They believe that images of gay families on television, however benign, are an affront to the sensibilities of most American families. They want sex education to vilify all premarital sexual activity. They are, in short, trying their damnedest to bring shame back as a restraint on sexual expression, believing that shame penalties would promote a revival of a common moral sensibility.

Leonard Kass, writing in a conservative journal in 1997, calls for a new culture of "courtship" that would educate young people to sublimate sexual desire rather than express it. The race for pleasure and immediate gratification has, he says, overtaken "the virtues of character, self-restraint, and respect for cultural hierarchies." True sex education," he argues, "is an education of the heart. . . . The energy of sexual desire, if properly sublimated, is transformable into genuine and lofty longings —not only for love and romance but for all the other higher human yearnings."[9] And Wendy Shalit's 2000 book, *Return to Modesty*, calls upon us to bring back codes of female virtue and male honor. Young women have been duped into believing that they must have sex at an early age in order to be desirable, she argues, but these "hook-ups" are generally devoid of emotion or true feeling. Who is to blame? she asks rhetorically. Sex education professionals, "cultural exhibitionists" in the mass media that glamorize promiscuity, the general relaxation of cultural standards, and permissive parents, she answers. Gone are the traditional forms of modesty and public rules that told "nice" boys to respect girls who said "no." We must, she urges, quickly bring these standards back.[10]

Conservatives, I would argue, offer exceedingly simple solutions to complex issues, solutions that see the world in black and white rather than true-to-life grays. They have little interest in helping girls and women to know their bodies and their desires or in giving them tools to help them negotiate intimate relations. And, frequently, their response to the young man or woman struggling with same-sex desires, who is in search of a community of like-minded others, is to try to "convert" them to heterosexuality. They fail to see that while individuals may use knowledge at times to make unwise choices, at least they have the capacity to make choices rather than not make them at all.

How a society imagines its sexual order, defines what is proper behavior and what is not, and envisions manhood and womanhood says a lot about how it treats its citizens in many other aspects of their lives. Today, those European nations with the most generous welfare states are also the ones that provide the fullest rights to sexual minorities and offer the most comprehensive forms of sex education. In the United States attacks on the social welfare of the poor have accompanied attacks on gay and lesbian civil rights and the promotion of abstinence-only sex education. Whether a society tolerates sexual diversity, values those who do not conform to the dominant sexual/gender order, and sees sexual knowledge as positive is a pretty good indicator of whether it protects its weakest citizens.

Conservatives figured this out quickly: they see the status of homosexuality as an indicator of the "moral temperature" of the larger culture, and they know that attitudes toward homosexuality, and nonmarital sexuality in general, have gotten steadily more liberal over the past few decades. Most Americans believe that some form of legal status should be granted to gay and lesbian relationships, and that men and women should be treated equally on the job and in the family. And just as the gulf between men and women has narrowed over my lifetime, so are the heterosexual and homosexual worlds far less divided than they were even a decade ago. This alarms the enemies of sexual dissidence, who see the normalization of homosexuality as part of a larger problem: our growing acceptance of nonmarital, nonprocreative sexualities, the sexualization of our culture, the decline of standards and moral certainties, and the supposed death of "the family."

Once the "legal underpinnings for marriage are destroyed," Dr. James Dobson warns, anything goes.[11] Historically, this spokesman for the religious right suggests, "the definition of marriage has rested on a bedrock of tradition, legal precedent, theology and the overwhelming support of the people." After the introduction of same-sex marriage, he warns, conjuring up what anthropologist Gayle Rubin once called "the domino system of sexual peril," the definition of family will be up for grabs, giving way to "group marriage, or marriage between relatives, or marriage between adults and children" and even between "a man and his donkey." The fact that a conservative religious spokesman would make such claims is not all that surprising; for the last three decades the religious right has made all manner of claims about the immorality, and even bestiality, of homosexuality. What is new and startling is the fact that such a spokesman has the ear of the White House and is considered a reputable representative of a constituency with vast political influence. Thanks to the rhetoric of Dobson and his ilk, some have come to believe that sanctioning same-sex relationships may weaken their own marriages.

But the truth is that for at least two hundred years heterosexuals have been busily transforming marriage into a voluntary relationship based on love, rather than an arrangement based on economic necessity or cultural compulsion. As historian Stephanie Coontz puts it, "Gays and lesbians didn't spearhead that revolution: heterosexuals did."[12] During the past few decades, voluntaristic, negotiable intimate arrangements have become the norm: a woman can choose to be the main breadwinner, a husband can stay at home with the children, and gay and lesbians couples can build relationships and families. While most Americans welcome these changes and the egalitarianism they imply, others are more ambivalent, lamenting the tyranny of choice and the loss of certainty.

In times of uncertainty, disputes over sexual behavior often become the vehicles for displacing social anxieties. This certainly seems to be the case today, when economic globalization is radically reshaping how we work and how we live, and virulent strains of politicized religious fundamentalism at home and abroad are challenging our sense of security. "It is precisely at times such as these, when we live with the possibility of unthinkable destruction, that people are likely to become dangerously crazy about sexuality," Gayle Rubin wrote presciently in 1984.[13] She was writing at the dawn of the AIDS epidemic, when the conservative backlash against sexual liberalization was beginning to achieve public prominence. "Just say no" was touted as a means of dealing with AIDS and other sexually transmitted diseases, and a burgeoning movement for abstinence-only sex education was making its way into American school systems.

To some, Rubin cautioned, "sexuality may seem to be an unimportant topic, a frivolous diversion from the more critical problems of war, disease, racism, famine, or nuclear annihilation"—and, we must add today, terrorism. But "in times of uncertainty," she noted, "disputes over sexual behavior often become the vehicles for displacing social anxieties." Today, as political leaders mine the growing sense of unease many of us feel, fanning our fears and offering up false promises in place of the difficult decisions that lay ahead, these words should give us pause.

PART I

Up from Shame

In the 1970s, young activists introduced a new vocabulary and set of concepts for understanding sexuality: the boundaries separating heterosexuality and homosexuality were, they suggested, permeable; homosexuality was a matter of identification, and not simply desire. One could be a lesbian by being "woman identified," developing "lesbian consciousness," making women central to one's life, and not giving oneself over to men. Gay people were not failed men and women, they were rebels against an oppressive system; if left to their own desires, most individuals would reject the constraints of both homosexual and heterosexual labels. "Coming out" was the central strategy of a movement dedicated to reducing homosexual shame. If shameful feelings lead us to hide from sight, activists urged anyone who had ever felt homosexual desires to declare them proudly. Suddenly, many people were faced with a choice about whether to be with women or men, and even those who had never entertained the idea of homosexuality were forced to scrutinize the nature of their attractions. Women's sexuality, in particular, seemed fluid, up for grabs; the heterosexual imperative was profoundly shaken.

In the 1980s, I was living in San Francisco and meeting people who had come out during the previous decade, inspired by these visions of self-transformation. I became very interested in speaking with women who had been shaped by feminist ideas at the moment in which they were fresh and heretofore unspoken, and in documenting some of the different ways these individuals made use of these ideas as they came to define themselves as lesbians. Building a new world was a messy process, and constructing a collective identity around something as fluid and indeterminate as desire was tricky at best. What is a lesbian? Are lesbians united by a common set of desires, their same-sex practices, or by a sense of themselves as outcasts?

"Shapes of Desire" tells the story of three different women who became lesbians in this heady, shape-shifting time. While they shared a belief in the importance of coming out, of declaring their desires openly and proudly, the meaning of such identifications varied, and some women experienced their homosexuality as highly driven; others much more as a conscious choice. In this early article, I began to try to tease out what I saw as a tension between the public rhetoric of lesbian activists, who tried to build a unified, normative definition of lesbianism, and the private experiences of individuals, who identified with this culture to varying degrees. This article emerged out of research for my first book, *Sex and Sensibility*, and was very much rooted in my queer world of San Francisco, where everyone, it seemed, was searching for an identity, trying on new identities, and then casting them off.

But even in freewheeling San Francisco, discussions of what lesbians actually did between the sheets were few and far between, and the fact that there might be myriad differences, sexual or otherwise, among us was a difficult subject to raise in public. We were expected to pay allegiance to some mythical lesbian "community," and be happy, shame-free representatives of gay life. But residues of shame persisted. Shame wasn't built in a day, and it couldn't be torn down in one day either. Young lesbian activists may have built safe spaces to nurture a different way of being, but most of us maintained ties with our families of origin, and we continued to reside in a culture where compulsory heterosexuality and antisex attitudes reigned supreme.

After the initial euphoria of "coming out" faded, some women began to ask whether some lesbians were more "authentic" than others. They came to imagine that the "true" lesbian experienced strongly felt homosexual desires and a strong sense of being different or deviant, and suggested that many women who came out "through feminism" were actually straight women who had become lesbians once the movement made it sexy. Oddly, some began to wonder whether it had gotten "too easy" to be gay. Lesbians, it turned out, were capable of wielding shame as a weapon, too, and many of those who were unapologetic about "politically incorrect" desires and practices—for men, for pornographic literature, for anonymous sex—were summarily chastised and sometimes even excluded from the club. (Let it be known that the now overused term "politically correct" began with us, as a somewhat ironic jab at those who would police the boundaries of the Lesbian Nation.)

In the quest for clearer boundaries to separate "us" from "them," highly rigid definitions of lesbianism that excluded all but the most dedicated were promoted, and even biological explanations for homosexuality, which had been the target of feminists' and gay liberationists' ire, gained new currency in the 1980s. Fading was the dream of liberating society by releasing "the homosexual in everyone." Within a few short years, the liberationist impulse, to explode the categories, was replaced by the desire to consolidate our communities and prevent disaffection from the ranks. Homosexuality was no longer a potential that existed in everyone: an "ethnic model" of homosexuality, resembling what feminist sociologist Mary McIntosh once called the "homosexual role," but freed from some of the taint of stigma, was born.

Interpretations of why the early liberationist impulse gave way to a more conservative understanding of sexuality vary. Some suggest it is the inevitable evolution of identity-based politics. As the argument goes, homosexuals could only define themselves collectively by becoming not-heterosexuals, hardening the boundaries around the group, and reinforcing the homo-hetero divide. Life cycle changes certainly played a role as well: as the baby boomers aged, the youthful enthusiasm of a movement in which all things seemed possible was beginning to fade. Certainly the original vision of gay liberation, which imagined that once we stripped off the labels, deep down we'd all be pretty much the same under the skin, was itself flawed; individual differences persisted, shaping sexual desire and intimate possibilities. And the pervasive fear of sexuality in our culture, sanctified by religious belief, did not easily fade away.

Into this highly charged atmosphere emerged what has come to be known as the "sex debates," a series of fiery public discussions, erupting first in New York, and then rippling across the country. At a normally genteel gathering of feminists at Barnard College in 1982, huge battles around the subject of sexuality divided feminists. On one side were those who opposed pornography and prostitution, and who saw sexuality as the locus of women's oppression; on the other side were those who saw sexual exploration in all its forms as central to women's liberation. Lesbians, who could be found on both sides of the divide, grappled with a series of related questions: Could one be a lesbian and still relate to men on occasion? Are sex workers members of our community, or traitors to the cause? And what shall we make of women who enjoy "unfeminist" forms of sexuality, such as sadomasochism? Such controversies challenged normative understandings of lesbianism as a "hand holding society," as sexpert Susie Bright put it, and gave rise to an unprecedented public discussion of lesbian sexuality.

In the "Year of the Lustful Lesbian," I profile Bright and JoAnn Loulan, two early crusaders for lesbian sexual literacy, who became synonymous with the unabashed discussion of lesbian sexuality that began in the 1980s. Susie Bright was the bad girl, who courted controversy and was unapologetic about ruffling feathers wherever she could find them; Loulan, the milder mannered of the two, used the language of therapeutic psychology to clear away sexual reticence. Their efforts to kick away lesbian sexual shame were pretty gutsy in a culture that was highly ambivalent about women's sexual autonomy at best. The sexperts also expressed a new willingness to embrace commercial representations of women, such as pornography, and see them as part of the heritage of lesbianism rather than as evidence of its exploitation. They helped to awaken a new interest in lesbian "representation," and called upon us to see lesbianism as a sexual identity first and foremost, rather than a form of female bonding and resistance.

Coming out was the centerpiece of the gay/lesbian movement. Closely linked to it were efforts to write lesbian and gay history, create gay and lesbian art, and circulate cultural evidence of gay lives, powered by an extraordinary degree of commitment on the part of mainly volunteer activists. Rather than make inroads into a commercial culture they considered to be tainted by the profit motive, many activists set out to create their own cultural forms. Music was an important site for critical analysis and cultural innovation. Early second-wave feminists saw the music industry as a boys' club, and rock 'n' roll as male-defined music that puts women down and maintains heterosexism. And yet women's alienation from this music has existed alongside their sheer enjoyment of it.

The dominant cultural model for girls in my youth was the romance script: we were supposed to fawn over teen idols and read love comics, and idealize surrendering to a dominant male pursuer. Rock 'n' roll, in contrast, emphasizes themes of separation—breaking loose—and however male-oriented the music was, for many girls of my generation, it was thrilling and subversive. In "Rock against Romance" I recall that rock 'n' roll gave me and other girls a space to imagine alternative conceptions of femininity. Even as a young fan I understood this unconsciously. Music became an alternative way of knowing and a route to self-knowledge and empowerment, a way of reading between the lines and listening to a different set of lyrics.

As a music fan, I've often been intrigued by the ways that subcultures, and especially minority and working class cultures, become grist for the commercial hit machines. Cool hunters prowl the downtown clubs in search of cutting-edge talent, and kids are all too eager to sign on the dotted line to cash in. The music industry is, after all, a route to upward mobility as well as a source of entertainment and cash, and subcultures and commercial culture exist in symbiotic relationship to one another. Subcultures, and the social movements with which they are often aligned, seek cultural power, and recognition; the culture industries seek innovative products and new markets. If there is money to be made, voracious corporations will certainly figure out how to make it, feeding upon subcultures, and spitting them out when they're through.

By the 1990s, some out lesbian performers were able to straddle both worlds, maintaining their subcultural popularity while "going mainstream," as I show in "Crossover Dreams." I discuss the tension between the counterculture and the mainstream, and how some out lesbian musicians such as k.d. lang and the Indigo Girls began to break through into mainstream popularity, sometimes pledging allegiance to the subcultures in which they were nurtured, while also achieving commercial appeal. But does the appearance of out gay/lesbian performers really strike a blow against "compulsory heterosexuality"? Is "visibility" a good thing? Some might suggest that television shows like *Will and Grace* and even *Queer Eye for the Straight Guy* have contributed toward shattering the silence around homosexuality in our culture, bringing images of (domesticated) gay and lesbian life into the living rooms of millions of Americans. Natalie Brugmann, the k.d. lang fan I describe at the beginning of "Crossover Dreams," would no doubt agree with this claim. But at the same time, visibility can't be equated with liberation in any simplistic way. The greater visibility of gender and sexual "minorities" challenges the belief that the world is neatly divided into male and female, heterosexual and homosexual, but it also reinforces our assumption that these categories are real and enduring.

Our growing appreciation of the "constructed" nature of gender and sexual arrangements—the fact that they are not somehow written in stone, permanent for all time, or embedded in our bodies or essential selves—has made possible an unprecedented degree of self-awareness and choice about how to live our lives. But it has also meant that there is a fundamental instability in the categories that we have unified around. The success of the gay and lesbian movement, for example, means that it is more and more difficult to locate the gay/lesbian "community," defined as a set of shared values and sensibilities, because it is so pervasive, de-centered, everywhere and nowhere. The transparency of categories such as "gay" and "lesbian," and even "man" and "woman," have also been called into question.

Once many women believed that they could construct a collective no-tion of what it meant to be a lesbian, and build institutions that could permanently consolidate that vision. By the 1990s, that hope was se-verely shaken: it became difficult to speak of lesbian identity, culture, politics, or even sexuality in singular terms. In "Sisters and Queers," I describe this "decentering" of lesbian feminism, and the contestation of meanings it implies. The article was written on the heels of a new queer radicalism, when a group of younger activists tried to rethink the as-sumptions of gay and lesbian identity politics—notions of who belongs in our community, how we define ourselves, and to what ends. Who is a lesbian? Are women who love other women but who are not self-iden-tified as lesbian members of our tribe? What about lesbian-identified bisexuals? Or women who were born male? The category "lesbian" did not represent as stable or unitary an identity as we once thought.

As a somewhat naïve young academic, when I first gave this paper at a number of conferences, I was roundly chastised by women who had come out through feminism, for being insufficiently appreciative of the contributions of lesbian feminism. A disclaimer: I was born at the tail end of the baby boom, and I have one foot planted in the liberationist 1970s, and another in the deconstructionist 1990s. As a nonathlete and a rock 'n' roll devotee, I often found myself out of sync with much of what passed as "lesbian culture": earnest folk music, feminist spiritual-ity, and softball. It seemed to me that lesbian feminism had spawned a culture that was fairly narrowly defined (as many women of color also suggested), but then I've always been skeptical about the capacity of any one identity to characterize the complexity of my own life. If the claims I made in "Sisters and Queers" are far less controversial today, it is because much of what I described in that article has come to pass.

Queer communities today are even more decentered, fragmented, and filled with a multitude of micro-subcultures defined on the basis of a plethora of different gender and sexual preferences than I could ever have imagined—and often the differences among these micro-subcul-tures are as great as those that separate the straight and gay world. The quest for clear boundaries that separate "us" from "them" has proven fruitless, and there is today growing tolerance for those who transgress those boundaries—tolerance that often extends even to those who came out as lesbians in the heady days of feminism and gay liberation, who have since changed their minds, and have chosen to make their lives with men—Susie Bright and JoAnn Loulan among them. Though lesbians may be the flavor of the month when it comes to hip dramas on cable television, we are no longer the vanguard of gender/sexual dissidence. The lesbians and gay men in the suburban community where I now live, predominantly middle class baby boomers in long-term relationships, fade gently into the woodwork. Much like their straight neighbors, the most pressing issues on their minds are the quality of their children's educations and the robustness of their property values—and the right to marry. Meanwhile, transgender activists, among others, are challenging the very binary conceptions of gender upon which we had staked our claims to identity.

Surrounded by all of the extraordinary cultural ferment and self-invention occurring in our communities over the past few decades, it's easy to imagine that shame has been undone once and for all. Yet it persists, making its way into our hearts and minds at inopportune moments, and causing us to hide aspects of our lives that others might find unpalatable. The big difference is that today, in contrast to even a few decades ago, the association of sexuality, particularly homosexuality, with shame is no longer unquestioned. Today the promoters of shame must rally behind political slogans and religious posturing to be heard above the fray of a commercialized culture that mocks sexual repression and positions its spokespersons as humorless prudes. Theirs is a defensive kind of shame. For this we must thank those who have worked so hard to expand the range of intimate possibilities.

1

Shapes of Desire

Are lesbians united by a shared sexual orientation, by their same-sex desires? Do they hold in common the experience of having engaged in sexual activity or having had close, passionate relationships with members of the same sex? Or are they bound together simply by their sense of themselves as outcasts or as rebels against heterosexual society?

The boundaries separating the group called "lesbians" from the rest of women are not at all clearly or immutably marked. Historically, lesbians constitute a group whose central characteristic is debatable and changing, a group about which there is little consensus. For example, there have always been women who have had sexual/romantic relationships with other women who have not labeled themselves on that basis. There have also been women—bisexuals, transsexuals, and others—whose actual sexual fantasies or practices don't fit the common social definition of lesbianism but who nonetheless identify as lesbians. There are many possible configurations of the relationship among desire, behavior, and identity—the possibilities far exceed the capacity of social categories to describe them.

Like ethnic communities, lesbian/gay boundaries, identities, and cultures are negotiated, defined, and produced. The history of lesbian social worlds is in part the story of this production of boundaries, identities, and cultures. These symbolic struggles construct female homosexuality as a social reality; they create images, myths, and fantasies of lesbian love, desire, and fulfillment; and they shape the composition of the group of women called lesbians.

For most of this century, medical experts have been the primary definers of lesbian existence. Medical discourses labeled homosexuality as a "condition," associated it with gender nonconformity, and constructed lesbians and heterosexual women as two distinct groups. Lesbianism, in the medical conception, is concrete and objective, a condition of being that has clear boundaries. It is something to be "discovered," something that always exists in the individual. Subjected to the power of such definitions, individuals defined themselves according to these understandings and organized subcultures to support homosexual desire.

In the 1970s, lesbians and gay men introduced a new vocabulary and set of concepts for understanding homosexuality, suggesting that the boundaries separating heterosexuality and homosexuality were in fact permeable. Lesbianism was a matter of identification, not simply desire. One could be a lesbian by becoming "woman identified," developing "lesbian consciousness," making women central to one's life, and not giving oneself over to men. Lesbians were not "failed women": they were rebels against an oppressive sex/gender system, the vanguard of women's liberation. One could be a lesbian and a woman too. Indeed, rather than posing a threat to one's womanhood, lesbianism strengthened and enhanced it.

The movement from "old gay" to "new gay" signifies the transition from a world in which medicalized conceptions of homosexuality were virtually undisputed to one in which they were roundly challenged, from a time when lesbians occupied a particular deviant social role, focused upon homosexual desires, to a time when lesbianism became an identity, a conscious basis for self-construction. It marks a movement toward greater consciousness with regard to lesbianism in particular, and to sexualities in general.

From Old Gay to New

Women of the baby boom, who reached adolescence and young adulthood during the 1960s and 1970s, found themselves poised between two different accounts of lesbianism. The dominant definition of "the lesbian" was a woman with a medical condition or psychological aberration, an isolated individual divorced from the rest of the world. An emergent account considered her to be a woman who made "a lifestyle choice linked with a sense of personal identity, a product of multiple influences rather than traceable to a single cause."[1]

Curious about variations in identities among those women who actually came out as lesbians during this period, a time when American society was in a period of great social ferment and gender and sexual norms

"Yantra #22" by Tee Corinne, 1982. Reprinted with permission.

were being publicly contested, I collected the life stories of twenty-five women in their thirties and forties who came out as lesbians between the late 1960s and the mid-1970s.[2] I wanted to gain a sense of the relationship between the social category "lesbian" and the variations among women who identified with that category at a particular historical moment when the meaning of lesbianism was highly contested. I also wanted to consider how their sense of self may have changed over time.

What I found was that lesbian-identified women of the baby boom shared a strong belief in the value of claiming a lesbian identity. But while "coming out" provided individuals with a "progress narrative" that legitimated and ordered the lesbian experience, the process of identification was a heterogeneous one. So pervasive among women of this age group was this narrative structure that when I asked them how they would describe their sexual identity, most responded by launching into their "coming out" story, which typically began with early childhood and moved chronologically through time to the present.[3]

Yet they held a variety of understandings of what coming out actually meant. To some women, becoming a lesbian meant "coming home," reengaging with what they believed to be their authentic self and acknowledging the desires they had long embraced in secret. It permitted them to adopt a surface identity as a lesbian to match the deep sense of difference they already possessed.[4] To others, coming out meant "discovering" their lesbianism. For these women, desire was often not the primary determinant of a lesbian identification; their deep identification as lesbian was preceded by an identification with lesbianism as a sociosexual category. For still others—for women whose sexuality was relatively fluid and inchoate—becoming a lesbian meant solidifying both personal and social identities simultaneously. Illustrating these different meanings, here are the stories of three lesbian-identified women of the baby boom generation.

Barb Yerba: "Just the Way I Am"

Forty-two-year-old Barb Yerba was born in 1949 to a lower-middle-class Italian family in New York. She thinks of herself as straddling the "old gay" and "new gay" worlds because she had same-sex experiences before the late 1960s, when the lesbian/gay movements expanded the social space open to lesbians and gay men: "I was sort of an old lesbian. To be an old lesbian meant you were out before feminism. I wasn't out to anyone but myself. But I knew when I was eight years old. I probably knew much earlier." Barb experienced desires for other girls early in life, acting upon these desires in isolation, often thinking that she was "the only one." She thinks of herself as having been a tomboy. "I never played with dolls and hardly ever played with girls. I wore boys' clothes at age eight or nine." At fifteen, Barb had a first sexual experience with another girl. It was 1962. At the time, she had no words to describe her feelings.

As an adolescent, she was vaguely aware of the existence of other lesbians, though unaware of the existence of an organized subculture. In recent years, she has made a hobby of collecting lesbian pulp novels, the dime-store fiction sold during the 1950s and 1960s, featuring lurid covers and titles such as *Odd Girl Out* and *Strange Sisters*. These tales of lust, intrigue, and secrecy, of being young and confused and a social misfit, remind her of her own adolescence, of "being young and out of control, having all these feelings, and having no place to go to talk about them." Being a lesbian, she says, was a "long stream of unfinished business." Like the characters in her pulp novels, she says, she felt a mixture of fear and exhilaration: "I felt the very same kind of dichotomy. On the one hand, I felt at peace with myself emotionally. This is home. There's this quote from *The Price of Salt*. 'Nobody had to tell her that this was the way it was supposed to be.' This is home after all these years. I knew that this was what I wanted, but I knew that it was a really bad thing." She feels that she has always been a lesbian, that it was not at all a matter of choice. To become a lesbian, she simply "discovered" what was already there.

Barb's first girlfriend "turned straight" after a few years. "She repressed all that stuff." But Barb couldn't. "I never had any doubts." In high school, Barb befriended Lore, the first "flesh-and-blood" lesbian she had ever met. One day, Lore looked Barb in the eye and said: "You are a lesbian." At the time, Barb says, she scoffed at the allegation, "but it planted some sort of seed." Yet claiming a lesbian identity in a social sense, beginning to self-identify as a member of a stigmatized group, was not an easy task. She was sent to a psychiatrist, who told her that she had "trouble relating to people" and prescribed tranquilizers for her to take. Through her teens and early twenties, Barb had a series of relationships with women, but never claimed a lesbian identity in a public sense—until a particular incident provided the catalyst for her coming out.

In 1970, while in college, she was living with a girlfriend and several other people in a communal house in upstate New York. One morning, she awoke to hear her roommates discussing whether the presence of Barb and her girlfriend were "warping the household." That was, she said, "the straw that broke the camel's back." Soon after, Barb became involved with a radical lesbian political group. Her first meeting, in

1971, was "like the messiah had come." "There were all these people who were like me. They were all my age. They were lesbians. I quickly realized I was a feminist as well as a lesbian." Becoming a feminist meant that she could begin to think of her lesbianism in positive terms. It also meant that she could think of her femaleness and her lesbianism as compatible, rather than conflicting. It gave her a sense that she could have a social as well as a personal identity as a lesbian. Barb says that she would be a lesbian regardless of these historical changes, but she imagines that she would have been forced to lead a far more secretive, far more unhappy life.

Barb's narrative exhibits many elements of the "dominant" account; she sees her lesbianism as an orientation that was fixed at birth or in early childhood. Adolescent girls vary in the extent to which they know their desires. Some are not at all aware of sexual feelings, heterosexual or homosexual, whereas others, like Barb, are deeply conscious of them.[5] Girls who are aware of their sexual feelings early on often experience their adolescence as a period in which their embodied sexual desire is simultaneously elicited and denigrated by the dominant culture. One can imagine that lesbian desires typically find no reflection in either the dominant culture or within adolescent peer groups. Indeed, as we have seen, Barb experienced herself as virtually alone in her desires, having no one to discuss them with. She talked about "knowing" she was a lesbian very early on, by age eight, even before she had words to describe her feelings.[6]

Barb identified her desires for girls and women at a relatively early age and felt these desires to be powerful and unwavering. When I asked Barb why she is a lesbian, she replied, "Its just the way I am." Indeed, she found the question itself rather curious. Barb sees her adolescent experiences of difference and her eventual homosexuality on a continuum. Her personal identity as a lesbian, she says, was never really in question. As she grew older and began to affiliate with the lesbian community, these connections gave her a social identity as well, a sense of direction and purpose that went beyond the self and a way to counter some of the stigma in the dominant culture. She spoke of the important role that the lesbian community played in allowing her to normalize her sexuality.

But the fact that she experienced her lesbian desires early in life has played a formative role in shaping her sense of self and the meaning her lesbianism holds for her. Indeed, Barb's identity account resembles the "old gay" account, insofar as the experience of secrecy and stigma looms large for those who spent their formative years "managing" their stigma, carefully determining which parts of the self they would reveal to others. (Recall Barb's comments that she felt like an "old gay" woman because she had lived much of her adult life in the closet.) Because of these experiences, like women of an earlier generation, Barb tended to accentuate the differences between herself and heterosexual women, viewing lesbians and heterosexuals as two distinct categories. She thinks of lesbianism in essentialist terms, as something that is innate, unchangeable, and believes that the only "real" lesbians are "born" lesbians—women like her who have little choice in the matter of their sexuality. ⚘

Margaret Berg: "Coming Out through Feminism"

Margaret Berg had always thought of lesbianism as something that was involuntary; it was an orientation that one either did or did not "have." But when she was in her early twenties, she became aware of the possibility of constructing her own sexuality and choosing lesbianism. As Margaret describes her history, she was one of those women who "came out through feminism."

She grew up in Brooklyn, New York, a red-diaper baby, the daughter of Jewish leftist activists. To be a woman in the 1950s and 1960s, even a middle-class white woman, she said, was to grow up with the profound sense of oneself as a second-class citizen. Margaret spoke of the fact that she had to feign underachievement in school in order to catch a husband. She said that she experienced her heterosexual relationships as largely unsatisfying. "I had all the feelings about men that we all had —we thought they were like zombies. I felt that I took care of all the men I was involved with. I felt like I was much stronger than they were. I felt like I gave much more than I got." She recalls, "We were growing up in a world that was so invalidating of women. I straightened my hair, I was ambivalent about being smart, my physics teacher told my parents: 'She's doing fine for a girl.' "[7]

The women's movement emerged in the late 1960s and gave voice to this alienation, situating these feelings in the context of women's oppression. Margaret compares her exposure to feminism in 1969 to coming out of a cave. "Feminism," she said, was "the most exciting and validating thing that had happened in our lives." It allowed her and others to resolve the dissonance they felt between cultural codes and subjective experience.[8] Within the context of the movement Margaret developed an analysis and vocabulary for these feelings and began to see her problems in gendered terms for the first time. She began to believe that she had devalued herself as a woman and underestimated the importance of her female relationships.

Because of their growing idealization of other women, made possible by feminism, women like Margaret withdrew from primary relationships with men. This was less a conscious decision than the product of the growing separation between men's and women's social and political worlds, at least among the young, predominantly middle-class members of what was loosely called the "movement." At the time, she was romantically involved with a man, but as her women friends became more and more central, he became more peripheral. With time, she recalls, "Most of my friends were women, all of my friends were feminists, men were not part of my life. It was all very seamless."

When Margaret became involved in her first lesbian relationship, she said, "The only gay women I knew (and we wouldn't call ourselves gay) were my friends and myself." Margaret met a woman, Jennifer, who eventually moved into her apartment. The world they traveled in was that of liberated sexuality and free use of drugs. There was, she says, "a real sense of barriers breaking." She was drawn to Jennifer as a kindred spirit, an equal. "There was a certain reflection of myself I found in her." Margaret recalls that Jennifer had "much more self-consciously identified homoerotic feelings," whereas hers were more about sexual experimentation and rebellion.

In an effort to try to make sense of her feelings and to find support for them, Margaret began to attend a women's consciousness-raising group devoted to discussing questions of sexuality. Practically overnight, through the influence of gay liberation and lesbian feminism, Margaret's feminist consciousness-raising group transformed itself into a coming-out group. In that group, Margaret was socialized into the lesbian world. She began to think of herself as a lesbian and call herself one. "There was a normative sense about discovering women and male domination and how disgusting men could be. Not to be a lesbian was stupid, masochistic."

She goes on:

Something called "lesbian consciousness" developed in our heads. We talked about "coming out" every four or five weeks. That term started having more and more ramifications as our lives changed. Not just making love with a woman for the first time—but every new situation where you experienced and/or revealed yourself as gay.

Within the context of a coming-out group, Margaret carved out a place for herself within the lesbian subculture. Earlier, coming out had referred almost exclusively to the process of disclosure. But now women who had never experienced themselves as deeply and irrevocably different, but who shared a sense of alienation from gender and sexual norms, could also claim lesbian identities by developing "gay consciousness." In the discourse of lesbian feminism, feminism and lesbianism were conflated. Lesbianism was revisioned to signify not simply a sexual preference, but a way for women to gain strength and confidence, to bond with other women.

But the political strategy of coming out to others as a means of establishing unity often had the contradictory effect of making differences among women more apparent, and the tension between identity and difference within the coming-out group soon became apparent. Margaret describes the "experiential gap" separating women who were "entering a first gay relationship" and those who were "coming out of the closet" in her coming-out group.

One woman was quite involved with a man and left almost immediately—it was never clear exactly why she had joined the group, except that she felt good about women. Another woman pulled out because she felt there was a "bisexual" orientation to the group. . . . Her "coming out" was very different from the rest of ours. She wasn't entering a first gay relationship; rather, she was coming out of "the closet;" entering a gay community and acquiring pride in an analysis of who she is. . . . There was a real experiential gap between her and the rest of the group. We had no understanding of the bar scene, of role-playing, of the whole range of experience of an "old gay." I'm sure a lot of this inexperience translated into moralistic arrogance—we were a good deal less than understanding when she called her lovers "girls."

Here we see a clash of cultures and two different visions of lesbianism: the old dyke world, which valorized gender roles, and the emergent lesbian feminist culture, which rejected gendered coupledom in favor of the communalized sensuality of the group circle dance.

> We all went to our first gay women's dance together. I was very scared by a number of older women dressed sort of mannishly. Not scared that they'd do anything to me, but wary of being identified with them. I was very relieved when a group of women . . . showed up and we all danced together in a big friendly circle. That was my first exposure to a kind of joyful sensuality that I've come to associate with women's dances. Looking around and seeing a lot of gay women enjoying themselves and each other helped me let go of a lot of my fears and validated the possibilities for growth and pleasure in the relationship with J.

The old gay world conceptualized lesbianism as desire; the new gay world reconceptualized it as "woman identification." Margaret sees the differences primarily in generational terms, evidencing the extent to which other distinctions may have been less salient at the time. For younger women, becoming a lesbian was a matter of developing "lesbian consciousness," developing a personal sense of self as lesbian. For these women, becoming a lesbian, developing a personal identity as a lesbian, was not really in question, but living as one, developing a social identity, was. But these differences were not solely intergenerational; they also divided women of the baby boom cohort.

Margaret grappled with figuring out her place in the lesbian world. Coming out, she acknowledges, is "an incredibly hard process." She alludes to the conflict between "old gay" and "new gay" conceptions of lesbianism.

> Coming out is an incredibly hard process; many women think there's some magic leap into gayness—that you suddenly lose all fears, doubts, heterosexual feelings. Others are afraid that they weren't "born gay." Come-out groups help women deal with all of those feelings. The existence of the Lesbian Mothers' Group brought home to us that women are not born lesbians; that women who were both wives and mothers could decide to live with and love other women.

After experiencing some doubts about whether or not she herself was "really" a lesbian, Margaret concluded that even seemingly gender-normative women—wives and mothers—can be lesbians.

Her story suggests that some women used the rhetoric of coming out to claim authenticity and gain membership in the lesbian world. Clearly, this was a very different path to lesbianism from that taken by women whose personal sense of self as lesbian was not really in question, for whom coming out meant coming out of the "closet." If women such as Barb thought of their lesbianism primarily as internally driven, for Margaret and other "elective" lesbians the adoption of lesbianism as a social identity often preceded the consolidation of lesbianism as personal identity. Unlike Barb, Margaret did not trace her lesbianism to early childhood experiences or to having the experience of being "not heterosexual" early on—even if she expressed alienation from heterosexual gender stereotypes. She reported that her sexual interest in men was often conflicted, motivated more by accommodation to male needs and social expectations than by her own desires.

Margaret also differs from Barb in her high degree of self-reflexivity. In general, she framed her lesbianism as the development of "lesbian consciousness"—a political rather than a sexual choice to be involved with women rather than men. Because of her history, Margaret believes that any woman can choose to be a lesbian. However, she recognizes there are different "types" of lesbians, women who exercise greater and lesser degrees of choice.

Joan Salton: "It's an Emotional Thing"

Forty-six-year-old Joan Salton grew up in the Midwest, the daughter of school teachers. She describes herself as a tomboy as a child. "I was always interested in the things that boys did, not really interested in playing with dolls, the whole works." She remembers herself as a "horny kid" who was interested in sexual experimentation and had sexual experiences with boys at an early age. She became sexually active with boys at age sixteen and with girls at eighteen.

Like many girls her age, she gained her early knowledge of lesbianism from pulp novels and from the literature of psychopathology, and recalls the images she found in books in the library.

I suppose the people they talked about in those books were much less weird than the descriptions made them out to be. They were really distorted, looking at things under the microscope without any perception of what the person under the lenses was feeling. I didn't relate to that stuff, but I knew all of the words—dyke, lesbian—and I knew it meant me.

Early on, Joan had what she describes as "better" sex with men than with women. But with women, she says, she felt a "depth of emotion" that she "couldn't feel with men." When she reached her early twenties she began to call herself a lesbian, even as she continued to have affairs with men, though she did not consider them to be "serious." Becoming involved with men, she said, was "sexually possible but emotionally not . . . There are some people for whom being a lesbian means something real different. For me it is a passionate lust for women, emotional intensity I feel only with women." Still, along those lines, Joan acknowledges, she made certain choices. "I dumped a guy who really loved me and who I had great sex with, and . . . for a long time afterwards, I sort of regretted it, because after that I had a really hard time finding a woman with whom I had such good sex. But I knew that I couldn't love him. I didn't feel anything for him emotionally." With time, her fragile sense of lesbianism became more solidified, and she came to have little interest in heterosexuality. This coincided, not coincidentally, with the rise of the gay liberation movement, in which she became public as a lesbian, first as an early gay liberation activist, then as a lesbian feminist.

"It was a time of great social ferment," she recalls. "There was a tremendous amount of feeling behind it. It was a time of connecting a lot of ideas with a lot of feelings." It was about affirming identities that were despised by members of the dominant culture and throwing them back in their faces. For Joan, lesbianism was always at least in part about the rejection of social norms—both inside and outside of the lesbian subculture. "There's a part of me that always wants to throw things in for shock value and stir them up a bit." She was a renegade of sorts, even within the movement; once she had an affair with a gay man who was also a gay liberation activist. Her rejection of the norms of the movement was motivated at least in part by a recognition of the partiality of sexual identifications. Joan was always very conscious of the fact that her own desires do not conform neatly with binary sexual categories, homosexual and heterosexual.

When asked whether her lesbianism is a choice, Joan replied, "Yes," adding, "but I'm not straight." Joan feels that her lesbianism is a choice insofar as she could choose to deny what she "really" felt. She could choose to be with men if she wished to fit in, but she has made a choice that fitting in is less important than being "who she is."

> What's choice? Is choice what makes you happy? No, I am not a born lesbian. I know I was able to have okay relationships with men, and good sex with men. I also know that nothing compares to being with a woman, emotionally or sexually. So is it a choice? I don't know. . . . Maybe for me [lesbianism] was 80 percent internal compulsion in a certain direction, and 20 percent choice, and maybe for other people it is half and half or something.

She is not like other lesbians, insofar as she was not "born" one, she says. Yet she sees herself as more sexually driven to women than many women who call themselves lesbians, particularly many who came out in the context of feminism. Indeed, she was involved with "one of those women" through the 1970s and was sexually dissatisfied for a long time. Whereas lesbianism was for Joan about passionate sexuality, for her girlfriend, she said, it was about bonding with other women. "It was about making a domestic relationship, making a life together where neither person dominated the other. It was about having a more equal relationship at home where one could be comfortable and not feel squashed by the other person."

As we saw earlier, Barb described her personal identity as a lesbian as preceding her affiliation with lesbianism as a social category, whereas Margaret said the opposite: Her affiliation with the lesbian category preceded her consolidation of a sense of "deep" identity. For Joan, separating out the personal and social aspects of lesbian identification and isolating which "came first" is impossible. She talked about her lesbianism in terms of elements that were chosen and elements that were not, and she remained conscious of a disjunction between "doing" and "being," between engaging in homosexual acts and claiming a homosexual identity.

Joan's lesbianism is a choice insofar as acting upon her desires and claiming a lesbian identity are chosen, since originally she experienced her desires as being at least partly fluid and changing. But at the same time, she is cognizant of the fact that her adoption of a social identity as a lesbian "organized" these desires, diminishing her earlier bisexual inclinations. She began the process of identity formation with a sense of

sexual difference that was relatively inchoate, embracing a lesbian identity with some uncertainty, seeing it as a strategic act rather than as a
firm expression of who she "is."

Making Sense of Accounts

Barb, Margaret, and Joan each represent an alternative account of lesbian identity. Although certainly not an exhaustive sample of different
ways of "being" lesbian, their stories illustrate how lesbian identification
presented a solution, a symbolic resolution of a problem each woman
faced at a particular historical moment.

For Barb, becoming a lesbian meant that she could affiliate with the
social category lesbian, disclose that affiliation to others, and build a
social world around the desires she had for so long kept private. For
Margaret, becoming a lesbian was largely a matter of developing a personal sense of self as a lesbian to match her affiliation with lesbianism
as a social category. She did not have a closet—a subjective sense of herself as highly deviant—to overcome; she was not highly driven toward
women in a sexual sense. Finally, Joan combined elements of both
Barb's and Margaret's stories. Like Barb, she began the process of identity formation with a sense of sexual difference, but she differed from
Barb in that her sense of difference was initially relatively inchoate and
unformed. She recognized homosexual desires relatively early, but these
coexisted with heterosexual desires. Joan saw her embrace of the social
category "lesbian" as a strategic act, motivated at least in part by her
deeply felt desires for other women, rather than as a firm expression of
who she "is."

Through interacting with other self-identified lesbians and by gaining
access to different accounts, these women formed a sense of personal
and social identity. These accounts were derived from the dominant culture and from lesbian/gay subcultures. A woman coming of age in the
late 1960s and early 1970s had access to a wider array of accounts and
ways of being a lesbian than women from earlier generations, when
sexual knowledge came almost exclusively from the medical discourse.
However, this does not imply that all individuals had an open-ended
ability to reconstruct themselves as they pleased.[9] Indeed, each woman
brought to the coming-out process a sense of self that was already partially formed.

Individuals' early experiences of difference or similarity in relation to the dominant heterosexual culture figured prominently in their narratives. Their feelings of difference were often related to the age at which they became conscious of their desires for other girls and women. The early-developing lesbian, such as Barb, seemed to incorporate a greater sense of "differentness" within her sense of self. Margaret and other later-developing lesbians were often very conscious of this, whether or not they named it as such. They were also conscious of how they differed from women who had come out before feminism and gay liberation. "Old dykes," particularly those who were very visibly butch, symbolized for them what they might become if they shunned heterosexuality, but they also embodied a kind of protofeminism, a willingness to go against the social grain.

Coming out can be seen, then, as two distinct but overlapping processes: the development of a personal identity as lesbian, or individuation, and the development of a social identity as lesbian, or disclosure.[10] Most analyses of "coming out" focus on the process of disclosure, assuming that the person is fully individuated before disclosure occurs. But for many women, as I have shown, the process of individuation follows disclosure. For others, individuation and disclosure occur simultaneously, each influencing the other

What these life stories reveal, to quote Karla Jay and Joanne Glasgow, is that "the word lesbian is not an identity with predictable content . . . it is a position from which to speak."[11] Individuals bring to the process of sexual identity formation a sense of self that is at least partly formed, and they use the available accounts, or repertoires of meaning, to make sense of this self. These images, or accounts, are themselves historical constructions. As women construct their identities they are acutely aware of those around them, and they select images to emulate or reject, fitting themselves into different lesbian worlds.

2

The Year of the Lustful Lesbian

> In living amorously together, two women may eventually discover
> that their mutual attraction is not basically sensual. What woman
> would not blush to seek out her amie only for sensual pleasures?
> —Colette, *The Pure and the Impure*

> Woman has sex organs just about everywhere. The geography of
> her pleasure is much more diversified, more multiple in its differ-
> ences, more subtle, more complex than is imagined.
> —Luce Irigaray

Women don't tend to attract all that much attention in the
gay male ghetto. But when six-foot Susie Bright, in high heels and a
slinky cocktail dress, turns the corner and saunters toward the Castro
Theatre, the dozen or so men perched in a café sipping after-work cock-
tails let out a flurry of catcalls. "Susie, Susie!" they yell, as she adjusts
her schoolmarm glasses, smiles politely, and marches up the street. It is
the 1989 San Francisco Lesbian and Gay Film Festival, the gay community's answer to Cannes. Dozens of women, most of them in their twenties and early thirties, are milling around outside the theater, frantically
trying to scare up tickets, while hundreds scurry inside, packing the cavernous hall. It has all the trappings of an event writ large, right down to
the theater marquee, which reads, in giant bold letters: SUSIE BRIGHT!
ALL GIRL ACTION!

Thirty-year-old Susie "Sexpert," a sort of lesbian cross between Dr.
Ruth and Al Goldstein (of *Screw* magazine fame), has become a familiar face in this neighborhood, hawking vibrators and other sex toys,
reviewing videos for *Penthouse Forum,* and for five years editing *On
Our Backs,* the first and largest national lesbian sex magazine. She has
emerged, through no small effort of her own, as perhaps the most visible leader of a movement to create a public erotic culture for lesbians.

Cover of *On Our Backs: Entertainment For the Adventurous Lesbian*,
Summer 1985.

Inside the red velvet deco-kitsch auditorium, the fifteen-hundred-strong audience is guided through a ninety-minute cinematic tour of sleazy straight porn, big-budget Hollywood productions, and home-grown lesbian-made videos, in search of images of lesbian sex. The audience watches with rapt attention. There are few men in attendance —a fact underscored by the high-pitched titters emanating from the crowd at various points during the evening, proof that the voyeur role is one to which women are not yet accustomed. It is an evening of strange juxtapositions. A bored housewife is pinned to the bathroom floor by a female maintenance worker who ends up servicing more than the kitchen sink. Two French schoolgirls fondle each other in the bushes. The lovers of *Desert Hearts* learn their way around each other's bodies. Bright punctuates the movie clips with a narrative mix of feminist theory and porn-film history. Midway through the evening, she calls on the audience to acknowledge the work of all "the wonderful porn actresses," who, she says, are "part of our lesbian erotic heritage."

Several years earlier, those would have been fighting words. Feminists tarred pornography as evidence of the degradation of women. Women Against Pornography and its national affiliates organized slide shows of violent antifemale images and widely publicized junkets through urban porn districts. The equation of pornography and violence, resting on the belief that women's complicity in that world was the result of coercion, or of "false consciousness" at the very least, was simple yet powerful.[1] For many women porn seemed to symbolize the fear that stalked them through the routines of daily life, from their interactions with strangers on dimly lit streets to their relationships with men at work and, all too often, at home.

That Susie Sexpert found receptive ears in this crowd is a signal of political shifts in feminist and lesbian culture. There is an increasing reassessment of an earlier feminist orthodoxy from the 1970s that held all sexual representations of women to be degrading. At the same time, there is a burgeoning lesbian conversation that sets itself apart from earlier feminist critiques, brandishing sexual representation to make its point. In the aftermath of the "sex debates" that roiled feminists in the early 1980s, and in an age of AIDS and sexual limits, censorship battles, and injunctions to "just say no," a growing chorus is arguing that women should seek sexual freedoms rather than reject them. Through their writings and speeches, films and videos, self-proclaimed "sexperts" such as Susie Bright and JoAnn Loulan are telling lesbians to reject deeply rooted patterns of female socialization and begin the next phase of their unfinished sexual revolution.

In the final part of the program at the Castro Theatre, Bright shows a series of clips from recent lesbian-made porn, seeming to offer them up as the crowning achievements of the last twenty-five years of film erotica—arty pastiches and campy romps which recall the humor (and limited production values) of early straight porn. "You're the frenzied generation," she teases the audience, mocking 1970s lesbian-made "erotica" for substituting images of flowers, seashells, and gentle female embraces for rough-and-ready sex. "Tenderness, gentleness, and reciprocity are really nice qualities in and of themselves," says Bright. "People would give their eyeteeth to have those qualities in their sex life, just to have someone be sweet to them. It's just that they don't have much fire because there's no passion, or conflict."

In *Clips*, a classic porn narrative is given a lesbian twist as a leggy blonde (who also happens to be the publisher of *On Our Backs*), dressed in a pale pink negligee and stockings, is sprawled out on a mauve La-Z-Boy armchair trying to tempt her partner away from the television set by masturbating. The butch, reading the business news, suitably attired in striped shirt, suspenders, and pants, remains uninterested. Microphones veer off course, and the acting is self-conscious. But as the femme fingers a large clear dildo the audience remains engaged. By the time the butch disrobes, the femme has come single-handedly, in an acrobatic feat which may go down in cinematic history as the definitive "G-spot ejaculation." It is an obvious play on the male cum shot, the hallmark of straight porn films, and a parody of the convention that says that the cum shot reveals real arousal in men. It is also an attempt to signify lesbian sexual prowess. See, the video says, we can wield our sexuality as a source of power rather than victimization.

If the scene tonight is any indication, it appears that Bright has gained a host of new converts to the cause. Some stalwart feminist bookstores still refuse to carry lesbian porn, and the appearance of leather-clad lesbian sadomasochists at women's music festivals can cause a stir. But the fiery battles have flickered out, the antiporn organizations have—for the most part—closed shop, and Susie Sexpert, in her slinky black dress, has emerged as a viable, even respectable, lesbian spokesperson. On this sultry summer night, the once inevitable feminist pickets are noticeable only by their absence; the ideological debates and emotional clashes of the past have faded to a distant memory.

If a lesbian sexual revolution is in the making, its most recent phase began in the early 1980s, when some women, primarily in New York and San Francisco, began to question the literal fashion in which many pornographic images were being interpreted by many feminists. Certainly, they admitted, violence against women was a pervasive fact in our society. But hadn't all the attention on sexual danger minimized the possibility of pleasure? They criticized the blanket equation of objectification with violence and proclaimed that "feminist porn" was not a contradiction in terms.

The polarized battles raged on in the pages of feminist publications and in public clashes—sex radicals branded their antiporn, anti-s/m opponents as good girls, who in turn tarred the bad girls as antifeminist and tried unsuccessfully to codify their views into law.[2] For lesbians, who could be found on both sides of the fray, these debates held a forceful, if ambiguous, resonance. Visual representations of lesbianism, from the early sexologists onward, have been uniformly one-dimensional, depicting lesbians as either sexless spinsters or mannish characters who stalked innocent women and seduced them into their ways. In contemporary popular culture, pornographic images were primarily responsible for linking lesbians indelibly with their sexuality.

Responding to this legacy, in the 1970s, feminists tended to downplay the queerness of lesbianism. "Men who are obsessed with sex are convinced that lesbians are obsessed with sex. Actually, like other women, lesbians are obsessed with love and fidelity," declared poet Judy Grahn.[3] Lesbians were not crazed perverts but very good friends—and the vanguard of the feminist movement to boot. The downplaying of sexuality was strategically brilliant, allowing lesbians to claim legitimacy and space in a homophobic culture, and at the same time recruit converts to the cause. If lesbianism was redefined as woman-identification, in some sense anyone could be a lesbian—you needn't even touch another woman where it counted (though it helped). What was once feminism's "lavender menace" became its vanguard.

The public desexualization of lesbianism emerged out of the realization that for lesbians, unlike gay men, sexual orientation was an insuf-ficient basis on which to build a culture and a politic. This echoed a tendency among some feminists to see sexual liberation as the undoing of women's liberation, as a male invention, a "phallic" concept that bore little relationship to the actual experience of women, rarely as goal-directed, and orgasm-centered, as men. When lesbian feminists af-firmed the erotic publicly, they did so in a holistic sense, in the words of poet Audre Lorde, as the creative energy or "life force of women."

But as Susie Bright and other heirs to the "pro-sex" wing of the sex wars see it, in defining sexuality as male and lesbianism as a blow against the patriarchy, desire—and all its wayward incorrigibility—

seemed to drop out of the picture. Down-and-dirty public discussions of sexual practice were skirted in favor of talk of eroticism, friendship, and softer pleasantries. The specificity of lesbian existence—as a *sexual* identity—seemed to get lost. "The traditional notion of femininity as gentle and nurturing creates the stereotype that lesbianism is just a hand-holding society," Bright says. "Lesbians don't have sex, the story goes. Or if they do, it is this really tiresome affair—five minutes of cunnilingus on each side, with a little timer nearby, and lots of talking about your feelings and your career." In *On Our Backs* and in Bright's lesbian-sex road show "All Girl Action," that vision of politicized sex serves as the dramatic foil.

"Entertainment for the Adventurous Lesbian"

Heralding 1984 as the "Year of the Lustful Lesbian," trumpeting "sexual freedom, respect, and empowerment for lesbians," and featuring erotic stories, graphic illustrations, and unmitigated boldness, *On Our Backs* appeared on the stands announcing itself as "Entertainment for the Adventurous Lesbian," gleefully ruffling some prudish feminist feathers in the service of sexual libertarianism—right down to its name, a not-so-subtle play on the radical feminist publication *off our backs*. It was a family affair, of sorts. Susie Bright was working at the local women's sex-toy shop when she got to know publishers Nan Kinney and Debi Sundahl (who were girlfriends). She contributed a tongue-in-cheek column that probed the ins and outs of dildos and vibrators. Other friends took photographs, wrote erotic stories. Early reader response was effusive, if not overwhelming.

Bright, the daughter of a prominent linguistics scholar and herself a former antiporn activist, quickly became the flamboyant and eloquent mouthpiece of the magazine's philosophy. Each installment of her column, "Toys for Us," a compendium of safe-sex tips, sex-toy consumer reports, and lesbian trend-watching, featured a different photograph of her, somewhere between goofy and sexy. Susie sucking her finger. Susie raising her T-shirt over her head. Susie getting a piercing. If many lesbian feminists scorned celebrityhood, at least in theory, on the grounds that it was unsisterly and elitist, Bright courted it. She quickly mastered the art of the media bite, with pithy quotes like "penetration is only as heterosexual as kissing," and told the press on more than one occasion

Cover of *On Our Backs: Entertainment For the Adventurous Lesbian*, Summer 1984.

that she believed that her mother had never had sex after Susie, an only child, was conceived. Bright also played bit parts in several porn films, including the Mitchell Brothers' safe-sex feature, *Behind the Green Door II*. In German director Monika Treut's 1989 film, *The Virgin Machine*, she played a caricature of herself: a fast-talking, bright-eyed sex-pert expounding on the virtues of dildos and vibrators. She even got up before a packed lecture hall to ask the intellectual savant Susan Sontag what she thought of lesbian porn. "The shocked expression on her face," says Bright, "made it well worth the effort." More than anything else, it is controversy, she says, that gets her "hot."[4]

In the fall of 1988, an article assessing the state of lesbian life in the 1980s appeared in *On Our Backs,* along with three drawings by cartoonist Alison Bechdel. The first showed a demure woman in skirt and saddle shoes clutching a copy of "The Ladder," the newsletter of the prefeminist lesbian organization Daughters of Bilitis; the second was of a cigarette-smoking hippie dyke circa 1973, a woman's symbol around her neck, a copy of *off our backs* stuffed in her overalls pocket. The final image was of a woman in black leather and cowboy boots, a heavy industrial chain around her miniskirt, holding a copy of *On Our Backs,* as if to say: we represent the lesbian of today—sexy, self-assured, and ready for action.

The editors of *On Our Backs* are supremely conscious of their place in history. It is, some say, a revisionist one, which pits renegade sex "radicals" against their bad "feminist" mothers and, in the process, simplifies the complexity of lesbian history, which was never quite as sexless as they make it out to be. But complexity doesn't sell magazines; provocation does, though perhaps not quite as many as *On Our Backs'* editors would like. In the five years since it began, circulation has grown modestly but steadily, to almost ten thousand paid subscribers (and possibly as many as twenty thousand unpaid ones, the editors are quick to point out), making the magazine perhaps the most widely circulated lesbian publication in the nation. Other lesbian sex magazines, such as *Bad Attitude, Power Exchange,* and *Outrageous Women,* also cropped up, but none ever equaled *On Our Backs'* influence, which far exceeds the numbers.[5]

While 1970s feminist "erotica" distanced itself from porn in both form and content, *On Our Backs* tries to subvert the genre on its own terms. Yet the magazine has a sort of homey look, hardly the glossy stuff of big-budget commercial magazines, and pale by comparison to most gay men's porn rags. Indeed, the most noteworthy thing about it, some have remarked, may be its very existence. Most lesbian-made porn shows the lesbian as the subject as well as the object of desire. Bright scoffs at the suggestion that most women prefer the sublimated masochism of romance to explicit pornographic material; the feminist view that porn embodies a male gaze to which women cannot possibly respond, she believes, is misguided. It was in commercial pornography that she herself first found images of lesbians that were exciting, realistic, and at times even funny—"wild s/m lesbians, aggressive biker-chick lesbians, nymphomaniacs who couldn't get enough"—images of sexual infantilism, wayward desire, aggressiveness, and fantasy, repressed in popular and in feminist culture. These images led her to believe that the problem is not porn per se, as her feminist predecessors had charged, but who controls it. Women objectify other women—whether they admit it or not.

Bright wants to take these feminist critiques and turn them on their heads. She'll admit that commercial porn, filled with blond WASPs with perfect figures and lesbian sex that is rigid and formulaic, doesn't do justice to women, who are rarely shown as powerful subjects of desire. Mainstream pornography never found out, she says, "that people are very subversive in their likes and dislikes." But she discards the conviction that capitalism cheapens sexuality by offering up a vision of good orgasms in exchange for the debasement of women. Porn's failings come from the fact that it is made by men, with male consumers in mind; its production, therefore, should be seized by those who have been disenfranchised from it—women. Magazines such as *On Our Backs,* Bright says, derive from the same self-help impulse as the feminist health-care movement. "What that movement tried to do for women's health," she says, *On Our Backs* attempts to do for sex. "Everyone assumes we started the magazine because we're nymphomaniacs. They had no idea it was a big political statement."

But if it is political, it is politics of a postmodern stripe. Politics, for second-wave feminists, meant a search for authenticity and truth, the communication of the reality of women's lives, and the forging of community. Politics, *On Our Backs* style, places fantasy above reality, artifice and style above the "truth," and individual desire above community rules. The magazine is less an attempt to convey what "lesbians really do" than to depict fantasies never fully realized. Rather than reassuring women with soft, sweet sensuality, as did 1970s lesbian erotica (and the new genre of heterosexual "feminist" porn produced by Candida Royalle and others), *On Our Backs* goes out of its way to be daring, pushing up against the parameters of politically correct fantasy, reappropriating the imagery of heterosexual, gay male, and prefeminist lesbian culture, and transposing them into the lesbian context.

And while the magazine has not radically redefined the boundaries of conventional beauty—young, femme, white, typically svelte models predominate—it has sometimes made gallant efforts to do so. *On Our*

Backs ran a "Bulldagger of the Month" photograph in its first issue, an image that was a far cry from the *Penthouse* ideal. In June 1990, the magazine featured a layout of three voluptuous women over sixty. "We don't show nontraditional images because we're trying to be politically correct," says Bright. "We do it because they're hot."

In fact, whether or not something is hot—at least in the eyes of its editors—is pretty much the sole criterion for what gets published. Since one woman's nightmare may be the next woman's fantasy, anything, or just about anything, goes. If feminists held up lesbian sex as the favorable alternative to an oppressive heterosexuality, in Bright's book all orgasms are created equal and all are good. This conviction, perhaps more than any other, lies at the base of Bright's view of lesbian sex. The extreme pluralism it implies often raises the hackles of even those who are mostly sympathetic to the project of creating a lesbian sexual culture, and feminist critics have accused her and others of failing to question the relationship between porn and sexual violence, and sexism in general. Black women, in particular, have said that she and other "sexperts" fail to acknowledge the historical associations of sexualized images of black women. But then subtle distinctions, as one critic put it, are not Bright's forte. Anything less than total freedom, says Bright, tarring feminist censors with the same brush as official thought policemen like Senator Jesse Helms, is "totalitarian piggery." After all, what counts in the end is pleasure, isn't it?

The Eisenhower of Lesbian Sex

If Bright represents an in-your-face sexual libertarianism, JoAnn Loulan may be greatly responsible for its widespread dissemination to the more faint of heart. Bright relies on shock value, championing the most outrageous images just to push buttons and stretch the boundaries of acceptable sexuality; Loulan, in her early forties, is the more respectable go-between, melding lesbian feminist sensibilities and 1980s therapy-speak into the brave new world of lesbian sexual abandon. While the pages of *On Our Backs* depict a fragmented world, filled with anonymous sexual encounters and forbidden fantasies, the archetypal reader lurking behind JoAnn Loulan's sexual primers is a Midwestern dyke, possibly coupled, whose sex life is on the rocks. She is someone probably not unlike Loulan herself, whose small frame, shoulder-length permed hair, and impish face present a package as different from Bright as one can imagine. "Compared to Susie Bright, I'm your grandma," says Loulan, whose folksy persona and comfortable suburban existence (she lives outside San Francisco with her young son) once prompted Susie Bright to call her the "Eisenhower of Lesbian Sex." Loulan's books —*Lesbian Sex, Lesbian Passion,* and *The Lesbian Erotic Dance*—are consistent best-sellers at women's bookstores throughout the country.

When cartoonist Kris Kovick illustrated an article Loulan wrote for *Out/Look* magazine, she pictured her in a short skirt, wielding two giant pom-poms and yelling, "Give me a *c*, give me a *u*, give me an *n*, give me a *t*," a reference to the last section of Loulan's book *Lesbian Sex*, entitled "Be Your Own Camp Director," which features a variety of "homework exercises" ("imagine yourself very small, and crawl up inside your own vagina").[6] Loulan would gladly assume the role of lesbian sex cheerleader. This folksiness has allowed her to get away with all manner of statements which might otherwise be considered blasphemous.

It's no coincidence that Susie Bright and JoAnn Loulan have both emerged in the San Francisco Bay Area, known for its tolerance of sexual nonconformity, home of a graduate program in sexology, clearinghouse for sexual information, and institutional mooring for the profession of sexology on the West Coast. Humanistic sexology melds Masters and Johnson–style therapy with human-potential philosophy. According to sociologist Janice Irvine, author of a study of sexology, *Disorders of Desire,* one of the cornerstones of the profession is a belief in the essential similarity of male and female sexuality. When some feminists argued in the early 1970s that orgasm was a male invention, sexologists dedicated themselves to the goal of teaching women to have more and better orgasms.[7]

Loulan, who emerged out of this sexual model, first seized upon the idea of bringing lesbian sex to the masses while she was teaching healthcare professionals at the University of California Medical School in the mid-1970s, an experience she calls "sex boot camp." She says, "I was appalled at the way medical professionals talked about sex, in such dry, clinical terms," and she was troubled by the lack of knowledge about lesbians. "All the models we had were heterosexual."[8] In 1975 she took a six-month course taught by a variety of liberal sex therapists and educators, some of whom were gay. Tee Corinne and Pat Califia, two veteran lesbian sex experts, were her teachers. It sparked her crusade for lesbian sexual literacy. She began working as a private sex therapist, mainly counseling lesbians, giving occasional talks in the community. At first, she got lots of flak for talking about sex out loud; the ones who weren't angry were usually embarrassed. But her blend of stand-up comedy and sex therapy eventually caught on.

Today she delivers about twenty talks a year and is a veritable star on the lesbian lecture circuit, having sold over a hundred thousand books to lesbians who find their sex lives lacking. On her 1988 tour, which featured a talk titled "An Evening of Provocative Comedy and Lesbian Sex Education," Loulan wore a long, flowing gown, matching pantyhose, big hair, and dangly earrings, and proceeded to outline the archetypal lesbian relationship. First comes the LIP (Lesbian Insanity Phase), in which you don't get out of bed for months on end; which often leads to MIP (Moving In Phase), in which you begin to merge but end up arguing about whose pictures to hang on the wall; which frequently declines to LBD (Lesbian Bed Death), in which a yeast infection is an excuse not to have sex for six months, which can end up turning into six years.

Onstage, this was all presented with the help of mime. There was the "going down on your lover" routine, the "coming out to the neighbors at the bus stop" mime, and the "stimulating the clitoris" scene, among others. In the final part of the evening, Loulan coaxed a volunteer onstage for a twenty-minute demonstration of "safer sex," which involved the placement of a dental dam on a fully clothed woman as Loulan pointed and announced, "That's your pussy, this is your clitoris, and here is your asshole." Some criticize her folksy manner, contending that she talks down to her audience. Loulan admits that she is not a particularly profound thinker. "Being esoteric is all well and good and interesting, but when do you plant the corn and when do you pick it? I want to know a little bit of the background and information of how I got here, but I really want to know what I can do with the pain that I'm in." This matter-of-factness, coupled with her concessions to feminist ideology, allows her to make anonymous sex, role-playing, and s/m fantasy palatable to even the most dyed-in-the-wool sexual ideologue.

"There is magic in this process of becoming fully identified with our lesbian selves," Loulan writes in *Lesbian Sex*. "For so long we have given our sex lives away to the closest person, family member or government. We don't have to do that anymore. . . . You can have what you want out of sex." The basic premise of the book, and of much of Loulan's work, is not particularly original: lesbians are caught in a double bind. They are raised in a culture that teaches women that they cannot be sexual. At the same time, they learn that their identity is determined by their sexual partner. This creates a great deal of anxiety and ambivalence, particularly in a homophobic society, as they are torn between being "good girls" and claiming a lesbian (read: sexual) identity. Following the behavioral model in which she was trained, Loulan believes that "if you change one part of the whole, the rest will change." It is an optimistic vision. Far from waiting until after the revolution, you can fight homophobia now—by having a good fuck.

About lesbian self-esteem Loulan has written: "I do not understand not wanting to have labels—the truth is, if you eat pussy, you eat pussy." On difficulty with dating: "Don't say 'would you like to go on a date?' if you mean 'would you like to fuck?'" And on sexual reticence: "We trap ourselves with shoulds. Sex should be sacred. Sex should be a spiritual union between two people. I don't know about you, but I have done some things during sex that are not all that sacred, and I wouldn't particularly say my spirit was unified with the other woman. I got off."

Her 1987 book, *Lesbian Passion: Loving Ourselves and Loving Each Other,* was culled from a series of Loulan's talks and includes fifty pages of sex homework.[9] "I like to make real practical applications," writes Loulan. The book continues many of the earlier themes of *Lesbian Sex* in a somewhat talkier style, punctuated with the ever-present language of the "recovery" movement. In a chapter titled "Healing the Child Within," Loulan insists that many of us have "an inner child with a broken heart," afraid to show her vulnerability, and she even admits that "many of us feel we have a little boy inside." There is a continuum between active physical child abuse and "inner child abuse," she reminds her readers, "your heart wasn't necessarily broken from incidents of incest or the death of a parent . . . it might have been something as normal as leaving home for kindergarten." We are all, in a sense, abused. Unlike many feminists, however, she draws a distinction between consensual and nonconsensual abuse. Referring to the often vitriolic lesbian debates about s/m, she writes: "We have a history of going after each other like crabs in a bucket. The sex wars, particularly around s/m, are just another way to divide us. I'd like the wars to be dialogues." She believes that the feminist position (which saw s/m as an example of violence against women) was overstated; the women who are against s/m are "torturing" the women who are into s/m. Still, Loulan wonders whether s/m isn't just another form of "getting stoned," seeking thrills and escaping from intimacy, and laments the fact that "a lot of younger women are becoming indoctrinated into it."

If many prosex activists of the early 1980s had a vision of sexuality that acknowledged danger along with pleasure, in the "sex wars" which ensued, the sides were often loudly polarized, pitting "bad girls" against "good girls," libertarian sex radicals against prudes. If there was any middle ground, any acknowledgment of the emotional pain which many women associate with sex, even as they desire it, it was hardly spoken. JoAnn Loulan, one might say, recognized that market and cornered it. By equating lesbian sexual prudishness with sexism and homophobia, placing a value on individual sexual expression, and acknowledging the pain that many women associate with sex, Loulan is able to mediate between feminist "prosex" and "antisex" positions, carving out some comfortable, if at times shaky, middle ground.

"Some women enjoy giving up control to someone they know and love," she writes, singing the praises of dildos and harnesses. "Some people say, now that's really male-identified. I say why not? Why should men be the only ones who get to put something into a woman's vagina and still keep two hands free?" She is a good girl who occasionally harbors bad thoughts, a prudish Ohioan with libertarian impulses. While she finds a kindred spirit in Susie Bright's work, Loulan believes that "sex radicals" often wrongly frame sex in terms of a political battle pitting the whores against the prudes. Loulan isn't looking for any battles; she believes that sex should be roundly depoliticized. She offers good old-fashioned American individualism, in new therapeutic clothing.

Her 1990 book, *The Lesbian Erotic Dance,* is a rethinking of butch-femme roles, an aspect of sexual orientation unique to lesbians which, she believes, has been trampled underfoot by homophobia.[10] The feminist insistence that roles were male-identified and retrograde, Loulan writes, was a product of lesbians' shame about being visible. The problem is, she writes, "In the lesbian community you can walk into any group and say something about butch-femme and everyone knows what you're talking about. It's a lesbian cultural phenomenon, but when you sit down and ask what those words mean, no one knows. We all know what it means on an emotional level, but we don't have language to explain it to one another." For a woman who has made her career as a sex therapist, it is perhaps ironic that Loulan has railed on more than one occasion against the "tyranny of orgasm," admitted that "most people in the world are sexual a small percentage of their lives," and suggested that lesbians' sexual identity "overemphasizes sex." If pushed, she might even say that lesbians' problems don't really center on sex at all; sexual problems are simply symptomatic of other difficulties. But in the end the liberal therapist in Loulan wins out. "There's a new paradigm being talked about, a new language being created," she writes. "It's all part of a process which is revolutionizing lesbian sexual practice. We're more willing to talk about sex, more willing to express it, and that's important."

Can Lesbians Sleep with Men?

While Loulan dedicates *Lesbian Passion* "to lesbians everywhere" who must "band together in our clan," Bright walks a fine line between celebrating the lesbian community and mocking it. For Bright, the discussion began early in 1975, when she was in college and lesbian separatism was at a fever pitch. She never identified with separatism, in large part because of her bisexuality, which many women around her assumed to be simply a phase in her coming-out process, and a political affront. "I had been wearing dyke buttons since I was fifteen, but slept with men and women the whole time," she recalls. "I used to get into terrible sobbing fights with women over bisexuality. I knew that the way those women characterized sex with men was stupid—the qualities people were talking about could apply to men or women."

Though she never stopped calling herself bisexual, she started calling herself lesbian because she wasn't having sex with men, not because she wasn't attracted to them. "They were just kind of out of the picture. I had a very busy little lesbian life," she recalls. But the controversy reared its head again a few years later, when, in an interview with a San Francisco gay paper, she was quoted as saying that it was all right for lesbians to sleep with men. The response this time, she says, was much more favorable than ten years earlier. "A lot of lesbians called me up and confided in me that they were having a secret affair with some guy, or that they had had a one-night stand two years ago, or a secret marriage." Still, many women remain leery.

In 1990, when writer Jan Clausen published an article in *Out/Look* that attested to her newfound relationship with a man and defended her right to retain her lesbian citizenship, a flood of letters to the lesbian/gay quarterly called her a traitor to the cause. Even as there is increasing acknowledgment of sexual difference among lesbians, bisexuality is still taboo in many quarters. Lesbians who sleep with men (termed "hasbians" by the feminist publication *off our backs*) are often seen as turncoats, betraying their lesbian sisters and unable to deal with their "true" desires. Some have even been accused of importing AIDS into lesbian communities. For ideological as well as personal reasons, the desire for sexual consistency remains strong.

Because bisexuality may call into question the notion of sexual identity as necessarily being fixed, consistent, and either homosexual or heterosexual, it makes some lesbians uneasy. In a society where heterosexuality is the norm and lesbianism is still stigmatized, bisexual boundary crossings often lead to hurt feelings, as when a woman is left by her female lover for a man. Particularly suspect, and confusing, are women like Bright who sleep with men but maintain a lesbian identity, navigating the turbulent waters of two often contending worlds.

In this debate, as in others, JoAnn Loulan assumes the mediator's role. "Lesbian identity goes much deeper than our genitals," she admits. "For some lesbians, sex with men is a wonderful adjunct to their ongoing sexual relating to women." She recognizes that discussions about lesbians sleeping with men may be coded debates about the loss of community and meaning of lesbian identity, the generational lament of baby boomers who are now finding their once supportive communities gone, transformed into fragmented couples and isolated individuals without firm mooring. "It's harder to be a lesbian these days," writes Loulan. "We're not hanging out together, supporting each other as much. As you get older, it's harder and harder to date."

Bright, however, will hear no such thing. She likens these fears to a "horrible *Titanic* paranoia" in which "there are only six lesbians left on the life raft, and if we lose one more person, we're all going to sink." She adds, "It's only threatening to those who are insecure, who feel as though we're losing our community." This she finds curious, as she's convinced that there are more lesbians, of all ages, coming out now than ever before. "It makes the period I came out in seem like small potatoes."

For her own part, in June 1990, after admitting to her readers that she had gotten pregnant "the old-fashioned way," she gave birth to a baby girl, silencing her critics' contention that "real" lesbians do it through insemination. "I lay on a waterbed with a real live man, someone whose genes and fatherly temperament I've been admiring for some time," she wrote in *On Our Backs*. "It was the first day of my ovulation and I remember visualizing the sperm being sucked into my cervix like a honey vacuum. It was thrilling. So many women are having babies on their own," she wrote, "with women spouses, men friends, and every other newfangled family support. It's rewarding to talk about when you dispense with the old stereotypes."

These old stereotypes have a lot to do with sexual boundaries. While some would like to narrow the definition of "lesbian" to those who limit their sexual practice to women, Bright would like nothing more than to erase the boundaries, admit anyone into the club who wishes to be a member, even those who occasionally embrace phalluses—of either the rubber or the human variety.

She is one of a growing number of intellectuals and activists who have begun to call on gay people to subvert the medical categories, to deconstruct the notion of homosexuality, to begin to speak of "practices" rather than identities. In the pages of *On Our Backs*, Bright exhorted her readers to "start talking about what we do instead of who we supposedly are. Don't say 'I'm an s/m lesbian,' when you could be saying, 'I fantasize about eating out my manicurist on the bathroom floor with her mouth gagged by a rubber ball,' or, 'I pinch my nipples when I masturbate until they're hard as points,' or, 'Fist me until the sweat drips off my lip.' Isn't that much more enlightening?" Calling herself a lesbian while living a bisexual life, championing the rights of sexual minorities of all sorts while writing columns for a heterosexual porn magazine—and viewing it all as perfectly consistent—Bright herself is perhaps the best exemplar of a post-Stonewall, post–identity-lesbian politics that has little respect for sexual borders or good behavior.

As JoAnn Loulan, Susie Bright, and others announced the onset of a lesbian "sexual revolution," some observers wondered whether lesbians were picking up where gay men had left off. Relatively unscathed by the AIDS crisis—if reports were accurate that woman-to-woman AIDS transmission was rare—lesbians seemed uniquely poised to reclaim female pleasure. And many did. Lesbians, critic Cindy Patton wrote, "have adapted the hanky code of sexual options, and the randy attitudes that go with them, from gay male culture," and may represent the reinforcements for a sexual-liberation movement badly damaged by the right wing and AIDS. "We got off on fighting back, while gay men got off on putting out," she wrote. "But sex is political, and sex lib theory rings false without some good, sweaty praxis."[11]

Some activists tried to build a renewed interest in prefeminist lesbian culture and reverse the feminist insistence that butch-femme roles were simply reflections of patriarchal values. Butch-femme relationships —"strong, fierce lovemaking: deep, strong givings and takings, erotic play challenges, calculated teasings," wrote Joan Nestle, "were complex erotic statements, not phony heterosexual replicas."[12] Like butch-femme roles, s/m embodied sex as performance, a far cry from the sun-dappled, hand-holding images of the past, providing an endless supply of fantasy images and a gendered archetype for the sort of erotic tension required by the emerging model of lesbian sex.

Lesbian sadomasochists took their cause to numerous conferences, forums, music festivals, consolidating themselves as beleaguered minorities within a minority, and mobilizing new recruits, leading s/m advocate Gayle Rubin to report that in 1982 there were about as many sadomasochists in most lesbian communities as there were radical feminists in 1970. By 1990 there were organizations for s/m lesbians in at least fourteen cities across the nation, with names like "Bound and Determined" (Hadley, Massachusetts), "Power and Trust" (Portland, Oregon), "Southern Kink" (Decatur, Georgia), and "Urania" (Somerville, Massachusetts). San Francisco's "Outcasts" vowed, in the words of Pat Califia, to be "male-identified, objectifying, pornographic, noisy and undignified," and claimed as many as a hundred members.[13]

In a striking historical irony, sadomasochists made dykes with dildos, once pathologized as man-hating perverts, hip. They represented a sort of class revolt—the rising up of a less "civilized" working-class sexuality against middle-class, "ladylike" feminist norms. Drawing on the iconography of prefeminist lesbianism, gay male culture, and heterosexual porn, this lesbian sexual fringe introduced a new vocabulary of lesbian desire, a world of dildos and harnesses, butch and femme, tops and bottoms, lust and intrigue—symbols of a queer female culture and reminders of a lesbian past that, for all intents and purposes, had disappeared from public view by the 1970s.

By the end of that decade, sadomasochism had crept into the vocabulary of "vanilla" culture, as some lesbian therapists began to prescribe a diet of sexual dominance and submission to guard against the stultifying effects of the much-touted "Lesbian Bed Death"; more and more women experimented with butch-femme and other forms of sexual role playing, or at least talked and wrote about it. Mail orders for harnesses and dildos skyrocketed, propelled by a new lesbian market; and a new playfulness about sexuality came into view in urban areas with large gay populations, especially among younger lesbians, who embraced dolled-up dyke fashion and new dance clubs that featured miniskirted go-go dancers. If their older sisters claimed power by renouncing lipstick, coquettishness, and even pornography, by 1990 many lesbians asserted their sexual power by reclaiming them, and by withholding access from the conventional male beholder.

But some cautioned against overstating the extent of the revolution. Throughout the nation, women wrote outraged letters to lesbian and gay newspapers, scoffing at the suggestion that lesbians had any intention of mimicking the sexual excesses of their gay brothers. And as many lesbian therapists could tell you, for all but a feisty sexual fringe the sexual revolution was probably more about changes in representations of sexuality than about changes in behavior.

"If you read *On Our Backs,* you think that things are changing rapidly," cautions Seattle therapist Elizabeth Rae Larson, "but it's important to recognize that few people actually do what appears in its pages." Most of her clients, she says, "are overwhelmed when handed stuff like that. It bears no resemblance at all to what they are doing." Like the pronouncements of a society-wide sexual revolution in the 1960s and 1970s, the notion that a lesbian sexual revolution is occurring today, she and others contend, may be exaggerated. Old patterns die hard. The combined effect of a still conservative dominant culture and the deep roots of individual sexual patterns make behavioral change slow.

On Our Backs and other sexual materials may "provide comfort," but all the dildos, harnesses, and new sexual techniques in the world, says therapist Larson, probably won't alter patterns that are "deeply rooted in the fact of being a woman, and being gay in this society." Because sex is so private in our culture, particularly lesbian sex, the few public representations which do exist tend to dominate the scene, distorting our perception of actual change. The growing visibility of lesbian-made representations of lesbian sexuality, and the rise of a sexual fringe, may be more indicative of the fact that a sexually active vanguard is becoming more visible than that such attitudes and practices are trickling down to the grass roots.

This realization has led some to ask whether the new model of the "lustful lesbian" may be leading to a "pleasure imperative" that is insidious in its own right. "It's great and it's playful, but it's not the only way," says therapist Marny Hall, warning of the arrival of a new set of standards. Writing in 1988 in the radical feminist journal *Sinister Wisdom,* Marilyn Frye chided lesbians for answering questionnaires that ask us "how frequently we 'have sex,'" contending that "they are leading women to become dissatisfied with ourselves and with our relationships because we don't 'have sex' enough." In a dig against Loulan and other sexperts, she proclaimed: "We are so dissatisfied that we keep a small army of therapists in business trying to help us 'have sex' more."

Hall agrees: "There's a fundamental problem with hooking our identity onto genital sex. What I would like our identity to be hooked to is our incredible ability to reinvent ourselves. That is our great strength." She is not alone in her ambivalence. Today, most lesbians will admit that while porn may have made a big splash within the lesbian community, if the truth be known, it has never really taken off. In San Francisco, the lesbian strip shows, so popular for a year or two, have exhausted their audience and closed. Even Susie Bright has left *On Our Backs* to devote herself to writing and mothering.

The sexperts have revealed a partial truth: that women are not as different from men as many feminists had asserted the decade before—though neither are they identical, as the resistance to the "lesbian sexual revolution" attests. While many women welcome the advent of a new prosex lesbian culture and applaud the license it affords, others hold out for a "kinder, gentler" alternative free of domination, subordination, and pleasure imperatives.

3

Rock against Romance

As far as I'm concerned, being any gender is a drag.

—Patti Smith

Recently I watched the PBS series *The History of Rock and Roll* for a second time. The first time I saw the documentary, I was captivated by the story of how, in the 1950s and 1960s, white male youth found a vision of a different way of life in black rhythm and blues, and how music often transgresses social boundaries that otherwise seem impassable. As *The History of Rock and Roll* shows, white kids in this country appreciated black music, enacting a kind of cultural desegregation even before the legal barriers separating the races were lifted. This time, while watching the documentary, I imagined myself as a young girl listening to the music of my youth. I tried to re-create the reactions I had to rock 'n' roll and think through its gender politics. In doing so, I couldn't help but reflect upon the ways girls and women have often been understood in relationship to rock.

The dominant image—at least for those of us who grew up in the sixties and seventies—is of Beatle-crazed girls and swooning groupies, uncritical, desiring masses. In the feminist take on this story, female rock fans are engaged in the affirmation of a fantasized, omnipotent masculinity. When *Ms.* asked in 1974: "Can a Feminist Love the World's Greatest Rock 'n' roll Band," Robin Morgan replied that feminists who listened to the Rolling Stones had adopted a "male style" that would destroy the women's movement.[1] Female rock fans are, in other words, dupes of men, prisoners of lust, or both. I, for one, couldn't find myself in any of these images.

I came of age in the early seventies, in a towering Bronx apartment building filled with working-class and lower-middle-class people united only by their mutual envy of those who had more. During this transitional moment of gender relations, images of female rage filled the media, and talk of feminism was in the air. Some of this talk had trickled down to my world. Mothers like mine who had become full-time housewives were encouraging their daughters to go to college and pursue careers. Still, the codes of femininity that valued catching a man over all else were pervasive in the culture at large. We girls were expected to enjoy "love comics," syrupy tales of fawning girls waiting for their knights in shining armor, or love ballads sung by clean-cut crooners.

From an early age I knew that love comics and teen crooners were not my cup of tea. My mother served as an example of what was in store if I lived by these codes of femininity: a woman whose visions of bliss clashed with the reality of a failed marriage. At the same time, many of my fantasies of rapture involved my favorite female English teacher—those knights in shining armor were nowhere to be found. Little that I saw around me in popular culture resonated with these desires and fears—until, that is, I found rock 'n' roll. Rock spoke to the alienation I felt from my parents and their world. It put me in touch with an image of a different way of life, and gave me a space to imagine alternative visions of gender.

As psychoanalyst Ethel Person suggests, men and women pursue self-realization through passionate quests. For women "the passionate quest is almost always predominantly interpersonal in nature, and generally involves romantic love, while for men," she says, "it is more often heroic, the pursuit of achievement or power." This gendered dichotomy, in which "men favor power over love and women achieve power through love," is reflected in mainstream popular culture and encapsulated in the romance narrative.[2] For second-wave feminists, romance was a form of ideology, a myth that kept women down. As feminist firebrand Shulamith Firestone put it: "Romanticism is a cultural tool of male power to keep women from knowing their condition." Women, she says, "may be duped, but men are quite conscious of this as a valuable manipulative technique."[3]

More recently, some feminists have attempted to reclaim romance as a hidden pleasure of femininity—reconsidering romance novels, sixties girl group lyrics, even love letters (cultural forms earlier renounced as evidence of women's entrapment) to be examples of female resistance.[4] Early feminist critiques of romance, which ignored how women actually feel and think about the popular culture they consume, it is true, were rather simplistic. Nonetheless, the standard romance narrative reinforces the view that women can only achieve full self-realization through merger with an Other. Men are subjected to no such expectations, and indeed are urged to break loose from Mom, wives, girlfriends, in order to become fully human. On balance, the romance "script" reinforces inequalities between men and women.

Instead of rehabilitating romance, I would like to reclaim rock 'n' roll, or at least explain how women have used rock to resist the expectations embedded in romance. Twenty years ago, critic Ellen Willis proclaimed the pleasures—and paradoxes—that rock held for female fans. "Music that boldly and aggressively laid out what the singer wanted, loved, hated—as good rock 'n' roll did," wrote Willis, "challenged me to do the same, and so even when the content was anti-woman, anti-sexual, in a sense anti-human, the form encouraged my struggle for liberation."[5] Yet the emerging history of rock, exemplified by video documentaries and myriad books, focuses upon how its modes of performance embodied male rebellion. Missing is an explanation of how and why young women, in historian Alice Echols' words, "harnessed rock's subversive and rebellious possibilities"—if not typically as active participants in the production of the music, then surely as consumers and fans.[6]

What meanings does rock embody for female fans? The meaning of all music is communicated on a number of different levels: there is the music, its rhythms, hooks, and melodies; there are the lyrics, most of which are barely recognizable; and there is the image, the look of the artists, conveyed through performance, music packaging, and, increasingly, music videos. These three aspects—the music, the lyrics, the image—cannot be separated out, as they work together to communicate a range of meanings, ideas, and emotions to audiences. At the same time, audiences are complex, shifting entities, comprised of different groups who interpret the music in multiple ways, often in ways that go against their intended meanings.

As a young rock 'n' roll fan in the 1970s, I knew that the music was typically made by young men, and spoke for and about male experience. (There was no more glaring reminder of this than when I went to a Rolling Stones show in 1976, only to witness the band straddling an enormous stage complete with giant inflatable penis and Tarzan rope for Mick Jagger.) Yet at a time when feminism was barely visible in the culture at large, I found in this music something unexpected: a nascent feminist message, an invitation to rebel against the visions of girlhood laid out before me.

Pleasure and Power

Music allows us to participate in "imagined forms of democracy and desire," writes critic Simon Frith. Twenty years after feminist critiques of rock first surfaced, he is responding to the brave new world of globalization, cultural fragmentation and "active" audiences. Our experience of music, of music making and music listening, he says, "is best understood as an experience of self-in-process." Frith describes how he has found pleasure in black music and gay music, or female music, though he clearly does not identify as black or gay or female.[7] Music, he suggests, knows no borders: it can be enjoyed by any and all, regardless of race, or religion, or gender.

Music in its purest sense *is* fundamentally a democratic art form—at least in principle. Music offers possibilities in fantasy that few of us can actually realize in our daily lives. But where hierarchies rule, those pleasures are always connected to power and dominance; relations of power shape the contexts of production and reception. Our fantasies take the contents of our everyday lives, the ways in which we feel powerful and the ways we feel weak, and play on those realities, bending and shaping them, often in unpredictable ways. Sometimes the experience of appreciating and listening to music allows us to resist that which we cannot resist in "reality"—the limitations of gender, for example. Girls' attraction to rock 'n' roll should be understood at least partially in these terms.

Girls' fiction and magazines typically convey the belief that the most important goal in life is to fall in love.[8] Romance permits a transcendence of the mundane through the rapturous embrace of love. It is through the romantic quest that the inner experiences and needs of individuals is mutually recognized and validated, and through which, potentially, both individuals are transformed. But this transcendence is founded upon inequality: in the standard romance narrative, boys/men become empowered sexual subjects and girls/women emerge as little more than sexual objects.

If the romance myth is predicated on female passivity, it also assumes heterosexuality. It can never admit that girls may in fact be aroused by other girls, or even that two girls might prefer each other's company. Indeed, it is the pursuit of the male fantasy object that sets females against each other. As cultural critic Angela McRobbie describes British girls' magazines, "No story ever ends with two girls alone together and enjoying each other's company." They cancel out completely any possibility other than the romantic one between girl and boy. Indeed, that admission would threaten the central tension that drives the narrative.[9]

If girls' popular culture proclaims that self-realization comes through merger with a (male) Other, boys' culture is its antithesis. The images available to boys and young men—in television, magazines, and pop music—emphasize separation, autonomy, and power. Rock 'n' roll, exemplifies this quest. Rock, Simon Reynolds and Joy Press write, is "fueled by a violent fervor to cut loose." "The born-to-run impulse of the Rolling Stones, the warrior comrade in arms (the Clash), the omnipotent (the Doors, gangsta rap)" are all "ways in which the male rebel has dramatized himself against the feminine."[10] A classic example from the sixties is The Who song, "A Legal Matter," where the hero feels his willpower enfeebled by the "household fog" of furnishings, baby clothes, marriage, and the like. As Reynolds and Press suggest, throughout the sixties, "male wildness is dramatized against female domestication."

This isn't to say that romantic narratives don't make their way into rock 'n' roll. Indeed, as Reynolds and Press argue, the psychedelic tradition—including such performers as Pink Floyd, Brian Eno, along with later ambient/techno music—engages in a mystical identification with the feminine. This rock tradition speaks of "longing to be enfolded and subsumed," exemplified by oceanic and cosmic imagery. But the *dominant* trope of rock emphasizes separation, not surrender.

Rock as a discourse, a way of knowing the world, operates largely in relation and in opposition to the traditionally female value of relationality—epitomized by the romance narrative. While romance values merger with an Other, rock glorifies separation. Through rock 'n' roll, girls have been able to resist the cultural idealization of hegemonic femininity. Rock has offered girls and women a vision of power, an alternative to the romance "script"; girls' attraction to rock 'n' roll, then, has a lot to do with gender transgression. As a teenager, I think I knew this intuitively. I didn't want to be confined to boys, marriage, and babies. I wanted more. Given the choice between dependence and autonomy, romance and rock 'n' roll, I chose the latter.

Ambivalent Pleasures

A preoccupation with romance was certainly reflected in the popular culture of my youth. Girls' magazines such as *Seventeen* carried the following message: girls must devote their lives to the quest for romance, for the "right" boy. She must go to all lengths to catch him. This search for rapture is inevitably accompanied by enormous anxiety and a loss of autonomy. Will he find me attractive? Will he still love me tomorrow? Popular culture told us to be obsessed with finding, falling in love with, and keeping boys, and to dream about rather than participate in life.

I was, instead, devoted to bands from "the British Invasion." My best friend Lisa and I snatched up the records of The Who, the Rolling Stones, and the Kinks. We sneered at our friends who preferred more acceptable mass-culture creations like the Monkees or the Partridge Family. In high school we sometimes cut class early to head downtown to see our favorite bands, waiting on line for hours to buy tickets. When The Who played Madison Square Garden in 1974, Lisa and I managed to score two tickets. For months I waited in anticipation of that night, our first live show. The concert itself was rather disappointing—the pot smoke was so thick we could barely see, and our seats were so far from the stage that we could hardly hear the music. But in a way, it didn't really matter. We were there for the experience.

What did I identify with in this music? The Who was a rather odd choice for a fourteen-year-old girl. *Quadrophenia,* perhaps my favorite Who album, was the ultimate paen to teen male angst. A "concept album," it told the story of Jimmy, an alienated working-class lad who gobbles up amphetamines to escape his claustrophobic family. In search of salvation, he flees to the seaside and enters the world of mods and rockers, and drugs, sex, and rock 'n' roll. This is the classic male dream of escape.

For me the appeal of the music was less about the expression of desire than the formation of an identity. I was a good girl who wanted to be bad. Loud, rhythmic music produced by scraggly young white men put me in touch with an image of a different way of life, one that was a long way from home. For me, the pleasures of rock were integrally related to identification with a sense of power that was only available to boys, and the feeling that through that music, I was subverting those gender barriers at least a little bit.

Like those British lads, I felt trapped within the shabby gentility of the aspiring middle class, captive in my parents' home. When Roger Daltrey had the gall to sing "Why don't you all just f-f-fade away?" and fantasize himself as a snotty-nosed teenager on a train to Brighton, I was carried along with the ride—even if in reality I lacked the means of escape. Listening to it was a kind of protofeminist act, enacting a secret rebellion at a time when a more overt rebellion was out of the question. During hot summer nights, Lisa and I went to shows in Central Park at least three times a week. At times we weren't even picky about what we went to see. We wanted to luxuriate in the aggressive loudness of the music. We wanted to get out of the house, and away from the watchful eyes of our hyperprotective parents—even if our fathers dutifully drove their cars to pick us up after the shows were over, shattering our illusions of teenage rebellion.

The dominant "reading" of girls and rock 'n' roll suggests that they are less interested in the music than in dreaming about their favorite male performers. Using this line of argument, some have suggested that the early Beatles appealed mainly to girls, and that when rock 'n' roll got heavier, and headier, more male—with the rise of The Rolling Stones and others—girls lost their interest in it. This doesn't describe my experience. I loved loud, thrashing rock 'n' roll. I wasn't one of those girls who stared at my favorite male rock stars dreamily, imagining that one day I'd fall into their arms. Anyway, Pete Townsend, my favorite member of The Who, wasn't much of a heartbrob.

I didn't necessarily want to *be* a guy, or even want to date them, but I did fantasize, perhaps unconsciously, about possessing their power. If my embrace of rock was at least partly a revolt against my mother, it was also a revolt against the gender system that trapped her. Seventies' mass culture, filled with sugary-sweet images of functional families in consumer-driven ecstasy, or teenage girls and boys rapt in romantic bliss, was, I believed, downright disingenuous. In choosing rock over romance, The Who over teenybopper idols like Bobby Sherman, I was resisting normative expectations of how girls are supposed to be. Rather than buy into the cultural idealization of female dependence, I opted, in fantasy if not reality, for autonomy.

Rock glorified masculinity and simultaneously suggested that it was fraught with contradictions; it reinforced hegemonic notions of gender and revealed that they were a lie. From the mid-sixties on, even as they cockily strutted their stuff, male rockers like Mick Jagger toyed with androgyny and sex role reversal, wearing lipstick, feather boas, and carrying on rudely with their band mates. David Bowie turned this subversion into an art form, flaunting sexually ambiguous alter egos such as Ziggy Stardust and Aladdin Sane. I loved it. Rock 'n' roll gave me a space to imagine alternative visions of gender when there were few other possibilities for resistance. It also spoke to my own budding lesbianism.

But at the same time, I knew, deep down, that my favorite performers, Pete Townsend, David Bowie, and the rest, weren't really singing to me. Rock 'n' roll in its classic form was produced by and for young men. As Reynolds and Press point out, female rock fans were "written out of the rock 'n' roll script." At some point, sometime after the mid-seventies, I became very self-conscious of this fact, and of my love of rock. I hid my Rolling Stones lest I be charged with "false consciousness"—listening to the oppressor's music—and I tried, with little success, to listen to feminist folk, or "women's music"; it failed to move me. It seemed to me at the time that feminist music, rooted in the folk tradition of social protest, relinquished the power of rock and embodied a rather limited conception of femininity, declaring power chords, teenage angst, and even gender ambiguity off-limits. If "cock rock" embodied power, autonomy, and self-invention, women who listened to the Rolling Stones, some feminist leaders warned, embodied a "male style" that would destroy the movement. That meant that the most exciting music, as Ellen Willis noted, was reserved exclusively for the boys.

Faced with this ambivalence, the feminist rock fan learned to change the pronouns of lyrics in her head, imagining herself in the role of the active, knowing male listener—or she simply denied her femaleness. This was not an unfamiliar strategy. Feminist theorist Jane Flax described the conflicts facing women in a world of limited options: women can either "be loved and nurtured and remained tied to the mother, or be autonomous and externally successful, and be like a man."[11]

Changing Femininities

Young women who are looking around for cultural representations that reflect their experiences are in a less conflicted position today than girls of my generation were twenty years ago. They are no longer forced to choose between a discourse of romance that glorifies surrender or a dis-

"Kimo and Tracy 1989," photo by Jessica Tanzer.

course of rock that idealizes autonomy. They have a much greater variety of different images of gender available to them in music, and in popular culture generally.

For example, during the past couple of decades a growing number of female artists have come to use the conventions of rock to rewrite the romance script. Gone are the blissful images of romance; a new self-consciousness about romance is evident. It began with women's involvement in the punk scene in mid-1970s New York and London, and with protopunk pioneers like Patti Smith, who wore men's ties and white shirts and famously said, "As far as I'm concerned, being any gender is a drag." Inspired by her example and by punk's bad attitude, women embraced punk's do-it-yourself esthetic, irreverent sensibility, and breakneck speed, forming bands such as The Raincoats, X-Ray Specs, and The Slits in England.

As one account put it: "The Slits' aggressive and confrontational sound was most definitely their own: the foundation was a stuttering, stumbling rhythm pounded out with grim determination, choppy guitar chords on maximum fuzz (and always ever-so-slightly off-key) scratched through the racket at irregular intervals like jagged shards of cut glass;

and undulating over the whole live, solid mass came . . . signature wobbly, screeching wails and yelps."[12] In one of their songs, "Typical Girls," they sang with typical punk irony: "Typical girls / She's a femme fatale / Typical girls / Stand by their men / Typical girls / Learn how to act shocked [. . .] Who invented typical girls? Who's putting out the new, improved model / There's another marketing ploy / Typical girl gets the typical boy."[13]

Taking a cue from punk's irreverent attitude, and rooted in a "post-feminist" sensibility, female rock stars in the 1990s, including Polly Harvey, Hole, and Liz Phair openly struggled with the pleasures and perils of relationships with the opposite sex. Liz Phair's 1993 album, *Exile in Guyville,* was a response to the Rolling Stones' album *Exile on Main Street* and featured nineteen songs, many of them scathing, about heterosexual relationships and game-playing. Writing in *Salon,* critic Cynthia Joyce recalled: "While most music takes you back to the time when you first heard it, somehow 'Exile in Guyville' retroactively defined my every romantic milestone, crystallizing each event so that the album became for me the diary I never kept. I'm sure I was hearing 'The Divorce Song' when I drove with my friend / lover to a Tennessee motel room during a long and revealing road trip ('It's harder to be friends and lovers / and you shouldn't try to mix the two / cause if you do it and you're still unhappy / then you know that the problem is you') even if it was two years before the album came out."[14] Lesser-known female bands, such as Columbus, Ohio's Scrawl, sang the lyrics: "He cleaned up / she took him back / he fucked up / she kicked him out," repeated over and over at an ever increasing pace. "If I were a boy and I found out that my girlfriend was listening intently to Scrawl's 'Travel On Rider,'" critic Gina Arnold wrote, "I'd take a good long hard look at my relationship, and try to figure out what was bugging her."[15]

Times have certainly changed. k.d. lang and Melissa Etheridge have become lesbian cover girls. Ani diFranco's sexual ambiguity—which teeters across the boundaries of identity as she sings of love, lust, and failed relationships with both men and women—won her a huge following.[16] Bands like Bikini Kill, Team Dresch, and Luscious Jackson embody an empowered female sexuality that takes its cue from Madonna but dispenses with her contrived postures. While the Britney Spearses of the music world will probably never completely fade away, in terms of a small but growing sector of popular music the dominant gender codes, including passive stereotypes of femininity, are withering away—

along with the hegemony of romance and its glorification of women's surrender.

In mass-produced girls' fiction, a similar pattern is evident. "The girl is no longer the victim of romance," writes Angela McRobbie. "She is no longer a slave to love. . . . There is love and there is sex and there are boys, but the conventionally coded meta-narratives of romance, which could only create a neurotically dependent female subject, have gone for good." McRobbie suggests that patterns of meaning which were once emblematic of the experience of teenage femininity, such as romance, have disappeared, replaced by a more "diffuse femininity."[17]

How can we explain the ferment that is now taking place in rock 'n' roll, and the unprecedented entry of a new generation of savvy, sophisticated female performers and fans? We must look at how feminism has changed—and is changing—our culture. On the heels of the feminist movement, female performers and fans have become commercially important properties and markets, giving both musicians and fans new power. The artists are not necessarily self-proclaimed feminists. Indeed, many are explicitly not. (Polly Harvey, among the most angst-filled of the bunch, is a case in point.) But in some ways, that's irrelevant. For the very existence of these artists is made possible by feminism. Girls do not want to be represented in a humiliating way. They are not dependent upon boys for their own sense of identity.

Young women coming out as lesbians today are much more likely to see their sexuality as inherently acceptable, even respectable, than women of my generation. They can learn about lesbian lives in women's studies courses, feminist fiction, and, increasingly, in mass-produced popular culture, such as the television show *Ellen,* or the music of the Indigo Girls. They do not feel a sense of loyalty to feminist or women's culture, as did many women of my generation. Rather than listen to feminist musicians recording on alternative record labels, young feminists today listen to women musicians who draw on lesbian/feminist imagery but perform for a mass audience. This may explain the popularity of the Lilith Fair, the roaming festival of mainstream girl pop, featuring the likes of Sarah McLachlan, Sinead O'Connor, and Erykah Badu. Young women today have a much greater sense of entitlement than we did; they believe that they deserve to be represented in mainstream culture, and they are making it happen.[18]

We are certainly not "talkin' about a revolution" here. For every empowered young woman there are many others who suffer from material and other forms of deprivation. The recording industry is, for all intents and purposes, still in the hands of men. But things are changing, slowly —but significantly. In the world of popular music, a growing number of female performers have been able to use the system to their advantage, openly incorporating gender rebellion into their art. Consequently, young women looking for popular culture that reflects their lives are no longer caught between two unsatisfying alternatives: a world of romance that embodies female dependence, and a world of rock 'n' roll that glorifies male separation. They have a greater variety of images of femininity available to them.

If this story poses a challenge to the emergent narrative of rock history that makes female rebellion relatively invisible, it is also a rejoinder to the feminist view that rock and feminism are necessarily at odds. Certainly rock 'n' roll, in its classic form, embodies male values of autonomy and separation. But for many female fans, rock has also been a source of gender rebellion. Increasingly, this rebellious spirit is reflected in the music itself. But even before the recent wave of "women in rock," some of us used rock to enact a secret gender rebellion. The history of rock should also include the story of girls like me, whose lives were saved by rock 'n' roll.

4

Crossover Dreams
Lesbianism and Popular Music

Twenty-two-year-old Natalie Brugmann of Rochester Hills, Michigan, has never heard of "women's music" or *On Our Backs* magazine. She attends a monthly gay coffeehouse in Detroit, twenty miles away, when she can get to it, though she much prefers riding her motorcycle or going hunting. But Natalie remembers, as if it were yesterday, the day, six years earlier, when she spotted performer k.d. lang on a late-night TV talk show, with a butch haircut, a man's Western suit, and no makeup. "I took one look at k.d.," she says, "and I said to myself: is that a guy or a girl? There was something about her attitude that I liked."

Natalie's room is filled with k.d. lang videos, promotional CD's, posters, autographed photos, T-shirts, and ticket stubs—paraphernalia she has collected through ads placed in magazines and bookstores. She finally got a chance to see her star in the flesh last year in Detroit, an experience she exclaims was "amazing."

Women like Natalie, primarily young lesbians, mob k.d. whenever she plays. When a fan club sponsored a video night at one of the oldest women's bars in San Francisco in 1990, the place was packed tighter than anyone could remember seeing it before. k.d. lang look-alikes wearing bolo ties danced the two-step with partners wearing cowgirl skirts. Others sat on the floor, transfixed by a large video screen, watching a collage of promotional videos and homemade footage assembled for the occasion. The glee in their faces, the longing for identification, were proof of how starved they were for celebrities to call their own.

Lesbians comprise what sociologist Herbert Gans has called a "taste public."[1] We are a heterogeneous group of individuals who, like all members of society, wish to see aspects of our lives reflected in the films, books, music, and other cultural goods we consume. We comprise a

Album cover "Absolute Torch and Twang" by k.d. lang and The Reclines, 1989.

partial culture, that is, we share some basic interests that separate us from the rest of society, but we also belong to mainstream society.[2] One would hardly know this from listening to popular music, however. Writing in 1990, pop critic Jon Savage noted that while "popular music acknowledges the sign of 'gayness,' there is not yet a whisper of female sexual autonomy, of lesbianism."[3] Because images of heterosexuality and, more specifically, female sexual accessibility, are central to pop music's appeal, out lesbians are not generally thought to be "crossover" material. Driven by big hits and anticipating the specter of meager sales (or outraged moralists), commercial record companies steer away from potential controversy.

A performer who makes her lesbianism known typically becomes categorized as a "lesbian artist," and is doomed to marginality. Consequently, performers, who labor under the competitive pressures of the market, engage in self-censorship, fashioning their words and images to achieve "universal" appeal, or at least what they interpret as such. The "crossover artist," who embraces lesbian identifications while achieving mainstream success, simultaneously acknowledging both lesbian marginality and membership in the dominant culture, such as k.d. lang, is a rare specimen indeed.

While images of heterosexuality dominate popular music, they do not go unchallenged. Women have always found ways to "read" popular music against the grain, by changing the pronouns of songs in their heads and projecting their fantasies of identification and desire upon female icons. In addition, out lesbians have for at least twenty years struggled for greater participation in popular music production, both by explicitly encoding lesbian references into their music and by using more implicit, ambiguous coding.

Sing This Song All Together

Lesbian performers have long participated in the creation of popular music in North America. However, the social movements of the seventies provided, for the first time, impetus for many women to openly incorporate their sexual identities into their creative work. In the early seventies, young women who "came out through feminism," as the saying went, attempted to transform lesbianism from a medical condition, or at best, a sexual "preference," into a collective identity that transcended rampant individualism and its excesses, as well as compulsory sexual and gender roles. Central to this movement was a belief in what Michel Foucault and others have called "reverse affirmation," the reclaiming and affirming of stigmatized identities, such as homosexuality.[4]

Lesbian feminism in the 1970s spawned a vibrant and visible lesbian culture, encouraging women to develop their own fiction, visual art, and music. "Women's music" was an important product of this period of cultural innovation. Though usually not explicitly lesbian, women's music was created and performed primarily by lesbian/feminists, who created popular music that drew upon lesbian/feminist iconography and imagery and dealt with themes that were of interest primarily to lesbian/feminists. Like other forms of women's culture at the time, women's music was imbued with a belief in a universal female sensibility, expressed in the idea of "woman-identification."[5]

This identity was defined, in large part, by its opposition to masculine forms of culture, such as mainstream rock and roll—"cock rock." In 1974, *Ms.* magazine asked "Can a Feminist Love the World's Greatest Rock and Roll Band?" and critic Robin Morgan replied with a resolute "No!" She warned that lesbian feminists who listened to the Rolling Stones were no better than those who advocated nonmonogamy and accepted transsexuals as allies: they had all adopted a "male style" that would destroy the movement.

Women's music also was rooted in the populist tradition of social protest and in the belief that small and simple was best.[6] For the American left, at least since the thirties, folk music provided an antidote to an alienated mass culture in which cultural objects became isolated from the communities and traditions that initially gave them shape and meaning. Women's music, which grew partially out of this left critique, sought to achieve a more authentic form of cultural expression for women, a goal that was embodied in the organization of the women's music industry itself. In addition to encouraging innovation in terms of musical content, women's music politicized the *process* of musical production.

Olivia, the pioneering women's record company formed in the early seventies, comprised the backbone of the women's music industry. Like most of the women's music industry, Olivia was founded on the belief that it was important to erase the distinctions between industry, performers, and audience—distinctions that were central to commercial music.[7] Even more important, perhaps, women's music sought to redress the fact that women in general, and lesbians in particular, had been shut out of positions of power in commercial music. Within alternative music organizations such as Olivia, women were offered opportunities —as performers, singers, producers, and promoters—not readily available to them. As singer-songwriter Holly Near explained in retrospect:

Women's music was not just music being done by women. It was music that was challenging the whole system, a little different from disco, a little different from David Bowie playing with androgyny. . . . We were dealing with a lot of issues David Bowie wasn't dealing with, questions his management wasn't asking. So it was not just the music. It was like taking a whole look at systems and societies and letting a music rise out of those systems.[8]

The vision of women's music was an ambitious one. In positively valuing women's (and lesbian) lives and accomplishments, and serving as an organizing tool, Olivia played an important role in the development of lesbian feminist culture. However, the narrow way in which women's music was defined—as music produced by, of, and for feminists—may have inadvertently limited its appeal.

Women of color charged that women's music had become firmly entrenched in what was, for the most part, a Euro-American tradition. Confirming their suspicions was the fact that albums and tours by black artists on women's music labels failed to attract much-needed sales. Criticism also came from women in punk who, like women's music artists, made a politics of disrupting gender and sexual codes, debunking "male" technique and expertise, and posing a critique of glamour.[9] But unlike women's music, punk refused to position itself as the affirmative expression of either feminism or gay liberation, and its brash style was at odds with the folkiness of women's music. As one of the founders of Boston's Rock Against Sexism, a cultural activist group comprised of "closet rock-and-roll fans" in the women's community, explained: "Women's music is really peaceful, not raunchy or angry; it doesn't really excite me or turn me on or get me energized."[10]

In the eighties, the viability of women's music was thrown into question by a crisis of identity. The "decentering" of lesbian feminism, related at least in part to generational changes and to the critique posed by women of color, called into question the prior belief that women's music could reflect an "essential" femaleness. The notion of identity constructed by a century of scientific "experts" implied that all lesbians were alike, united by a common deviance. Removing its basis in biology, lesbian feminists attempted to universalize the possibility of lesbian experience, but in its place they often created rigid ideological prescriptions about who belonged in the lesbian community, and what lesbian culture should look and sound like.[11]

In the end, women's music was revealed to be the expression of a

Cover of *Bitch: The women's Rock newsletter with bite!*, volume #22, 1988.

particular generation of activist women. But its undercapitalization prevented it from branching out into other directions. As sales lagged,
many women's music producers responded by moving away from their
lesbian-feminist roots.[12] In 1988, as Olivia Records celebrated its fif-
teenth anniversary with a series of concerts throughout the United
States, its records languished in the "women's music" section in the rear
of record stores, if they were there at all. But at that very moment, a
new generation of women performers was entering the mainstream.

Androgyny Goes Pop

In 1988, American music journalists proclaimed the arrival of a "new breed of women" in popular music. Tracy Chapman, k. d. lang, Michelle Shocked, the Indigo Girls, and Melissa Etheridge, among others, were noted for defying conventions of femininity in popular music and moving "back to the basics"—away from artifice and role-playing into authenticity. The reverse of an earlier embrace of androgyny by male pop stars like David Bowie, influenced by gay drag's tradition of artifice and costume, it was a movement that confounded the critics. "Neither their songs," one critic wrote, "nor the images they project, cater to stereotypical male fantasies of female pop singers." Another proclaimed: "The most astounding thing of all is that Tracy Chapman et al. even happened. Since when did the industry that insisted its strongest women play cartoon characters . . . allow a serious, powerful, flesh and blood female to stand firm on a concert stage?"[13] The answer, as any informed observer could see, was rather simple: the "new breed" of pop women emerged once the industry was convinced that they were marketable. Tracy Chapman became a household name in 1988, selling more than ten million albums because she was "just so real," according to an Elektra Records executive.

Subcultures have long fueled musical innovation: hugely successful commercial disco and house music, for example, had its origins in the black gay dance floors of Chicago and New York. Likewise, on the heels of the feminist movement, female performers and fans became commercially important "properties" and "markets," giving them a new position of power to define what they did and demand what they wanted. The trail was blazed by performers like Cyndi Lauper and Madonna, whose messages, though at times contradictory, affirmed an empowered female sexuality practically unseen in commercial pop. In 1983, Lauper released the single "Girls Just Want to Have Fun," described by Lisa Lewis as a "powerful cry for access to the privileged realm of male adolescent leisure and fun."[14] Madonna, probably *the* most successful female star of the contemporary period, exuded sexual power and invincibility, at times making allusions to lesbianism, as on her "Justify My Love" video, which was banned by MTV at the end of 1990.[15]

While there had been, at least since the early seventies, women in popular music who defied conventions of femininity—Patti Smith, Janis

Joplin, and Annie Lennox were among the most prominent figures—
what was new about the eighties wave of androgyny was that its proponents, though not always lesbian identified, tended to be rooted, at
least partially, in lesbian subcultures. Tracy Chapman made the rounds
in women's music festivals in 1986 and 1987, while Melissa Etheridge,
k. d. lang, Michelle Shocked, and the others knocked around lesbian
and "alternative" clubs in Austin, Atlanta, San Francisco, and New
York City.

Though influenced by feminism, and frequently by women's music,
they were convinced that it was necessary to work within the constraints of the industry to get their message across. They saw main-
streaming as an act no less subversive than the feminist disaffection
from the industry a decade earlier. Los Angeles–based singer-songwriter
Phranc, whose 1989 album *I Enjoy Being a Girl* sported her in a flat-
top haircut (alongside a blurb that sang her praises as a "little daughter
of bilitis"), toured as the opening act for the Smiths and other popular
postpunk acts, playing for mixed audiences because, she said, "it's important to reach out to the kids." As a member of 2 Nice Girls from
Austin, Texas, put it: "We don't want to be found only in the specialty
bin at the record store. We want to be in your face."[16]

But the most ambitious of these performers carefully constructed
their personae to assert a strong, sexually ambiguous female presence.
Studiously avoiding male pronouns in romantic ballads through the
subtleties of self-presentation, which were often indecipherable to those
who weren't cued into the codes, they made themselves objects of female as well as male desire. Swaggering in a man's Western suit, k. d.
lang proclaimed: "Yeah, sure, the boys can be attracted to me, the girls
can be attracted to me, your mother . . . your uncle, sure. It doesn't
really matter to me." On Michelle Shocked's 1989 album, *Captain
Swing*, one had to listen closely to "Sleep Keeps Me Awake" to make
out the fact that it was a love song to a woman. Even as they were
being applauded by the critics for their fresh, unencumbered simplicity
and their return to "honesty" and "naturalness," many of these artists
constructed their songs and their images with an ambiguity that at times
verged on camp.

The arrival of the new breed of androgynous women in pop in the
eighties, propelled in large part by an increasingly self-conscious lesbian
audience, suggested that some women could finally defy conventions
of femininity in popular music and still achieve mainstream success.

But typically, the classic dilemma persisted: a performer either became known as a "lesbian artist" and was doomed to marginality, or she watered down her lesbianism in order to appeal to a mass audience. In a rare acknowledgment of the lesbian roots of the late 1980s folk boom, Michelle Shocked, upon accepting the award for Folk Album of the Year at the 1989 New Music Awards in New York (nominated along with Phranc, Tracy Chapman, and the Indigo Girls), quipped, "This category should have been called 'Best Lesbian Vocalist.'" But she later complained to an interviewer about being lumped together with all the other emerging women performers, while others avoided the subject entirely, refusing to be interviewed by lesbian/gay or feminist publications. Lesbian performers were only "safe" (read: marketable) if their sexuality was muted—a woman singing a love song to another woman was still taboo.[17]

The Politics of Ambiguity

Some who had made an explicit politics of their lesbianism charged that the cultural revolution that had begun in the early 1970s had been stalled, gobbled up, and incorporated by "the industry." As Phranc sang:

> Everybody wants to be a folk singer. They want to be hip and trendy. They want to make sensitive videos and sing about politics. Androgyny is the ticket or at least it seems to be. Just don't wear a flat-top and mention sexuality, and girl you'll go far, you'll get a record contract and be a star.[18]

Women's music, which was created in the context of lesbian institutions and communities, had linked lesbian/feminist authorship to feminist content and audience. With the arrival of the "androgynous pop star," some argued that women's music had been replaced by music that blandly played with lesbian signifiers like clothes and hairstyle in order to gain commercial acceptance, but never really identified itself as lesbian.[19] Such criticisms were overstated and overlooked the fact that many of the new artists happened to be more talented than their more overtly political predecessors. Still, it was true that, shorn from its community base, lesbian music emerged in the mainstream as a series of floating signifiers, linked to feminist/lesbian sensibilities, but having no real loyalty or commitment to an organized subculture or movement.

Industry constraints were at least partially behind the apparent prohibition against "speaking" lesbianism. In the eighties, the belief in an undifferentiated mass market was replaced in favor of marketing appeals targeted to niches geared to specific racial, ethnic, and "lifestyle" groups of various sorts. Yet it was rare for a commercial record company to acknowledge the existence of the lesbian audience possessing a specific location and particular tastes. When record companies recognized the existence of such a market, they often saw it as a liability rather than as an asset. In marketing an out-lesbian musician such as Phranc, a spokesman for Island Records acknowledged that a performer who makes her lesbianism a central part of her act (that is, she mentions it at all) may have a "limited consumer base."[20]

But if many of these emerging performers were ambiguous about their identities, it was not simply because of industry constraints—it was also because, frequently, their identities *were* ambiguous. Historically, artists have often resisted the demands of identity politics, preferring instead to place their art above loyalties to any one particular group. In the eighties, the "decentering" of lesbian feminism called into question the tendency to make lesbianism a "dominant" or "master" identity. Audre Lorde wrote in 1979:

> As a Black lesbian feminist comfortable with the many different ingredients of my identity . . . I find I am constantly being encouraged to pluck out some one aspect of myself and present this as the meaningful whole, eclipsing or denying the other parts of self.[21]

Following from this, one can imagine that Tracy Chapman, a black woman, is a complex personality possessing commitments to more than just the lesbian community. So too is Michelle Shocked, who eventually became involved with a man. In the seventies, Holly Near often hid her bisexuality in order to appeal to a women's audience, in the interest of providing a united front. Ten years later, there appeared to be greater tolerance for ambiguity, and even a certain attraction to *not* really knowing the "truth."

Anyway, what *was* the truth? The eighties, after all, was a decade in which "pleasure," said critic Larry Grossberg, "was replacing understanding."[22] David Letterman, the American baby boomers' late-night talk-show host of choice, celebrated alienation with a mocking self-referentiality, as MTV blurred the boundaries of pop music and advertising. Quick-change, recombinant pop jumped from style to style, integrating new sounds and textures, new identities and images and blurring cultural categories of all sorts. A rap song sampled the theme from the television series *Gilligan's Island*; Peter Gabriel and Paul Simon borrowed from African traditional music. Comedian Sandra Bernhard mixed and matched identities, alluding at times to her lesbianism without ever really embracing it. "I would never make a declaration of anything," she proclaimed. "It's so stupid. Who even cares? It's so presumptuous."[23]

Indeed, for many audience members, particularly younger ones, it seemed, this ambiguity was part of the appeal. As one nineteen-year-old lesbian told me:

> I like "cock rock" and women's music. I like both. But I like mainstream women's music the best. Music that speaks to women but isn't only of women. . . . They don't use pronouns, proper nouns. To us that's cool. And we notice that men don't really listen to that music.

The fantasies lesbians construct about particular performers' identities, and about themselves in relation to these performers, are a collectively shaped and shared part of lesbian experience. Sexual ambiguity allows for the double appeal of the music—to the subculture as well as to the mass audience. It allows performers to communicate with lesbian and feminist members of its audience without pledging allegiance to the norms of the subcultures, or becoming spokespersons for them. It allows audience members to listen to music that they consider, secretly, to be lesbian, with the knowledge that millions of other people are also listening to it.

In the end, perhaps it was a testimony to the maturity of feminist and lesbian culture that performers, as well as members of their audience, no longer saw it necessary to make their lesbianism the central overriding feature of their work. In the eighties, as feminist styles were incorporated into popular culture and the boundaries between the mainstream and women's culture blurred, some performers found an unprecedented degree of freedom to construct their images, and their music, as they pleased.

But this strategy also had its limitations. While the new wave of women in pop achieved mass appeal beyond the already-converted audience of women's music, they were reliant on the existence of a savvy audience to read their codes. Young lesbians could finally see images in the mainstream that closely resembled them, but since lesbianism was still unspoken and since the vast majority lacked the necessary knowledge to cue into these codes, the heterosexual norm remained, for the most part, unchallenged.

Crossover Dreams, Marginal Realities?

In the early 1990s, a few women were able to "cross over" and achieve mainstream success as out lesbians, integrating their sexuality into their art without allowing it to become either *the* salient fact, or else barely acknowledged. k.d. lang and Melissa Etheridge, who had previously coded their sexuality as androgyny, came out as lesbians to great fanfare within lesbian/gay circles and even greater commercial success. Their coming out was highly significant, in part because it was certain to have a ripple effect, encouraging others to follow suit.

Still, it would be unwise to view this development as evidence of the unmitigated march of progress. While these artists were able to (partially) incorporate their lesbianism into their music and images, they did so only after they had achieved considerable commercial success. It was much more difficult, and perhaps even impossible, to do the opposite, to "cross over" from margin to mainstream, and come out while one's career was still in the early stages of development.

Moreover, as I have tried to show, the representation of lesbianism in popular music is a far more complex matter than the sum of individuals who "come out." Lesbian representation in popular music has occurred through the interaction between performers, music industry, and audiences. Artists attempt to achieve popularity while maximizing their creative autonomy, frequently against the imperatives of both the recording industry and a demanding public. The music industry, a source of both conservatism and innovation, tries to keep abreast of trends and emerging "taste publics" without alienating existing audience members. Audiences are constantly in flux, shaped by cultural trends and social movements (such as feminism and gay liberation) that create subcultures that in turn influence popular tastes.[24]

Furthermore, lesbian representation is not simply a matter of making lesbianism visible. Increasingly, as Biddy Martin has argued, the "irreducibly complex and contested nature of identity has itself been made more visible."[25] Women of the baby boom generation, the founders of women's music and culture, believed that they could construct a collective sense of what it meant to be a lesbian, and also develop representations of that collective identity. Many young lesbians today, much more aware of the limitations of identity politics, seemingly do not. While this indeterminacy is deeply troubling to many women, particularly those who once held the hope of constructing a lesbian-feminist movement that was culturally and ideologically unified, a "decentered" lesbian identity and culture may present new democratic potential. For one thing, many women who felt excluded by an earlier model of identity and culture now feel they can finally participate on their own terms.

During the last two decades, female pop stars, a good number of whom are lesbians, have worked within these constraints, utilizing different strategies to bring their message to an increasingly self-conscious and sophisticated female audience. The influence of feminism on mainstream culture has meant that many performers are able to exercise a greater degree of control over their image and their music. Popular music is today performed by self-identified lesbians, bisexual-and-proud types, and even straight women who aren't afraid to be (mis)identified as lesbians—k.d. lang, Tracy Chapman, Ani diFranco, Madonna, and Sleater-Kinney, to name a few—who draw upon lesbian iconography and/or subcultural sensibilities and address an audience that at least partially consists of lesbians. And while the dream of a body of music and art that expresses lesbian experience(s) openly and honestly has not yet come to pass in the mainstream, in the meantime lesbian performers and audiences are struggling in various ways to construct positions from which to speak that acknowledges both lesbian marginality and membership in the dominant culture.

5

Sisters and Queers
The Decentering of Lesbian Feminism

A mother of two boys told me that "in the old days," the 1970s, she could go to a particular place—a cafe or women's center, for example—to find the lesbian community in her medium-sized town. But by the late 1980s, when she broke up with a longtime lover, she went out searching again for that community and couldn't find it. Another woman I knew expressed fears about the number of lesbian friends she had lost to heterosexual conversions, having become convinced that more and more women were forsaking their lesbianism in exchange for what she saw as the greater public respectability afforded by living with men.

Lesbian feminism emerged out of the most radical sectors of the women's movement in the early 1970s. Young women who "came out through feminism," as the saying went, attempted to broaden the definition of lesbianism, to transform it from a medical condition, or at best, a sexual "preference," into a collective identity that transcended rampant individualism and its excesses as well as compulsory gender and sex roles. It was a movement that spawned the most vibrant and visible lesbian culture that had ever existed in this country.

But by the mid-1980s, the vision of a Lesbian Nation which would stand apart from the dominant culture, as a sort of haven in a heartless (male/heterosexual) world, began to appear ever more distant. In contrast to the previous decade, lesbian culture and community seemed placeless. This complaint was common, particularly among women who came of age during the previous decade, when becoming a lesbian meant coming into a community committed to some shared values. Philosopher Janice Raymond sounded the call of alarm in a women's studies journal in 1989: "We used to talk a lot about lesbianism as a political movement—back in the old days when lesbianism and feminism went together, and one heard the phrase lesbian feminism. Today we hear more about lesbian sadomasochism, lesbians having babies and everything lesbians need to know about sex."[1] As she and others explained it, the 1980s and 1990s brought a retrenchment from the radical visions of the previous decade. A triumphant conservatism had shattered previously cohesive lesbian communities.

While many of these assertions are unquestionably true, the death-of-community scenario cannot explain the apparent paradox that by 1990, in many urban centers, lesbian influence appeared to be nowhere *and* everywhere. In 1991 the *San Francisco Examiner* reported on the closing of the last lesbian bar in that city. How strange, the columnist noted, that "more lesbians than ever live in San Francisco but that the last lesbian bar was set to close." Bemoaning the loss of a "home base" for lesbians, the former owner of the bar said: "It's a victim of the lesbian community becoming more diverse. There is an absence of a lesbian community in the presence of a million lesbians."[2]

Reflecting this more decentered sense of community, today's lesbian "movement," if one can call it that, consists of a series of projects, often wildly disparate in approach, many of which incorporate radical and progressive elements. If the corner bar was once the only place in town, by the early 1990s in cities across the country there were lesbian parenting groups, support groups for women with cancer and other life-threatening diseases, new and often graphic sexual literature for lesbians, organizations for lesbian "career women" and lesbians of color, and mixed organizations where out lesbians played visible roles. What is new, I suggest, is the lack of any fundamental hegemonic logic or center to these projects.[3]

The once clear connection between lesbianism and feminism, in which the former was assumed to grow naturally out of the latter, is not all that clear today. Gone is the ideal of a culturally and ideologically unified Lesbian Nation. A series of challenges, largely from within lesbian communities themselves, has shaken many of the ordering principles of lesbian feminism. In the following, I want to explain this process of decentering. What does it mean? Why did it occur? And what might it tell us about the trajectory of identity-based movements?[4]

Identities and Movements

All movements engage identities, but in recent years "identity" has become a key term, signifying the sense in which the goal of movements is

Advertisement for One from American Express.

not only to mobilize identities toward some other end but also to act upon collective identities themselves. In the 1960s and 1970s, in response to the widespread perception of postwar social conformity, new social movements politicized the concern for autonomy and subjective identity, arguing for notions of political activity that challenged previously clear-cut distinctions between private and public, personal and political.[5]

Lesbian feminism, and the women's liberation movement in general, was committed to the goal of authenticity, to redefining and affirming the self. A movement such as this confounds the abstract universalism of theories such as Marxism or resource mobilization, which have typically conceptualized social movements as expressions of shared interests within a common structural location. In such theories, actors find their collective identities within a prevailing cultural model that is more or less fixed. The formation of collective identities is assumed to be relatively unproblematic, reflecting "essential" differences among persons that exist prior to mobilization. We refer, for example, to a supposedly unified subject such as the *women's* movement, searching for signs of collectivization and unity and downplaying evidence of discontinuities and ruptures.

Instead of assuming that collective identities simply reflect differences among persons that exist prior to their mobilization as a group, we need, I think, to look closely at the process by which movements remake identities. For it is through the process of mobilization that this sense of "groupness" is constructed and individual identities are reshaped.[6] New social movement theories that emerged in the 1980s in Europe come closer to being able to answer some of the questions posed by movements such as lesbian feminism: for example, how do people develop politicized group identities? How do these identities change over time? Rather than conceiving of movements as narrowly concerned with achieving material benefits, theorists such as Alain Touraine see them as struggles for the "management of historicity," for the "social management" of culture. In this framework, movements emerge not simply as the expression of needs narrowly defined but as needs rooted in self-conceptions, in identities.[7]

With this in mind, I want to reread the history of lesbian feminism as a series of identity reconstructions that are partial and strategic. A social movement organized around sexuality may seem a peculiar site for such an examination, since sexual desires and behavior tend to be viewed as presocial and unchanging. Over the past two decades, however, scholars have argued against such assumptions, claiming with respect to homosexuality that it is "socially constructed," that it is "situational, influenced and given meaning and character by its location in time and social space."[8]

Lesbian feminists took this constructionist critique very seriously. Indeed, they literally tried to remake lesbian life in this country by bringing together disaffected members of the homophile, gay liberation, and feminist movements, as well as unaffiliated women, to form autonomous lesbian organizations that would be part of the larger struggle for social and sexual freedom.[9] Yet in the end, I will argue, the movement failed to see the constructed, indeed fragile, nature of its own collective self-concepts.

Smashing the Categories

To my suggestion that lesbianism is becoming decentered, one could reply that the lesbian-feminist movement, consisting of hundreds of semi-autonomous small-scale efforts nationwide, was never centered. However, while it was never unified, it did have a hegemonic project. It was, first, an effort to reconstruct the category "lesbian," to wrest it from the definitions of the medical experts and broaden its meaning. It was, second, an attempt to forge a stable collective identity around that category and to develop institutions that would nurture that identity. And third, it sought to use those institutions as a base for the contestation of the dominant sex/gender system.

The medical model of homosexuality, dominant for most of the twentieth century, declared that sexuality is fixed at birth or in early childhood, an intractable property of the individual. The "old gay" prefeminist world, a series of semisecret subcultures located primarily in urban areas, formed in relation to the hegemonic belief that heterosexuality was natural and homosexuality an aberration. But for 1970s "new lesbians," the prefeminist world and the conviction that lesbians were failed women were no longer tenable or tolerable. In place of the belief in a lesbian essence or fixed minority identity signified by an inversion of gender, long synonymous with the image of lesbianism in the popular imagination, they substituted the universal possibility of "woman-identified" behavior.[10] As a popular saying went, "Feminism is the theory, lesbianism is the practice."

In critic Eve Sedgwick's terms, we see the "re-visioning, in female terms, of same-sex desire as being at the very definitional center of each gender, rather than occupying a cross-gender or liminal position between them. Thus women who loved women were seen as more female . . . than those whose desire crossed boundaries of gender. The axis of sexuality, in this view, was not only highly coextensive with the axis of gender but expressive of its most 'heightened essence.' "[11] Through encountering feminism, lesbianism straddled what Sedgwick has called "minoritizing" and "universalizing" strategies, that is, between fixing lesbians as a stable minority group and seeking to liberate the "lesbian" in every woman. Feminism provided the ideological glue that wedded these two sometimes contradictory impulses.

The movement could not have emerged without the second-wave feminist insight that gender roles are socially constructed, or without the gay liberationist application of that insight to sexuality. If the "exchange of women"—compulsory heterosexuality—was the bedrock of the sex/gender system, as Gayle Rubin and others argued, then women who made lives with other women were subverting the dominant order.[12] Jill Johnston and others declared that a "conspiracy of silence" insured that for most women "identity was presumed to be heterosexual unless proven otherwise. . . . There was no lesbian identity. There was lesbian activity." Expressing the feelings of many middle-class women of her generation, Johnston wrote in 1973: "For most of us the chasm between social validation and private needs was so wide and deep that the society overwhelmed us for any number of significant individual reasons. . . . We were all heterosexually identified and that's the way we thought of ourselves, even of course when doing otherwise."[13]

If homophobia on the part of heterosexual feminists and in society at large deterred many women from claiming a lesbian identity, collapsing the distinction between identification and desire minimized stigma and broadened the definition of lesbianism, transforming it into "female bonding," a more inclusive category, with which a larger number of middle-class women could identify. Indeed, there was historical precedent for this vision in the "passionate friendships" common among women of the eighteenth and nineteenth centuries.[14]

Lesbianism represented a sense of connectedness based on mutuality and similarity rather than difference. Ultimately, it was more than simply a matter of sex, poet Judy Grahn declared: "Men who are obsessed with sex are convinced that lesbians are obsessed with sex. Actually, like other women, lesbians are obsessed with love and fidelity."[15] The new, broadened definition of lesbianism resonated with many women who had long experienced their sexuality in relational rather than simply erotic terms, and who considered sexuality a relatively nonsalient aspect of identity and an insufficient basis upon which to organize a mass movement.

Centering lesbianism upon female relationality and identification, these "new lesbians" challenged medicalized conceptions that focused upon gender inversion and masculinized sexual desire. They blurred the boundary between gay and straight women and transformed lesbianism into a normative identity that over time came to have as much—and sometimes more—to do with lifestyle preferences (such as choice of dress or leisure pursuits) and ideological proclivities (anticonsumerist, countercultural identifications) as with sexual desires or practices.

This shift in meaning enabled many women who had never considered the possibility of claiming a lesbian lifestyle to leave their husbands and boyfriends—some for political reasons, others in expression of deeply rooted desires, many for both. It allowed many of those who lived primarily closeted lives to come out and declare their lesbianism openly. Never before had so much social space opened up so quickly to middle-class women who dared to defy deeply held social norms about their proper sexual place. As a result, the group of women who called themselves lesbians became increasingly heterogeneous, at least in terms of sexuality.

Remaking the Self

Historically, there have always been women who have had sexual/ romantic relationships with other women but have not assumed the label "lesbian." There have also been women whose actual sexual desires and practices don't fit the common social definition of lesbian-women, for example, those who identify as lesbian but who are bisexual in orientation and/or practice. There are many possible configurations of the relationship between desire, practice, and identity—many more such configurations than there are social categories to describe them.

Yet popular understandings of lesbianism assume a clear-cut relationship between sexual orientation/behavior and sexual identity. Lesbians are assumed to be women who are attracted exclusively to other women and who claim an identity on the basis of that attraction. But for many women, the relation between sexual orientation, sexual identity, and sexual practice is far from stable or uncomplicated.

Moreover, as I have suggested, such definitions change over time. Particularly before the advent of the lesbian-feminist movement, these definitions were situated primarily within the framework of medical expertise, which fixed lesbianism as a "condition" and made it synonymous with cross-gender, or mannish, attributes. It meant that a woman who took on a lesbian identity needed to overcome extreme social disapproval and formulate a favorable sense of herself that included a "deviant" sexuality.[16] Those who took on this identity during the pre-Stonewall era were more apt to be women who never developed stable identities as heterosexuals.

Often these women either had never had significant sexual and emotional relationships with men, or they related to men only in an effort to hide or deny their lesbianism. One such woman described her coming out in the following terms: "I fell in love with a woman when I was about fifteen or sixteen. I don't know whether I used the term lesbian then; I knew that I loved women, and that was where I was and where I wanted to be. I didn't fall in love with men."[17] In sociologist Barbara Ponse's terminology, she would be considered a "primary" lesbian—someone who identified homosexual feelings in herself before she understood their social significance, who did so at a relatively early age, and who experienced homosexuality less as a choice than as a compulsion. If the "old gay" world was largely comprised of women for whom lesbianism was "primary," lesbian feminists claimed that the pool of potential lesbians was much larger. Young lesbians in the early 1970s universalized the critique of compulsory heterosexuality and emphasized the possibility of coming out or "electing" lesbianism, proclaiming that it was the "feminist solution." Not only was the institution of heterosexuality constructed, activists argued, but so too were heterosexual desires. Because they were constructed, they reasoned, such desires could just as easily be reconstructed.

This fifty-two-year-old woman had been married for twenty-two years. Interviewed in the early 1970s, she described her coming out as follows:

> I began . . . to become involved with women's consciousness-raising groups, and I began to hear . . . of the idea of women being turned on to each other. It was the first time I heard about it in terms of people that I knew. . . . I was receptive but had no previous, immediate history. Like there was a part of me that had been thinking about it, and thinking, "Gee, that sounds like intellectually that's a good idea."[18]

The movement thus brought into the fold many "elective" lesbians like this woman, for whom relationships with men were often significant; some were married, some had long-term relationships with men with whom they felt they were in love and to whom they were sexually attracted. Nevertheless, they "discovered" women as sexual and emotional partners at some point, and came to identify as lesbians. Writing of this period several years later, a longtime activist recalled:

> Those of us who were active in 1971 and 72 witnessed the tremendous influx of formerly heterosexual women into the Lesbian Movement. They came by the thousands. Lesbians of this background now compose the very backbone of the Lesbian Movement. . . . We put the world of men on notice that we were out to give their wives and lovers a CHOICE. We got a bad reputation as "chauvinistic." Lesbian feminism was called an "expansionist philosophy"—meaning that we were out to politically seduce (read: awaken) all women. In the years that have followed, it seems ironic to this old-gay-never-married dyke, that some of the most ardent, anti-straight women . . . were 1971's HOUSEWIVES![19]

The distinction Ponse and others have drawn between "primary" and "elective" lesbians—who differ as to their accounts of the origins of their lesbianism, the meaning of lesbian activity and lesbian feelings, and their age of entry into the lesbian community—thus suggests very different paths through which women have arrived at lesbian identity. Drawing upon object-relations psychoanalytic theory, Beverly Burch argues that the "early" or primary lesbian incorporates a greater sense of "differentness" within her sense of self than the "later-developing" or elective lesbian.

"Primary" lesbians generally have to struggle to establish a positive sense of themselves as lesbians during adolescence, when other issues of social identity are being negotiated. Women who come out later in life, on the other hand, may have already negotiated other issues of social identity before they assume a "deviant" sexual identity. They may have established a sense of self as relatively "normal," at least in terms of their sexuality. Taking on a lesbian identity at this stage, says Burch, means coping with somewhat different issues. It may involve a sense of loss in terms of acceptability and social ease, but losing something one has had is an experience quite different from never having had it."[20]

Moreover, as I have suggested, historical evidence shows these sexual choices are shaped by class position. Women who joined public lesbian subcultures before Stonewall were more likely to be of working-class origin, due at least in part to the fact that they tended to be less concerned with losing social status. Women encouraged to "elect" lesbianism through exposure to feminism, by contrast, were more likely to come from the middle classes. With time, these and other preexisting, largely unspoken, differences in identity would pose thorny problems for the process of collectivization. Smashing the categories, it turned out, was a much simpler task than remaking the self.

Border Skirmishes

Twelve hundred women attended the first West Coast Lesbian-Feminist Conference, held in Los Angeles in June 1973. The goal of the conference was to unify lesbian feminists under a common program, but almost immediately the gathering was wracked by internal disagreements over the definition of lesbianism and, by extension, debates over who would be admitted. A male-to-female transsexual guitarist was shouted down by the crowd and prevented from performing. A prominent feminist writer and theorist was criticized for living with a man. Shortly after the conference, one woman's comment was telling: "If there was any point of unity it was that almost all lesbians are conscious of and hopeful for the development and existence of a lesbian-feminist culture/movement."[21] But a unified culture and movement implied a consensus on the meaning of lesbianism that did not exist.

During the early 1970s, such debates about who was a lesbian became commonplace throughout the country—at conferences, at women's music festivals, and within local communities. Border skirmishes around transsexualism, lesbians with boy children, bisexuality, and other issues deeply divided many lesbian events and communities. Symptomatic of the difficulty of defining the category "lesbian," they marked a growing preoccupation with fixing boundaries, making membership more exclusive, and hardening the notion of lesbian "difference."

The movement had earlier tried to broaden the base of lesbianism by loosening the boundaries around the group. But smashing some categories entailed the creation of others; identity politics requires defining an identity around which to mobilize. Boundary-setting became a preoccupation of the movement once it was faced with the challenge of insuring commitment and guarding against disaffection from the ranks, particularly in view of the preexisting differences among women that I earlier identified.

If early lesbian feminism emphasized the fluidity of identity categories and the importance of self-description, with time the definition narrowed:

lesbians were biological women who do not sleep with men and who embrace the lesbian label. If they shared certain values in common, foremost among them was their willingness to have lives apart from men. The growing symbolic importance of the notion of a "women's community" in the mid-to-late 1970s signified the importance of boundary definition.[22] It centered the movement upon a rejection of men and patriarchal society. It claimed that gender is the primary basis of lesbian identity (and that all other divisions are male-imposed), and argued that power was something imposed from without, by men. If power and hierarchy issues surfaced, members of the "women's community" saw this as the residue of patriarchy and male-identification, something that would fade away with time. If women within the community developed heterosexual desires, lesbians in the mid-to-late 1970s tended to see this as a sign that patriarchy had been insufficiently purged.

While the language of the movement was radically constructionist, at least in terms of sexuality, in practice it privileged the "primary" lesbian for whom desire, exclusively lesbian, was congruent with identity. Studying the lesbian community in a medium-sized southern city in the 1970s, Barbara Ponse described the "biographic norm" of lesbian communities as the "gay trajectory," popularly known as "coming out." Lesbians assumed that this process was unidirectional. In the highly politicized milieu of lesbian communities, one did not come out and then "go back in" without suffering the consequences of such a move. Ponse concluded that the fluidity and changeability of both identity and activity at the level of the individual "may elude classification within the frameworks of the paradigms of the lesbian world, which, like the dominant culture, assume a heterosexual-homosexual dichotomy."[23]

The movement also privileged white, middle-class women, for whom lesbianism represented both a sexual choice and an oppositional identity. But for many women of color, as well as white working-class women, the choices were never so clear and unambivalent. Women of color, in particular, often felt that they were forced to pick and choose among identities. Many resisted pressures to make lesbianism their "dominant" or "master" identity.

What was problematic, I believe, was not so much that boundary making took place—for it does in all identity-based movements—but that the discourse of the movement, rooted in notions of authenticity and inclusion, ran so completely counter to it. Lesbian feminism positioned itself as the expression of the aspirations of *all* women. Like other identity-based movements, it promised the realization of individual as well as collective identity, and saw the two as intimately linked. At its best, it provided women with the strength and support to proclaim their desires for one another. It allowed many to withdraw from difficult and often abusive situations and opened up social space never before possible in this country. But at its worst, it hardened the boundaries around lesbian communities, subsumed differences of race, class, and even sexual orientation, and set up rather rigid standards for living one's life.

Dilemmas of Identity

All identity-based movements have a tendency to fall into what Alberto Melucci has termed "integralism," the yearning for a totalizing identity, for a "master key which unlocks every door of reality." Integralism, says Melucci, rejects a pluralist and "disenchanted" attitude to life and encourages people to "turn their backs on complexity" and become incapable of recognizing difference.[24] Indeed, the contemporary sociological and historical literature on lesbian-feminist communities of the 1970s is rife with such observations.[25]

When sociologist Susan Krieger looked at "the dilemmas of identity" posed by a women's community in the Midwest in the mid-1970s, she found that individuals frequently experienced a loss of self, in which they felt either overwhelmed or abandoned by the community. While noting that "all social groups confront their members with this kind of conflict," Krieger admitted that "in some groups"—namely, those in which "the desire for personal affirmation from the group is great, and the complementary desire for assertion of individuality is also strong"— this experience is felt more intensely than in other groups and seems to occur more frequently.[26] Lesbian communities were often characterized by likeness, intimacy, and shared ideological orientation; they comprised women who were highly stigmatized. Krieger surmised that all these things contributed to the seeming difficulties their members had with maintaining their individuality amid pressures to merge and to become one with the community. Often this dynamic caused individuals to become more preoccupied with bolstering their own identities than with achieving political goals and led to internal struggles over who really belonged in the community.

While Krieger focused on gender as the primary basis of similarity within lesbian-feminist communities, one could also add race, class, and personal style to the mix. In many parts of the country, despite their efforts to free themselves from imposed social roles, subcultures often created new ones, prescribing sexual styles, political ideologies, and even standards of personal appearance that relatively few could successfully meet. This had the effect of excluding many women, particularly working-class women of all races, but also women who for any number of reasons may not have felt at home in the movement's countercultural milieu.

Particularly after the mid-1970s, many lesbian-feminist communities, scattered throughout the nation, became increasingly private enclaves. If earlier the movement tried to "smash the categories," substituting for the narrow, overly sexualized definitions of lesbianism a broad, normative definition that welcomed all women into the fold, over time these definitions themselves narrowed and became increasingly prescriptive. It is ironic, perhaps, that the very qualities that were once seen as a boon to the lesbian-feminist movement were coming to be viewed as seeds of its demise. Communities of intimacy, it turned out, were also communities of exclusion.

Individuals troubled by the inability of lesbian feminism to resolve the tension between identity and difference were faced with two basic options: they could reject identity as a basis for politics and strike out on their own, asserting their individual autonomy and personal difference. Or they could reshape identity politics and form new attachments that acknowledged "multiple" allegiances and the partial nature of lesbian identity. Indeed, as I will argue, both trends characterize the current phase of lesbian identity politics.

In the early 1980s, a series of structural and ideological shifts conspired to decenter the lesbian-feminist model of identity. First, the predominantly white and middle-class women who composed the base of the movement aged, underwent various life-cycle changes, and settled into careers and families of various stripes—often even heterosexual ones. Second, a growing revolt emerged from within: women of color, working-class women, and sexual minorities, three separate but overlapping groups, asserted their claims on lesbian identity politics. The next section focuses on these shifts, particularly on how sexual difference posed a challenge to lesbian-feminist constructions of identity.

Sex, Race, and the Decline of the Male Threat?

From the mid-1970s to the early 1980s, the most visible political campaigns undertaken by the feminist movement were against pornography and sexual violence against women. For many women, straight and gay, pornography symbolized male sexuality and power and the fear that stalked women through the ordinary routines of daily life, representing all that was anathema to the vision of a female sexuality that emphasized relationality and reciprocity rather than power and coercion.

But new voices emerged, charging that the radical feminist vision glossed over the real, persistent differences among women and that it idealized women's sexuality and their relationships with one another. These women argued that all the attention upon sexual danger had minimized the possibility of women's pleasure. Highly polarized battles raged in the pages of feminist publications, as "sex radicals" branded their antiporn, anti-s/m opponents as "good girls" and came to a head in the unlikely setting of a conference at Barnard College in 1982, when anti-s/m activists picketed a speak-out on "politically incorrect sex."[27]

These political clashes, which have come to be called the "sex debates" or "porn wars," rarely addressed the subject of lesbianism explicitly. But insofar as these debates called into question the normative basis of the lesbian-feminist model of identity, lesbianism was the salient subtext. Lesbian "sex radicals" charged that somewhere in the midst of defining sexuality as male, and lesbianism as a blow against the patriarchy, desire seemed to drop out of the picture. As "pro-sex" lesbians saw it, in all the talk about "woman identification" the specificity of lesbian existence as a sexual identity seemed to get lost. In response, some tried to reengage with the tradition of pre-Stonewall lesbianism, which they saw as unencumbered by feminist ideological prescriptions and rooted in working-class bar culture and butch-femme roles.[28] A burgeoning sexual literature reasserted the centrality of desire and sexuality in lesbian identity and culture. Rather than making the distinction between male and female sexualities the primary political cleavage (as radical feminists had done), it acknowledged the sexual diversity implicit within the lesbian category and often invoked, symbolically at least, the sexual license of an earlier moment in gay male culture.

For many women, the onset of the AIDS crisis, which occurred nearly simultaneously, made coalition building with gay men an even

Advertisement for General Electric Monogram Collection with a look inside the kitchen of John Dransfield and Geoffrey Ross, a gay couple.

more immediate task. Centering post-Stonewall lesbian identity upon the shared rejection of men and patriarchy, lesbians had earlier disengaged from a gay liberation movement that was largely blind to their needs. But the tide of homophobia unleashed by the AIDS crisis affected lesbians as well as gay men and served at times to sharpen the differences between lesbians and heterosexual women. As the withered body of the person with AIDS replaced the once-pervasive image of the all-powerful male oppressor, the sense of male threat that underlay lesbian-feminist politics diminished further.

Lesbians in many urban centers joined the ranks of such predominantly gay male organizations as ACT UP and Queer Nation, which engaged in public actions across the nation to increase lesbian/ gay visibility and puncture the "heterosexual assumption." Others attempted to construct sexualized subcultures that took their cue from an earlier era of gay male sexual experimentation. There were more co-ed gay bars, social events, and institutions. The new identifications between lesbians and gay men extended to personal style as well: clothing, music, and other forms of consumption.

By the late 1980s, even if relatively few women were directly touched by these developments, their effects could be felt in many lesbian communities. The break was largely, though not entirely, generational. An emergent lesbian politics acknowledged the relative autonomy of gender and sexuality, sexism and heterosexism. It suggested that lesbians shared with gay men a sense of "queerness," a nonnormative sexuality that transcends the binary distinction homosexual/ heterosexual to include all who feel disenfranchised by dominant sexual norms—lesbians and gay men, as well as bisexuals and transsexuals.[29]

As a partial replacement for "lesbian and gay," the term "queer" attempted to separate questions of sexuality from those of gender. But in terms of practice, this separation was incomplete. The new coexistence of gay men and women was often uneasy: ACT UP and Queer Nation chapters in many cities were marred by gender (and racial) conflicts. The new "co-sexual" queer culture could not compensate for real, persistent structural differences in style, ideology, and access to resources among men and women. This recurring problem suggested that while the new queer politics represented the assertion of a sexual difference that could not be assimilated into feminism, neither could gender be completely subsumed under sexuality. Despite their apparent commonalities, lesbians and gay men were often divided along much the same lines as heterosexual women and men.[30]

A less noisy but no less significant challenge to lesbian feminism came through the assertion of racial and ethnic identifications. At conferences and national meetings, women of color argued for the importance of acknowledging the divisions of race and class, which had long been subsumed in the interest of building a unified culture and movement. A series of influential anthologies challenged the feminist belief in the primacy of the sex/gender system and led to the development of autonomous black, Asian, and Latina lesbian-feminist organizations.[31]

If lesbian feminism often presented itself as a totalizing identity that would subsume differences of race, class, and ethnicity and pose a united front against patriarchal society, these challenges pointed toward an understanding of lesbianism as situated in a web of multiple oppressions and identities. Lesbians of color and lesbian sex radicals questioned the belief that lesbian life could ever stand completely outside of or apart from the structures of the patriarchal culture. They problematized the once uncontested relationship between lesbianism and feminism. And they shifted lesbian politics away from its almost exclusive focus upon the "male threat," toward a more diffuse notion of power and resistance, acknowledging that lesbians necessarily operate in a society marked by inequalities of class and race as well as of gender and sexuality.

Seventies Questions for Nineties Women

Some might interpret the scenario I have painted of the increasing spatial and ideological fragmentation of lesbian communities and the currently contested nature of the relationship between feminism and lesbianism as indicative of a "postfeminist" era. Certainly, the series of cultural shifts I have described break with an earlier moment of lesbian-feminist politics. They result in large part from the difficulties lesbians have faced in mobilizing around a sense of group difference, even as these cultural shifts are made possible by the construction of that very sense of difference.

I have argued that the lesbian-feminist movement found itself torn between two projects: between fixing lesbians as a stable minority group, and seeking to liberate the "lesbian" in every woman. As I suggested earlier, feminism provided the ideological glue that wedded these two sometimes contradictory impulses. It redefined lesbianism in more expansive, universal terms, constructing a lesbian culture founded upon resistance to gender and sexual norms. While it opened up the possibility of lesbian identification to greater numbers of women than ever before, it could ultimately only achieve unity through exclusion, though a gender separatism that hardened the boundaries around it.

Younger women today are trying to carve out lesbian identities at a moment when many of the apparent certainties of the past have eroded —the meaning of lesbianism, the relationship between lesbianism and feminism, and the political potential of identity politics. They recognize that while marginalized groups construct symbolic fictions of their experience as a means of self-validation, and that compulsory heterosexuality necessitates the construction of a lesbian/gay identity, identities are always simultaneously enabling and constraining. As one twenty-three-year-old New Yorker recently told me: "What I am is in many ways contradictory. I don't belong in the straight world, though I'm a white girl. . . . But I don't really belong in the feminist world because I read lesbian porn and refuse to go by a party line. On the other hand, I think I'm a feminist. It's a set of contradictions." Even as they integrate feminism into their daily lives, she and others reject the view that lesbianism is a feminist act, that any sexual identity is more authentic or unmediated than any other. In this sense, they are in fact "postfeminist," if that term is descriptive of the consciousness of women and men who, while holding their distance from feminist identities or politics, have been profoundly influenced by them. They simultaneously locate themselves inside and outside the dominant culture and feel a loyalty to a multiplicity of different projects, some of them feminist oriented, others more queer identified, many of them incorporating elements of both critiques. And they see themselves, and their lesbianism, as located in a complex world marked by racial, class, and sexual divisions.

Indeed, this indeterminacy is deeply troubling to many women, particularly those who once held out the hope of constructing a lesbian-feminist movement that was culturally and ideologically unified. But I want to suggest that today's more "decentered" movement may present new democratic potential. Many women who felt excluded by an earlier model of identity now feel that they can finally participate in politics on their own terms. As clashes over feminist issues such as abortion, sexual harassment, and pay equity heat up over the coming years, as they are likely to do, lesbians will be on the front lines, as they have always been—only this time they will be out as lesbians. Some will continue to organize primarily as lesbians. Others will continue to participate in movements that are not necessarily feminist at all, but have greater visibility than ever before.

This suggests that any unified conception of lesbian identity is reductive and ahistorical; collective identity is a production, a process. Stuart

Hall's comments on ethnic resistance are relevant here. In any politicization of marginal groups, he says, there are two phases. The first comprises a rediscovery of roots and implies a preoccupation with identity. Only when this "local" identity is in place can a consideration of more global questions and connections begin.[32] For many lesbians in this country, the first phase of this movement has already occurred. We may now be seeing the arrival of the second.

PART II

Shamed Again

*(Or a funny thing happened on the
way to the sexual revolution . . .)*

For a long time, we operated under the notion that gays and
lesbians were marching forward, making progress in the battle for inclusion, rights and cultural influence. Despite the ravages of AIDS, for
many of us it was easier to be queer than ever before. We had built
a powerful commercial infrastructure and a lively alternative to mainstream hetero-culture, based on the quintessentially American notion
that people could start all over again from scratch, that they could
make new lives, new families, even new societies by reinventing themselves. Over time, our communities grew, became more diversified and
visible, and branched out in a thousand unforeseen directions. And the
primary opposition to this seemingly unstoppable process of liberalization was little more than a mild irritant, a group of rag tag zealots who
showed up at gay rights marches spouting bible verses.

How terribly wrong we were. In the early 1990s, when I moved
north to Oregon, I met people who were desperately trying to respond
to the right, which was busily organizing in churches throughout the
state, assembling a well-oiled machine to oppose lesbian/gay civil rights.
While the national organizations of the right shied away from sexual politics, fearing it would divide their constituencies, organized homophobia
moved to the grassroots, and politicized religious conservatives ran can-
didates for school boards, sponsored local ballot measures against gay
rights, abortion and comprehensive sex education, and successfully took
over the Republican Party in many states. Dozens of antigay measures
appeared on state and local ballots across the country, some of which
garnered considerable support.

It was only then that I realized that conservatism wasn't an aberration, a fringe movement filled with conspiracy theory-spouting, bible-

thumping crackpots—though it certainly had its share of them. It was a movement steadily growing in numbers and power, at least since the late 1950s, when thousands of "ordinary" Americans—middle-class suburbanites dedicated to the notion that government and moral laxness are the root of all evil—were hard at work in the trenches, steadily building a culture and a political movement. It was a potent conservative cocktail—a movement dedicated to not only untrammeled modernization but also to turn-back-the-clock notions of morality, built upon evangelical Christianity, antipathy toward government, and privatized, sprawling landscapes.

In the 1990s, we began to witness some of the fruits of their efforts: a burgeoning network of evangelical Protestant churches politicized around abortion and homosexuality, unified by a national right-wing citizens lobby that was making powerful inroads into statewide Republican party organizations. In hundreds of communities nationwide, homosexuality became a catalyst for bitter conflict, as parents organized to squelch discussions of homosexuality in the classroom, and communities tried to prohibit civil rights for sexual minorities. In Oregon, I heard stories about the shock that some people experienced when their neighbors placed signs on their front lawn supporting antigay ordinances, and families who stopped their children from playing with kids whose parents stood on the other side of the issue. Few people, it seemed, knew any flesh and blood gay people, yet they became convinced that granting them civil rights was tantamount to tolerating the rising tide of individualism and social dislocation they saw all around them.

In 1997, when I began to interview people in a small community that had been split apart by the issue of gay rights, I met people who considered themselves to be good citizens and upstanding family members, who felt threatened by an invisible menace lurking in their community, a menace given a name and face by a grassroots organization and a rising evangelical movement. The lumber mills that had once formed the economic base of their town had all but closed, local stores had shut down, and young people were forced to move away to find jobs. I met people who were troubled by huge changes occurring all around them: the quickening pace of marital breakups, the decline of small communities, and the fact that faceless corporations seem to have more and more power to make decisions about what they will eat, how they will work, and where they will live. Some people became active against gay rights in order to try to do something to hold off these confusing challenges—

or so they thought. They truly wanted the best for their children and believed they were acting in their interest. For many of them, an image of youthful innocence and purity provided a feeling of security, of hope for the future, of faith in a world unsullied by unpleasant conflicts, and looming uncertainty.

Yet a number of things struck me as rather curious. For one thing, in many, if not most of the small communities where these campaigns gained the most support, there were few if any out gays and lesbians jockeying for rights and political power. Sociologists tell us that if the stigmatized respect the boundaries set up by the dominant group, stability is assured; if shamed and stigmatized, they are tolerated. But once the stigmatized begin to challenge dominant notions of normality, efforts to reinforce the supposed distinctions between the two groups quickly follow. If gays and lesbians begin to move toward normalization, becoming more openly visible members of churches, schools, and communities, and populating, in some small measure, the media airwaves, conservatives would mobilize against them. But few antigay activists I met in Oregon had ever met someone they knew to be homosexual: theirs, in other words, was a phantom enemy.

There were other curious aspects to these campaigns, it seemed to me as I sat in the spare living room of a timber worker who told me that he regularly donates money to the wealthy Heritage Foundation, which opposes public restrictions on corporate power, though he fears that he may lose his job due to corporate downsizing. Why would a timber worker who is on the edge of financial disaster give money to a wealthy foundation, or give a hoot about gay rights? Over the past twenty years, the conservative movement has managed to expand its base to so many people who share so few of the privileges of its core constituency of affluent Americans. In the parlance of political strategists, homophobia has been used as a "wedge" designed to bridge the split between economic conservatives who seek market reform and social conservatives whose goal is moral reform. Homophobic rhetoric attacks the status of lesbians and gays as a minority group deserving equal rights under the law, charging they are an undeserving special interest group that has won "special rights" by manipulating the system.

When I met them one on one, many of these righteous Christian soldiers seemed far less sure of themselves than their actions, and public pronouncements, would have suggested. They were vulnerable people, unable to come to terms with their own sense of shame, who displaced it onto others, as I discuss in "Revenge of the Shamed." Shame develops out of the infantile demand for control over the world, and unwillingness to accept neediness, and while it is often fused with antisex feelings, the source of shame is broader. Hoping to find a surrogate safety by bonding together against a stigmatized group, in this case gays and lesbians, conservative activists invoked cherished moral values they believe are under siege, but their own shame and their desire to hide from it, fueled their activism in large part. Antigay campaigns play on the fear of dependence and vulnerability, offering up false promises of control, self-restraint, and social segregation as the answer.

At the same time, antigay crusaders on the right have usurped the left's rhetoric of victimhood, arguing that *they*, not gays and lesbians, are the real victims of discrimination who deserve sympathy and redress. This strategy became clear when supporters of gay rights sponsored a travelling exhibit on Anne Frank, equating anti-Semitism with homophobia, in order to gain sympathy and public support. They argued that gays are a quasi-ethnic group, much like Jews, Italian Americans, and even African Americans, and like any ethnic group, they deserve civil rights protections and "tolerance." Conservative Christians responded that they were the rightful inheritors of the legacy of anti-Semitism. "Whose Memories, Whose Victimhood?" addresses the ways the memory of the Holocaust has been used—first by gays and lesbians, to claim moral authority by association with Holocaust victims, homosexuals among them, and then by conservative Christians, to deflect such claims and claim moral superiority for themselves.

In culture war battles such as these, the loop of blame and counterblame is seemingly endless, the emotional battles exaggerated by namecalling and by the media's search for explosive imagery. What could be more explosive than the image of Europe's murdered millions? Like others, I have been dismayed by tendencies, on the right and left, to use the Holocaust as a metaphor for evil. In a world in which morality is increasingly difficult to define, such language seems unavoidable: the Holocaust has emerged as the "ultimate evil" against which our relativistic culture defines itself. But some claims to victimhood are more justifiable than others: the Christian right's use of Holocaust imagery distorts the historical record and exploits the memory of the victims, my Jewish ancestors among them. Even gay claims to Holocaust memory are often overstated, I argue; we must be judicious in using incendiary language.

Such discussions are at least partly about twists and turns in identity politics, and how groups define themselves and make claims on that basis. The days when one could use the term "lesbian community" or even "gay community" and see that as an adequate way of describing where and how we live are over, as we saw in the first part of the book. The diversification of sexual identities has meant the decline of normative conceptions of sexual identity. Of course, the American lesbian/gay movement has long been divided between two impulses: the desire for citizenship and the desire for transgression, as historian Jeffrey Weeks once put it so well.[1] We have a citizenship movement that seeks civil rights protections, utilizing an ethnic understanding of homosexuality that imagines gay people as a fixed category that has little to do with heterosexuality. On the periphery of this is a movement for sexual transgression, which engages in in-your-face actions to deconstruct this ethnic understanding. Each has generated separate language, strategies, epistemologies, and understandings of homosexuality. The former seeks inclusion in the social order; the latter fundamentally challenges it. The former emphasizes the fight for equality (we're just like you and we want the same rights); the latter emphasizes difference (we're here, we're queer get used to it). Today, these tendencies toward political fragmentation have met a formidable enemy: the Christian right.

The attacks of the right have done more to unify gays and lesbians around the shared goal of lesbian and gay civil rights than any other development ever could, and the citizenship movement is gaining ground, as the groundswell of support for same-sex marriage suggests. The issue of marriage, for better or worse, has captured the imagination of many lesbians and gay men who never before saw themselves as activists. These are men and women who simply want to be considered part of the American mainstream. Their fight for inclusion in what is fundamentally a traditional institution is what makes the campaign simultaneously radical and conservative. Same-sex marriage advocates are saying to the world: our relationships are as legitimate as yours. In doing so, they're affirming the dominant view that some (but not all) sexual relationships deserve to be made legitimate. At the same time, they're expanding the definition of what kinds of relationships can rightly be seen as legitimate.

Still, we should be mindful of who gets left out if—and when— gay relationships enter what Gayle Rubin once called the "charmed circle" of legitimate sexuality.[2] Two decades ago, Rubin predicted that gender-conforming homosexuals, masculine-seeming men and feminine-acting women, in long-term committed relationships would become the eventual standard against which all other gays and lesbians would be measured, and that those who failed to conform to this standard would be meted out and punished. She was writing at a time when feminists were wracked by splits over pornography, sado-masochism, when gays and lesbians were coming to see their status as a kind of quasi-ethnic identity rather than a radical challenge to the rest of society, and imagining assimilation into the dominant culture as the answer to antigay prejudice.

At times, it seems that Rubin's predictions have largely come true. A few years ago, the Human Rights Campaign, one of the most influential gay/lesbian rights organizations, placed an ad in *USA Today* that featured a white lesbian couple, Jo and Teresa, with their three young children. The caption read: "A marriage license: Good for this family. Good for every family." Jo and Teresa have been together nineteen years and certainly deserve the kinds of protections that marriage offers. They are, as writer Andrew Sullivan puts it, "virtually normal."

For Sullivan, marriage should be the gay community's central concern, because it is the political equivalent of "coming out." Because homosexuality is associated with shame in Western societies, Sullivan explains, "the gay teenager learns . . . that that which would most give him meaning is mostly likely to destroy him in the eyes of others." Shame, in turn, leads to "distinctions between . . . sexual desire and . . . emotional longing . . . and to . . . anonymous and promiscuous sex than . . . committed relationships." But this promiscuous sexual ethic is, writes Sullivan, "infantilizing and liberating at the same time" and deepens the divide between gay and straight worlds.[3] Lesbian and gay subcultures, in other words, nurture sexual norms that distance gay and lesbian Americans from mainstream society.

In contrast to this shame-based sexuality of the lesbian and gay subculture, Sullivan argues, marriage is "noble" and "ennobling." Marriage would be personally and socially beneficial, according to Sullivan, because it would re-couple sex and intimacy (especially for gay men), and because it would admit gay men and lesbians into civilization's most civilizing institution. Marriage, notes Sullivan, "is the only political and cultural and spiritual institution that can truly liberate us from the shackles of marginalization and pathology." The right to marry, he suggests, would make family values lesbian and gay values, and mend the cultural divide that separates homosexuals and heterosexuals.

There is some truth to this, to be sure. Many gays and lesbians believe that the only thing standing between them and normality is their sexuality, which in the grand scheme of things is something quite insignificant. But the campaign for same-sex marriage, and the promotional efforts that buttress this position, which typically feature white middle class gay families who conform in most respects to the American norm, may also do us a disservice. They tend to homogenize and sanitize the great diversity of gay and lesbian life, downplaying the ways we differ from heterosexual families and in fact offer an alternative to heteronormativity. Moreover, some suggest, this politics of normalization reflects residual feelings of shame. "The queer stigma covers us all, at least in some contexts," Michael Warner wrote in *The Trouble with Normal*, published in 1999. "As a consequence, people try to protect their identities by repudiating mere sex."[4] Rather than defending homosexuality, he suggests, we should be targeting sexual shame.

This more radical position has been drowned out by the groundswell of support for same-sex marriage, which has only increased in response to right-wing campaigns against it. In "Make Room for Daddy," I ask: what are the sources of continuing antipathy toward homosexuality, and what might they tell us about changing forms of American masculinity? The essay documents some emergent homophobias circulating among conservative activists in campaigns against gay rights and, ten years later, against same-sex marriage. As feminist critiques of traditional masculinity make their way into conservative rhetoric and as men struggle to define a role that maintains male authority without sounding overly authoritarian, I show how new forms of homophobia have emerged that are compatible with conservatives' quest to be seen as "compassionate" protectors of the family.

The old certainties are falling away, a fact that is troubling to many people. In a world where the private is often public, and many of the old scripts are being rewritten, it's no longer possible to imagine that one will spend one's life living with one person, have only one job, or be able to exert total control over children's media consumption. This troubled my mother, who grappled with my choices—and my quest for independence—with a mixture of envy and revulsion. My mother was not a religious Christian, or even a particularly doctrinaire Jew, but she shared many of the fears that religious conservatives have recently given voice to, including the fear of loss of control over their children's hearts and minds, and their own sense of vulnerability. Zygmunt Bauman calls these "ambient fears"—capturing the sense in which our insecurities seem to rarely have a name or an explicit location. Instead, they float freely, leaving us feeling anxious and powerless.[5]

Yet if the truth be told, the list of contradictions embedded in conservatives' sexual politics is very long indeed. They rail against sex education, saying that condoms don't work, and call for abstinence-only education programs—which increase the chances of engaging in sex without protection, as studies have proven. They condemn extramarital sexuality, but practice little of the personal restraint they preach, as evidenced by numerous sex scandals involving preachers and conservative elected officials. They fume against the sexualization of America, but do little if anything to regulate an economy that ceaselessly transforms all manner of things, including bodies and pleasures, into potential sources of commercial value. They speak out against the sexualization of society and yet speak endlessly about sex, publicizing the very behaviors that they are trying to root out, much like the Victorians before them.

And when all is said and done, social conservatives fail to represent most Americans' views, and yet declare that they do. Decades ago, it may have been possible (though not easy) to compartmentalize one's life, and go to work, leave one's "private" life at home, and banish pregnant teachers, or lesbians and gay men from school classrooms. But this hiding took its toll, shattering families and communities, and most people would not really want to go back to it. The fact is that today, most heterosexuals are much more aware of the fact that sexuality comes in many different varieties. Even many kids know this. Living openly as a lesbian or a gay man, or as an unwed mother, need no longer entail estranging oneself from one's family, friends, and community. Most Americans believe these changes are for the good.

Nonetheless, social conservatives are doing their damnedest to "restore" supposedly timeless standards of behavior, and bring back shame as a vehicle for social control. By seeking to hide away aspects of human behavior that some find troubling, this strategy offers them temporary relief at best, and harms others in the process.

6

Revenge of the Shamed
The Christian Right's Emotional Culture War

The activists of the Christian right share a certainty that things have gone radically wrong and that traditional values, based upon a "strict father" morality, are the only sure way to correct those wrongs.[1] Their worldview is an extension of their image of the good family: good families value strength and obedience and do not tolerate weakness and dependence; they develop self-discipline in children by using rewards and punishments. Punishment is nurturing in that it teaches discipline, self-reliance, and respect for authority. In contrast, self-indulgence and lack of discipline lead to poverty, drug addiction, and a host of other problems—including homosexuality. They wish to restore rules, order, authority—structures that give shape and meaning to a world out of bounds and guide individual actions in a world of bewildering choices and changes. They wish to construct a conception of the world that is secure, unambiguous, where there are good people and bad people, and where they are clearly on the side of the good and the true.

Christian conservatives defend their moral visions in terms of religious beliefs: they understand truth in terms of an external, definable, and transcendent authority. They hold fairly consistent views on a cluster of issues such as abortion, gay rights, and welfare reform. And they define themselves against those who see truth as constantly in flux. On one level, this is evidence of a "culture war."[2] But on another level, their activism is more than a quest to repair the world, and transform culture: It is an effort to repair themselves, and in this it is a deeply personal quest. Conservative activists are not unique in this sense: social movements seek to change the world, gain concessions from the state, or alter the way that people view particular problems, but they almost

Cartoon by Matt Wuerker.

always embody expressive goals as well. By joining with other like-minded souls, individuals become activists to affirm both themselves and their vision of the world.[3]

While Christian conservatives are fond of speaking of their motives as a selfless commitment to higher authorities—family, nation, God—their activism offers the hope of self-realization as well. This quest for meaning encompasses emotional as well as cognitive dimensions as they try to construct a positive sense of themselves and their families as strong and independent, in contrast to weak, shameful others. Their activism is a reparative act.

The Emotional Culture War

In the early 1990s, dozens of small Oregon communities became the site of bitter battles over the issue of homosexuality when the Oregon Citizens Alliance (OCA), then an affiliate of the Christian Coalition, sponsored a ballot measure that sought to deny civil rights protections to lesbians and gay men.[4] A toned-down version of an earlier statewide measure that was narrowly defeated, this ballot measure brought the issue of homosexuality to rural Oregon in an unprecedented way. Neighbors debated with neighbors, husbands and wives disagreed, people wrote letters to the local paper, and homeowners placed signs on their lawns. At the time, I found the whole thing curious. Why did sexuality become such a salient issue in towns where lesbians and gay men were virtually absent, or at least invisible? How did various sectors of the targeted communities respond to this campaign?

To find out, I looked at what people said publicly in the debate about homosexuality in one small Oregon town during this period, tracking newspaper articles, letters to the editor, and published flyers and pamphlets. I also interviewed people who participated in these debates to try to figure out what homosexuality symbolized for people on a deeper level—both for those who sought to legislate against gay rights, for those who sought to defend these rights, and for those who were ambivalent on the matter. Among these interviewees were a number of local activists against gay rights, members of the OCA.[5] I wanted to "get into their heads" and figure out who they were, how they understood their world, and how a Christian conservative organization channels their discontent toward political ends.

During the course of my interviews, some people I met wept with joy in my presence, recounting how they found the Lord, and spinning elaborate tales of apocalyptic end-times. It quickly became clear to me that this was a movement with profound emotional dimensions. As sociologist James Jasper suggests, "Protest always combines strategic purpose, pleasures and pains in the doing, and a variety of emotions that both motivate and accompany action."[6] Recent literature on social movements has looked at such topics as the role of emotion in constructing collective identities and understandings of grievances and opportunities in motivating activism, and in creating a sense of community within social movements; the mobilization of emotions in the process of becoming a movement participant; and the emotional culture, rituals, work and rules of social movements—what one might call the "politics of feeling."[7]

Yet surprisingly little has been written about how the right taps into emotional needs. This is surprising in view of an earlier tradition of research that examined the psychological dimensions of right-wing activism, seeing such movements as an irrational playing out of paranoid fantasies or as disorganized, relatively spontaneous "panics."[8] Certainly, many movements embody irrational dimensions. But moral movements such as the contemporary Christian right, much like their counterparts on the left, are much more complex, and more organized, than this. We must move beyond the view of emotions and fantasy as "an unbridled irrationalism without any logic," writes cultural critic Linda Kintz.[9] Emotions do possess a logic, and movements give shape and public voice to those emotions.

The Logic of Emotions

Individuals come to know themselves through interactions with others; the self is a social construct.[10] It should come as no surprise that emotions, both positive and negative, are inseparable from social interactions. Individuals are continuously involved in a quest to abide by "feeling rules" in order to "protect face" and minimize the public display of negative emotions.[11]

Sociologist Thomas Scheff suggests that shame, a widespread, negative emotion, is the "premier social emotion," influencing all sorts of social interactions, often in unacknowledged ways. Shame differs from guilt—"something specific about which the self is critical."[12] In shame, "criticism or disapproval seems to emanate from "the other" and to envelop the whole self." It is the "social emotion" that arises from monitoring of one's own actions and viewing oneself from the standpoint of others.[13] In shame, hostility against the self is "experienced in the passive mode," causing individuals to feel "small, helpless and childish," vulnerable, victimized, rejected, passive, and not in control. Psychoanalytic literature suggests that individuals with soft self-boundaries, who are highly conscious of themselves in relation to others, are most prone to shame, and since shame is a painful emotion, the result of the perception of negative evaluations of the self by others, it tends to hide from view.[14]

There are two different types of shame: overt shame, in which an individual says "I am ashamed," where one's emotions are relatively accessible, and therefore less potent and destructive; and "bypassed shame," which begins with a perception of the negative evaluation of self where the individual is overly conscious of his/her self-image from the other's viewpoint. However, unlike the markers of overt, undifferentiated shame, which are often flagrant and obvious, those of bypassed shame may be subtle and covert. They include thought and speech that "takes a speeded up but repetitive quality" which might be seen as "obsessive." Typically, psychoanalyst Helen Lewis says, "Individuals repeat a story or series of stories, talking rapidly and fluently, but not quite to the point. They complain of endless internal replaying of a scene in which they felt criticized or in error." And they are distracted. Both types of shame create rigid and distorted reactions to reality, but because bypassed shame tends to be ignored it is becomes exceedingly destructive. The shamed person "avoids the shame before it can be completely experienced, through rapid thought, speech, or actions."[15] And she/he compensates for shame by displaying incessant thought, speech and/or action, and frequently by shows of "overt hostility" and retaliation.

My interviews suggest that the emotion of shame, particularly bypassed shame, figures prominently in the narratives of Christian conservative activists. Though my small sample makes any claims speculative —and I would not go so far as to suggest that there is a monolithic Christian right personality type—the role that shame plays in the emotional dispositions of the Christian right activists I spoke with seems undeniable. To make this argument, I provide examples of some recurring dynamics between myself and those I interviewed.

My second claim is that religious right organizations frame their appeals in order to mobilize shameful emotions toward political ends. In this the religious right is not unique. Indeed, during the past three decades, one of the primary goals of the lesbian/gay liberation movement has been to encourage people to "come out" and declare their sexual identifications proudly and publicly as a means of countering the shame and secrecy associated with homosexuality in our culture. The Christian right, in contrast, mobilizes around a felt sense of shame in its constituency, promising the hope of alleviating it, but its strategy of targeting other shamed populations (such as lesbians and gay men) in order to transform shame into rage provides temporary relief at best.

"They're Pointing Fingers at Us"

"I'm one of those nasty right wing nuts," says sixty-five-year-old Jeri Cooksson facetiously.[16] She distrusts me, sees me as an outsider, someone who's out to make her and her fellow activists look bad, yet at the same time she is pleased, flattered that I'm taking the time to ask for her opinions. Despite her initial hesitation to talk with me, Jeri held forth for several hours. "You know I don't usually talk to people like you," she tells me. "I don't think a whole lot of those people up at the university." For Jeri, university teachers are liberal, morally lax secular humanists who can't be trusted. She wonders whether I will portray her as a shrill, intolerant old biddy. Like most of the other activists I interviewed, she is guarded, leery of my intentions.

Though I did not originally set out to consider the field of emotions in relation to these interviews, in the course of speaking with my subjects, I was quickly struck by several recurring dynamics: their tendency to speak rapidly and obsessively, to the point where I could barely get a word in edgewise; their tendency to avert their eyes while they interacted with me; their unwillingness to openly acknowledge feelings of embarrassment; and their overriding feelings of victimization. These interactions led me to consider whether deep emotions might be at play, emotions that go far beyond the standard feelings of stress and anxiety that accompany many interview settings.

Sally Humphries, a forty-five-year-old mother of two, said in the middle of our interview, "I just feel beet red. I'm not an expert on any of this stuff, you know"—a response that in itself was not all that surprising in view of the fact that Sally, who had never finished high school, was talking one-on-one for the first time in her life (to her knowledge) with someone who held a doctorate. Still, at several points during the interview, she seemed overly concerned with what I thought of her and told me that she worried that I might think she "is crazy." Often during the course of these interviews, individuals exhibited thought and speech which took a speeded-up, repetitive, almost obsessive character. For example, in telling me that Christian right activists were labeled as "Nazis" during their Oregon campaign against gay rights, Erica Williams trailed off onto a discussion of a job she once held in Alaska.

> What they were doing is what the Nazis have done. They started with name calling. They didn't say, you're an evil person, you're taking all of our money. And they may not have ever had anything to do with anybody's money. And that's the way it began. The job I had in Alaska, after I was healed. I came outside, and my dear sister, now dead, could

never just say hello or goodbye. Somebody called her because they had her telephone number and asked if I would like this job as a historian. So she called me in Tucson and I came and we had this wonderful talk.

Erica Williams was an extreme case of the tendency of individuals to "spill over" a series of unorganized feelings and ideas. But when I observed variations of these patterns in nearly all of my interviews with religious conservatives, I began to wonder why this might be the case. What was I observing? Was it the function of the interview setting, the length of the interview, the subject matter, or my interviewees' psychological make-up?[17]

Eventually, I came to recognize many of these recurring dynamics as markers of shame. In her therapeutic practice, Helen Lewis noticed that shamed persons have a propensity to "spill over" relatively unorganized feelings and ideas and to repeat a story or series of stories, talking rapidly and fluently, but not quite to the point.[18] During the course of my interviews with religious conservatives, I became, analogous to a therapist, the person through which my subjects acted out their feelings of shame, and played out their "internal" conversations. Since Christian conservative activists define themselves against secular humanist elites, whom they believe to be destroying the nation's moral fabric, I became, by virtue of my academic position, a representative of that population and therefore the perfect foil against which they could define themselves.[19] This was less evident in *what* people said than by *how* they said it; the different behavioral cues in the course of our interactions were as important as the actual content of our conversations.

Psychoanalytic accounts suggest that the experience of shame often occurs in the form of imagery, of looking or being looked at. Shame "may also be played out in imagery of an internal auditory colloquy in which the whole self is condemned by the other," according to Helen Lewis.[20] Women may be more prone to shame because of their greater relationality and feelings of powerlessness. During the course of our interview, women were more likely to ask me if I thought they were "making any sense," whether they were "giving me what I wanted," whether they were being coherent. When Sally Humphries, who had just finished telling me about how she became "born again," became ashamed of what she had told me, worrying that it might signify that she is crazy, she implicated me as a participant in her "private theater."[21] As a witness to the subject's shame I became a shaming agent myself.

When asked how she would describe her religious beliefs, Erica Williams replied: "I'm a very conservative, Bible-believing Christian, one of those 'mean-spirited' ones." When I asked her if that is how she considers herself, she replied: "Well, that's what they describe people who are very conservative Christians: mean spirited." Which people? I asked her. "The people in the press, people around town," she replied. Has anyone in town ever called her these things? "Not to my face, no. But I'm sure they say it in private," she replied.

Christian conservative activists believe they are the innocent victims of numerous injustices. Living in an ostensibly secular society, they believe they are persecuted for their beliefs, as the following exchange suggests:

> *Craig Miller*: "Just because I believe in Jesus Christ, I don't think anyone should be pointing their finger at me."
> *Interviewer*: Is someone pointing their finger?
> *Craig*: Yeah, the left is very much doing that, you know?
> *Interviewer*: Who in particular?
> *Craig*: Everyone.

Similarly, when asked to describe the Oregon Citizens Alliance, Barney Wooten replied: "Mostly conservative, traditional-values people—we've been enormously demonized in this state. They label us as 'hateful' or 'bigoted' or 'narrow-minded.'" These activists frequently used the word "they" to refer to their enemies: *they* do this; *they* think that; *they* have an "agenda"; *they* are trying to "indoctrinate" people—responses that attest to the feeling that they are being victimized by a liberal, secular society.

It is true that Christian conservatives are sometimes vilified by the left and mocked by the media. Christian conservative views do not play well in a society steeped in the liberal pluralist we're-all-different ethos, an ethos consonant with commercial media imperatives. As sociologist Joshua Gamson shows in his study of tabloid television, when religious conservatives appear on tabloid talk shows, the "bigot becomes the freak": the audience and hosts often turn against antigay guests such as Paul Cameron, head of the right-wing Family Research Institute, turning those who impose antigay morality into "sick, ungodly, bigoted, un-American freaks."[22] The therapeutic-pluralism-turned-entertainment, he says, is much more sympathetic to liberal approaches to sexual nonconformity than to conservative condemnations of it. I found that a similar dynamic was true of the media in the small Oregon town I studied.

Still, religious conservatives tended to exaggerate the extent of their victimhood, often even staging confrontations that permitted them to claim they were being vilified by the left. For example, in the midst of the campaign against gay rights in Oregon in 1993, members of the OCA appeared in a "diversity awareness" parade in a nearby town, courting confrontation with gay rights supporters by appearing in a float depicting three family-values scenes. As the float went by, thousands of onlookers turned their backs, and a handful of people threw eggs at the float and attempted to block the route. The OCA responded with outrage: "Traditional Christianity is now the Evil Empire for the politically correct."[23] Religious conservatives usurped the left's rhetoric, redefining themselves in the language of interest group liberalism and identity politics, and shifting from an earlier notion of Christians as guardians of the status quo who represent the "moral majority," to the view that they are an oppressed minority comprised of social outcasts.[24] At the same time, they embrace a highly individualistic ethos that denies their feelings of shame.

"I've Fought My Demons on My Own"

The conservative activists I interviewed are people who have struggled against a variety of demons: poverty, drugs, family turmoil, illness; they lack education and sophistication, they misspeak, they use bad grammar, and they have never traveled abroad. And while they acknowledge, at times, having had drug habits, checkered work histories, and relationship problems, their discussions of these problems were always accompanied by explanations of how they struggled to overcome them. In psychoanalytic terms, shame is the opposite of autonomy.[25] To admit weakness is therefore to admit shame, something which few are willing to do.

Thirty-six-year-old Craig Miller talked about his drug addiction. "You know, I've had my share of problems and my share of downfalls in life," he told me. "And I've got no problem with that. Some people have tried to throw those in my face from time to time. And I've got no problems with my past and stuff. I've gotten in trouble with the law. But I learned some lessons from that." Like Craig, the conservative activists I interviewed were, on the whole, working folks who made good, who owned a little property and had some money in the bank. They embrace what sociologist Alan Wolfe calls a "middle class morality," striving to earn enough money so that they feel that their economic fate is in their own hands, but also trying to live by principles such as individual responsibility, the importance of family, obligations to others, and a belief in something outside oneself.[26]

At the same time, they live in an era of "declining fortunes," a time when many Americans' sense of entitlement to the trappings of middle-class life—home ownership, occupational security, mobility on the job, and a decent standard of living—is eroding.[27] Even as the stock market soars to unprecedented levels, and many industries enjoy the fruits of a globalizing economy, few of the postindustrial economy's winners are to be found among these conservative activists. At a time when the fastest growing sectors of the economy require mental labor, they work with their hands.

Jeri Cooksson described her family's changing economic fortunes. "We were poor. Very poor. My husband and I grew up in the depression. I've been very, very poor," she said. Jeri and her husband moved to Oregon from outhern California in 1968, looking for a better place to raise kids and work. Jack was a carpenter, like his father before him. Jeri was a full-time homemaker who occasionally worked outside the home once their kids got older, as a cashier at Sears, selling real estate on the side. She asks me if I have ever seen the movie *The Grapes of Wrath*. When I reply that I have, she tells me that it's the story of her husband's family. "He had a rough life, believe me." When he was in school, she says, his mother and father paid scant attention to his progress. "They never looked at one of his report cards . . . they didn't care. He was a good kid, he worked hard, he never did anything wrong. They didn't care whether he learned to spell or not."

Nonetheless, she told me, "We were happy, and responsible, and we took care of ourselves, and we loved each other. We didn't have a Little Beaver type family, no we didn't. But we stuck together, and we were independent and we took care of ourselves." Jeri shows me around her home, a modest but pleasant 1920s bungalow that she and her husband bought on the cheap and fixed up, located in the middle of town. They just redid the floors, and her husband installed new kitchen cabinets. The house means a lot to them. It is their security in old age, but more than that, it symbolizes how far they have come. When Jack retired they started a small janitorial service, cleaning offices around town. They work one or two nights a week to supplement their social security, and have additional income from two rental properties in town. "We've been very blessed because we earned every dime we got," she says proudly.

Though they had come to enjoy a bit of economic security and respectability, their hold on middle-class status remains tenuous, and there is shame in their voices when they speak of a past that lingers, shaping their sense of themselves. Many individuals held multiple jobs to make ends meet, and anxieties about future employment and about the fate of their children loom. Jeri, for example, spoke at great length about how she felt about the educational system and its declining standards. She believes the schools are selling her grandchildren short and expressed fears about the decline of her small timber community. Yet she reserved most of her wrath for those who are "taking advantage of the system," and collecting welfare at her "family's expense." She and other conservative activists feel themselves to be victimized as hardy individualists who have had to pull themselves up by their bootstraps, living in a society that coddles individuals and squelches self-reliance. Jeri, for example, is firmly committed to the belief in the possibility of upward mobility for all, and the notion that individuals, through hard work, strength, and family solidarity, can help themselves.

> I think, in this country, people should be hired or fired, or rented to or not rented to, or whatever, by whether or not they are going to take care of the property, or not take care of the property, pay the rent . . . not pay the rent, do the job . . . not do the job. If somebody is not capable of making it at the university, I don't think they should be let in, and make a special case for them, or any special privileges because he's black, or white, or green, or purple, or homosexual or not. He either passes the course and he can make it in there, or he can't. And if he can't, set up some special school to prepare him to go into that, you know. I can see where if somebody. . . . You don't have to say okay, this is school for black kids . . . this is school for kids that didn't quite make it in high school and needs a little more education before they go to university. Not lower the standards of the university, see what I mean?

Jeri sees herself as having achieved economic independence alone, with little help from the world beyond. She and other conservative activists feel that all around them, others face the same struggles but suffer few of the consequences; they are being coddled by society, receiving a variety of handouts and entitlements, and this is unfair. A belief in the loss of standards, as in the "dumbing down" of education, is a theme that comes up in conversations with conservative activists again and again. The state has intervened, fulfilling the role that family once played. It takes over the role of educating and socializing the child. It even takes over the role of providing for the child. A system of entitlements benefits the least deserving: the lazy, the slothful, the morally suspect. It has created, in their eyes, a dysfunctional society, filled with people who are trying to get something for nothing, who don't know the value of discipline and hard work. Individuals are no longer given incentives to work hard. Certain groups in society are taking advantage of the flaws in the system, and hardworking people pay the price. On one level, this is fairly predictable conservative rhetoric. But on another level, it plays into feelings of unacknowledged shame, and accounts for the rise of a rhetoric of victimhood that is now pervasive on the right.

The white, predominantly working-class religious conservatives I interviewed tend to see themselves as victims of forces beyond their control yet, at the same time, they are firmly committed to an individualistic ethos which suggests that they hold their destinies in their own hands. To be morally strong, they believe that one must be self-disciplined and self-denying. Moral flabbiness ultimately helps the forces of evil. Carried into the political realm, this moral system—with strength at the top of the list of values—leads to the belief that poverty, drug habits, and illegitimate children can be explained only as moral weakness and any discussion of social causes is irrelevant. Their individualism helps them deny their shame, but it also exacerbates it and prevents them from seeing the structural roots of their malaise. Consequently, they harbor a series of resentments against the world around them.

The Politics of Shame Reduction

In psychoanalytic understandings of shame, the loss of self-esteem drives the person to repair the loss. In Erving Goffman's terms, the individual wishes to "save face."[28] She/he wants to "right" a "wrong" and prevent the loss of self. But rage originating in shame is trapped or becomes "silent rage."[29] Social-movement leaders must articulate this sense of shame in order to transform it into focused rage; so the skilled organizers of the right have tapped into the "bypassed shame" of their audience and devise rhetoric that speaks to it and promises to alleviate it. If religious conservatives' shame is linked to a sense of victimhood, they are drawn to political rhetoric that identifies this victimhood, locates a cause, and offers them the possibility of seeing themselves as strong, independent beings. This rhetoric functions to permit shamed individuals to feel rage and to imagine themselves as members of a collective identity of similarly raged people. In the process, they affirm a sense of themselves as independent, as strong, and as bearers of the truth.

Aided by the belief that they are engaged in "culture war" for the preservation of American morality, Christian right activists imagine themselves as fighting the good fight. One of the best ways of creating solidarity among one's adherents is by using polarizing rhetoric that pits "us" against "them": insiders and outsiders, saints and sinners, purity within and danger and pollution without.[30] By imagining Christians as a group excluded from the culture, OCA leaders stoked the fires of the culture war, transforming a vague, amorphous sense of threat and dis-ease into an attribution of blame. "We're the 82nd airborne of the pro-family movement," Lon Mabon, the OCA's head, proclaimed. "We drop behind the enemy lines. We take the most casualties. We take the most hits."[31] This rhetoric worked on several levels. It played on a masculine fascination with war—what historian Richard Slotkin has called "regeneration through violence"—and the widespread belief in the coming apocalypse.[32] At the same time, it evoked the image of "good Christian soldiers" doing battle for the Lord, an image that appealed to evangelical Christians who saw themselves as excluded from the culture by liberals, homosexuals, and their secular-humanist cronies. And it lent an air of immediacy to the struggle: *they* were winning the battle for the hearts and minds of America. *We* must respond—swiftly and strongly. This is serious business, Mabon told conservative Christians throughout the state, we must not delay.

In an evil-filled world, Christian conservatives believe that only a blessed few can see through the moral murk and point the way to a better understanding of things on Earth. Those who have "a personal relationship with the Lord" are these people. They are the witnesses who testify against the ugliness they see around them, the troubadours who lead us back to our moral sensibilities, before it is too late. A sense of identity is founded upon "intimate familiarity," the re-creation of familial bonds among unrelated intimates.[33] In the pentecostal and charismatic congregations that comprise the base of the religious right, individuals are encouraged to express emotions in prayer. Religious right organizations draw upon these emotional bonds to mobilize believers to take action.

This sense of identity is constructed through opposition to Others—nonbelievers and sinners—over whom the shamed individual can triumph over or humiliate. Since shame is the function of a preoccupation with an "Other," shame reparation or reduction involves retaliation against an Other who, it is suggested, is the shame-agent. For Christian conservatives, homosexuality has during the past fifteen years served as the Other. Christians see gay people—affirming relationships that have no strings attached, no mutual duty and no guarantee of duration—as the antithesis of the good society, the embodiment of a world in which rules, order, self-discipline and stability are severely lacking. Christian Right organizations have sponsored a number of ballot initiatives designed to deny civil rights to lesbians and gay men. In 1994 there were over twenty antigay measures on state and local ballots, many of which garnered considerable support.[34]

In rural Oregon in the early 1990s, the OCA mounted a series of campaigns to amend local charters so that they "shall not make, pass, adopt, or enforce any ordinance, rule, regulation, policy or resolution that extends minority status, affirmative action, quotas, special class status, or any similar concepts, based on homosexuality or which establishes any categorical provision such as 'sexual orientation,' 'sexual preference,' or any similar provision which includes homosexuality."[35] Since the vast majority of these localities had never considered passing any such gay rights ordinances, or if they had done so they would have a negligible effect, these campaigns were largely symbolic. These campaigns were much more about consolidating a religious right collective identity than about effecting public policy.

When I asked Jeri Cooksson why she was active against gay rights she replied, fusing a belief in moral and medical contagion, "It's a lifestyle that is harmful to our country because it tears down family values, harmful to the individuals involved because it is unhealthy." According to "reputable studies," she says, people involved in homosexual activities are twelve times more likely to develop hepatitis B. During the local campaign against gay rights in Oregon in 1993–94, homosexual

Cartoon by Kirk Anderson 1992.

"atrocity tales" filled the press. The schools were infested with "militant, avowed homosexuals" who were teaching preschoolers that "masculine and feminine roles are not a matter of anatomy but of choice." If students or parents challenge such a view, one woman charged, they are met with "name calling, ridicule and half truths."[36] In another story, the middle school had invited two gay people to speak to their students about their lives. They were "practicing homosexuals who had AIDS" who presented their lives as perfectly natural and normal. When asked by one sixth-grader what they did sexually, they explicitly described some of their unconventional sexual activities, including fisting—or so it was claimed.

Clearly, the impressions OCA activists hold of gay people are rooted partly in misunderstanding of the Other. In diverse societies, Zygmunt Bauman writes, individuals are forced to live with those who may be different from themselves, but we construct defenses so that we do not have to come to really know them. Confronted with strangers on a daily basis, we are practiced in the "art of mismeeting and the avoidance of eye contact." We create social distances that evict from social space the Others who are otherwise within reach. We deny them admittance, and prevent ourselves from acquiring knowledge about them. But these evicted Others, in Bauman's words, continue to hover in the background of our perceptions, remaining "featureless, faceless."[37] Indeed, OCA activists' knowledge of homosexuality derived less from personal experience than from watching television, or from a one-time foray on a tour bus into San Francisco's Castro District, or from reading Christian right political materials. The superficiality of this contact allowed them to inflate their targets into folk devils who they imagined were posing a threat to their conception of the good society. By constructing the Other as an abstract category, they were able to separate the fate of gay people as a group from gay people as individuals. The lack of sustained contact and knowledge of homosexual culture bred feelings of repulsion and subdued hostility that were ready, given the right political rhetoric, to condense into hatred.[38]

Authoritarian individuals, according to Theodor Adorno, project their unacceptable feelings—especially sexual feelings—onto a minority group and thereby create a scapegoat. Once the group has been vilified, acting out one's rage against them becomes acceptable and logical. Indeed, some have suggested that antigay activists' fervor is fueled by their desire to compensate for their own homosexual desires. Perhaps this is true, but a more powerful explanation links shame to sexual desire in general. Sexual desires call up emotions—love, rage, shame— that are repressed in our sex-obsessed and sex-repressed culture. Advertising images and other forms of popular culture draw upon and elicit sexual feelings, and at the same time banish them from critical scrutiny and public discussion. Conservative Christians, like all Americans, experience sexual desires in a society that condemns their open expression. How can they not feel torn between conflicting impulses? Prominent evangelicals such as Jim Bakker and Jimmy Swaggart crusade against premarital sex and are caught with their pants down. In rural Oregon, rumors of preachers kicked out of congregations for sexual indiscretions abounded, and many people seemed to think that children in evangelical families were even more likely to transgress sexual and other norms.

Psychoanalytic theories suggest that shame is closely linked to sexual failure, and that masculinity is extremely fragile and always needs to be carefully fostered and protected.[39] Male homosexuality is particularly threatening because it calls "normal" masculinity, founded upon identification with the aggressive father, into question. Because desire is so powerful and prohibitions against nonnormative sexuality are so central to Christian orthodoxy, is it any wonder that people would seek to project one's unacceptable sexual feelings upon others and seek to punish those who openly flaunt these desires? It makes sense, then, that conservatives would seize upon the "homosexual problem" as a means of constituting themselves as a collective identity. In the antigay campaigns of the right, conservatives deploy homophobia in order to affirm a father-dominant social order; the shamed parties turn the tables, enacting a "triumphant sexual fantasy" that imagines "the Other" in shame.[40]

While OCA activists railed against homosexuality as a threat to the health and well-being of all, they often qualified their claims with professions of sympathy for individual gay people. "There's quite a few here in town. I've met several of them," said Jeri. "Very, very nice people. Extremely nice people." Barney Wooten tells me about gay people he works with, one of whom refuses to talk with him because of his beliefs. "He has more negative feelings about me than I do about him." But when it comes down to it, the conservative activists I speak with don't *really* know any living, breathing lesbians or gay men. Their descriptions are shot through with stereotypes, cardboard characterizations, and distortions. Homosexuals, Sally Humphries tells me, are "highly talented people, very artistic people," and since she considers herself artistic, she feels a particular affinity for them. She admits to having gay friends. "I'm drawn to them. They're into art and color. They're more caring sometimes."[41]

Christian love-the-sinner-hate-the-sin rhetoric permits OCA activists to hate gays and love them at the same time. While passing a ballot measure to prevent homosexual "special rights" might not change very much, Christian right activists believe it is a first step. Through their activism, they are taking a stand against the rise of a permissive society and are affirming a sense of themselves as strong and independent. They are assuming the role of parent, disciplining the moral flabbiness of those around them. Extending the metaphor of the child in need of discipline, they believe that homosexuals are wayward children, the children who got away, who need to be punished in order to get them back on track. It makes no logical sense that the government would come to protect their rights. Like a good child gone bad, they need to be shown a little tough love: sometimes you have to be cruel to be kind.

Christian conservatism and the activist projects with which it is associated may be less a distinct set of beliefs than a generalized "state of mind."[42] The conservative Christian activists I interviewed are people who have struggled against a variety of demons. A precarious sense of achievement fuels their quest for respectability. Yet shame and anxiety linger in their out-of-bounds world, a late-modern scenario in which the familiar structures of family, work, and community are rapidly being redefined, where women find themselves caught between competing loyalties to family and work, where communities are increasingly segmented, and where child abuse and other problems appear to be rising.

Christian conservatives strongly believe that good families value strength and obedience and do not tolerate weakness and dependence. In a just society, good families are rewarded and bad families punished. But all around them, they see those who face the same struggles as they do but who suffer few of the consequences. They imagine that they are being coddled by society, receiving a variety of handouts and entitlements, and they see this as unfair. A sense of resentment fuels their anger, and their activism. No one helped *me*. Why should *they* receive more? If some can receive handouts without working, the value of work is diminished. If homosexuality is affirmed along with heterosexuality, then the meaning of heterosexual marriage is diminished.

Through their activism, Christian conservatives construct a conception of the world that is secure and unambiguous, where their own lives and their own struggles have meaning and purpose, where they feel strong and powerful. Their activism is a reparative action that seeks to make the blurry clear, to classify clear, definable, morally inferior Others. The culture war, then, is about more than the realization of cognitive beliefs. There is a profound emotional dimension as well: a quest to transform shame into pride.

7

Whose Memories?
Whose Victimhood?

In recent years we have seen the proliferation of Holocaust stories. There are, of course, Jewish stories of the Holocaust, stories that describe the experience of destruction: families dragged from their homes and shipped to camps, communities emptied and herded into cattle cars, testimonies of personal trauma and collective horror. Though these stories share some commonalities, not the least of which are descriptions of sheer terror, they vary with the particular circumstances of the teller, along with the audience and the historical context of the telling.[1] Other groups tell Holocaust stories as well. Nations, for example, utilize Holocaust memories to serve political ends: deflecting charges of complicity, in the case of many European nations; or making moral claims to victimhood, in the case of Israel.[2]

Increasingly, stories about the Holocaust are told by those with little or no direct relationship to the historical events in question. Sectors of the far right in the United States and Europe are engaging in Holocaust denial, attempting to erase these memories altogether.[3] But far more commonplace than outright denial are acts of appropriation by social movement activists on the right and the left. Consider the following images: antiabortion activists call abortion mills "death camps" and refer to abortion as a contemporary holocaust; a feminist compares a survivor of rape to a survivor of Birkenau, the Nazi death camp; an exhibit in Atlanta describes the period of slavery as "The Black Holocaust"; members of an Oregon Christian right organization suggest that homosexuals were the backbone of the Nazi Party in Germany during World War II; gay activists suggest that the AIDS crisis is tantamount to a holocaust, faulting government bureaucrats for "Nazi-like" actions.[4] As these images suggest, fifty years after the end of World War II, the Holocaust has become a recurring theme and reference point for U.S. social movements, on both the right and the left. It has emerged as a "frame" through which identity-based movements construct reality and claim moral authority.

Since historical memories are always partial, fragmentary, and in dispute, these framing activities are necessarily subject to reinterpretation and political contestation. Who has rightful claim to these historical events and memories? Do these memories belong to the survivors and their descendants alone, or do other groups have the right to invoke Holocaust memories? Such questions arise in relation to all appropriations of historical memory; they are especially present in relation to the Holocaust, particularly at a time when the last survivors possessing firsthand memory of the period are dying out, and when some would deliberately manipulate historical memory to deny its occurrence.

Drawing upon movement literature and the writings of activists in the United States, in this essay I illustrate how the Holocaust has emerged as a social movement "frame" in two opposing movements, the lesbian/gay movement and the Christian right, and explore the meanings, and sets of associations, evoked by the Holocaust frame. Finally, I examine the ethical questions that arise when competing movements battle over the same frames, or symbolic territory. Uses of Holocaust memory by those who lack a direct connection to the historical events are, in effect, acts of appropriation. But all acts of appropriation, I will argue, are not equivalent.

Against the poststructuralist belief that texts, such as stories, take their meaning relationally within a global universe of interacting texts, an ethical approach to the appropriation of historical memories, particularly atrocity memories such as the Holocaust, distinguishes among claims on the basis of the social contexts within which texts are produced, and the uses to which they are put.[5] Here I distinguish between two different types of appropriation: *revisionism* (efforts to rewrite the history of the Holocaust, which make claims about a historical event) and *metaphor creation* (efforts to compare present events or experiences to those of the Holocaust). The distinction between these two rhetorical strategies, I will argue, is best understood in relation to the social contexts, such as contemporary social movements, in which Holocaust memories are deployed.

Framing Movements

To gain adherents and influence public opinion, social movements seek to define themselves. Interpretive work is central to this process of collective identity formation. This is certainly true of "new" social movements such as the feminist, lesbian/gay, and environmental movements, for whom changing cultural perceptions may be as central, or more central, than changing laws and policies.[6] But it may be equally true of movements on the right, which are also concerned with winning the battle for hearts and minds. All movements seek to define their boundaries and develop a sense of collective consciousness and identity. They wish to construct a conception of themselves that might appeal to potential adherents and aid the process of mobilization. William Gamson's analysis of the language necessary for collective political action concludes that mobilization requires constructing a sense of *injustice* (existing social arrangements are morally flawed), a sense of *identity* (a boundary between us and them), and a sense of *agency* (our involvement will make a difference).[7]

Social movements construct a sense of injustice, collective identity, and agency by engaging in "frame alignment processes." Movement leaders try to galvanize adherents through acts of cultural appropriation, in which they draw upon highly resonant themes and attempt to associate them with movement activities. They "frame" reality, simplifying the "world out there" by "selectively punctuating and encoding objects, situations, events, experiences, and sequences of actions within one's present or past environments."[8] Social movements use language and cultural symbols to mobilize and forge solidarity among potential adherents.

Historical memories are among these cultural symbols and representations and encompass a central, though relatively undertheorized element of movement framing activity. Sociologist Doug McAdam describes how the American civil rights movement became a "master protest frame" that was later appropriated by the women's liberation, gay rights, American Indian, farmworkers, and other movements during the 1960s and '70s.[9] Martin Luther King Jr.'s power as a leader was at least partly the product of his ability to appropriate and evoke highly resonant cultural themes, both from the southern black Baptist tradition, but also from American political culture more generally. Subsequent movements have framed their grievances by drawing upon

King's rhetoric and the discourse of "civil rights" he and others articulated.[10]

Since movements use historical memories to frame reality in ways that resonate with potential constituencies, perhaps it should come as no surprise that the Holocaust would figure prominently in the rhetoric of contemporary social movements. The Holocaust is an "atrocity tale" of wide cultural resonance. During the past two decades, the Holocaust has become "Americanized"; it has become a salient part of the American imagination, as exemplified by the erection of the Holocaust Museum in our nation's capital.[11] Increasingly, the Holocaust has become a universal symbol of injustice utilized by groups seeking to construct a sense of identity and agency.

Holocaust memories are evoked by groups seeking to claim victim status and name their enemies as perpetrators of genocide. Utilizing the symbolism of the Holocaust, social movement activists associate themselves with the victims of the Holocaust, thereby constructing a "protagonist identity field."[12] Conversely, they also construct "antagonist identity fields," likening their enemies to the perpetrators of genocide. Jeffrey Alexander suggests that binary oppositions or "homologies" such as these are a key feature of civil discourse in this country.[13] Through the use of binary discourse, citizens seek to associate themselves with such characteristics as "rationality," "equality," "autonomy," and "truth." They attempt to position their enemies as "irrational," "hierarchical," "dependent," and "dishonest." The Holocaust frame is particularly well suited to such moral identity claims since it is a historical template in which the distinction between good and evil is unambiguous.

For most of the postwar period, the historical memory of World War II, the "good war," was counterposed against the "evil empire" of communism. With the collapse of communism, the Holocaust has moved to center stage as the embodiment of radical evil. This frame is particularly appealing in an age in which politics in general, and social movements in particular, are mass mediated. The desire to dramatize and exaggerate conflicts derives in part from a need to play to the media, which is a primary target and audience for social movement activities in contemporary America.[14] Documenting the relationship between the antiwar movement of the 1960s and media coverage of that movement, Todd Gitlin suggests that the media concentrated on images of extremes, playing up the most dramatic, most radical elements of the student movement, thereby elevating marginalized leaders to positions of power. Post-sixties activists know that in order to gain media attention, dramatic images of conflict must be emphasized.[15]

Psychologists Lifton and Mitchell provide an additional explanation for the resonance of the Holocaust frame: the emergence of a an "apocalyptic self." After Hiroshima—and, one might add, the Holocaust— the "individual self," they suggest, "is threatened with being overwhelmed by, or dissolved into, the larger absurd death event." We see the emergence of an "apocalyptic self" that is "preoccupied with the nuclear end, haunted by images of mass killing and dying, and haunted by death in general."[16] This rhetoric is pervasive among sectors of the Christian right, in which a vision of the end of the world is seen as "a prelude to new spiritual achievement," such as the Second Coming of Christ. As the end of the century nears, many fundamentalists invoke the biblical prophecy that Jesus will appear, followed by Armageddon, a battle between good and evil, and by his one-thousand-year reign on Earth. One can also find apocalyptic rhetoric among some gay male and African American AIDS activists, who imagine their plight as a battle against the forces of evil conspiring against them.[17]

The Holocaust, then, has emerged as a familiar historical template evoking profound emotional associations. In our late modern age, when the moral boundaries separating good and evil are often amorphous, when the mediatization of political discourse results in the dominance of image-based politics, and when communism no longer exists as a clear-cut, visible enemy, the Holocaust stands out as an indisputable instance of immorality, evoking images of apocalypse. These factors have made it a resonant "collective action frame" for contemporary social movements in the United States.

The Holocaust first emerged as a central theme in lesbian/gay rhetoric in the early 1970s and has appeared in different forms during the past twenty-five years; it became a part of Christian right rhetoric somewhat later, and continues today. The appropriation of the same symbolic resources by two rival movements should not be surprising: the Christian right and the lesbian/gay movements exist in dialectical relationship with one another.[18] They are an "oppositional dyad" that helps to "constitute the internal identity of each group."[19] In the following, I specify how these claims operate in each movement, and how they have emerged and shifted over time.

They're Nazis, We're Jews

The Holocaust frame appeared in lesbian/gay rhetoric at three different moments: the early 1970s, in relation to the rise of the gay liberation movement; the early to mid-1980s, in response to the twin threats of the New Right and the AIDS epidemic; and the 1990s, in response to antigay ballot measures sponsored by Christian conservative organizations in several states. Gay activists have sought to revise the historical record to reflect the extent of gay victimhood during the Nazi period; they have also used the Holocaust as metaphor, comparing the plight of homosexuals today to the plight of victimized minorities during the German Reich. Through the use of the Holocaust frame, lesbians and gay men have positioned themselves as victims and situated their opponents—garden-variety homophobes, negligent AIDS bureaucrats, and Christian right antigay campaigners—as perpetrators.

Invoking the history of the Third Reich, contemporary lesbian and gay activists recall that the Nazi Party sought to "cleanse" German society of those groups that violated the tenets of Aryan purity and that were believed to pose a threat to national unity: Jews, gypsies, homosexuals, communists, and the disabled. Though the "final solution" targeted Jews for annihilation above all else, other marginalized groups were caught in the frenzy of purification. Among them were homosexual men, who were seen as a threat to the patriarchal family idealized by Nazism. A 1928 Nazi Party statement proclaimed: "Anyone who thinks of homosexual love is our enemy. We therefore reject any form of lewdness, especially homosexuality, because it robs us of our last chance to free our people from the bondage which now enslaves it."[20] Between 1933 and 1945, tens of thousands of homosexual men were sent to concentration camps, and perhaps 10,000 of them perished.[21]

In the early 1970s, the contemporary gay liberation movement in the United States and Europe adopted the pink triangle, the symbol worn by homosexual concentration camp prisoners during World War II, as a symbolic marker. Through such symbols, lesbian and gay activists recalled the historical memory of the Holocaust, exhorting them to "never forget" their slain brothers and sisters, and positioning themselves as the historical heirs of the lively pre–World War II homosexual rights movement that was extinguished by German aggression. At the same time, plays like *Bent* (1979) and books such as *Men of the Pink Triangle* were engaged in revising the historical record to reflect the suffering of gay men during that period.[22] This historical legacy was not lost on gay activists such as Harvey Milk, one of the leading figures of the post-Stonewall gay rights movement in the United States. Milk grew up in suburban Long Island, the child of middle-class Jews, and finished high school as news of the Holocaust reached the United States. According to his biographer, the destruction of European Jewry "touched Milk doubly" as a Jew and a gay man, and provided the inspiration for his eventual leadership of the gay rights movement.[23]

Gay liberationists frequently invoked the memory of the Holocaust to aid their goal of destigmatizing homosexuality. The term "homosexual" first emerged in the nineteenth century, in the context of modern medical and psychiatric knowledge that pathologized sexual deviance.[24] Despite the liberal intentions of many early sexologists, scientific categorizations on the basis of sexuality (along with race) became the basis for the creation of a special, stigmatized homosexual category. Gay liberationists enacted a "reverse affirmation," claiming the stigmatized category, and the sense of victimhood associated with it, as a means of destigmatizing the category. Casting themselves as victims permits a group to "dramatize [its] essential innocence."[25] By drawing parallels between contemporary lesbians and gay men, and the homosexual (and, by implication, Jewish) victims of Nazi genocide, activists deflected responsibility for stigma, suggesting that homosexuals were innocent victims of generalized prejudice, warning of the dangerous consequences of categorizing and stigmatizing groups on the basis of sexual or other differences.[26]

In the mid-1970s, as social conservatives became more proactive and the enemies of gay liberation more visible and tangible, the rhetoric of lesbian/gay activism shifted from *deflecting responsibility* for stigma to *assigning causes* for their victimization. As the Christian right mobilized to defend the "moral majority" against the supposed homosexual/feminist threat, lesbian/gay rhetoric frequently drew parallels between American conservativism and European fascism. Barry Dank, in an op-ed article in the *Los Angeles Times,* compared singer Anita Bryant to Adolph Hitler:

> Just as Hitler viewed the Jews as a powerful force that was polluting and destroying society, so do Bryant and her followers view homosexuals as social defilers. Hitler reduced the Jews to vermin who were infecting the master Aryan race. The Bryant brigade talks as though

homosexuals are alien perverts bent on destroying the fabric of Christian America.[27]

He went on to quote a spokesperson for the Anti-Defamation League: "There's a whole new cadre . . . around who are smart enough not to wear swastikas. They join the Klan now or create churches . . . but they're Nazis just the same."

Later, a more sophisticated version of this argument utilized the Freudo-Marxism of philosopher Herbert Marcuse to suggest that the sexual repression found in the middle-class family was fascist in character, and that homosexuals were the vanguard in a struggle against sexual repression. As Barry Adam suggested:

> Homosexuality for the New Right as for the Nazis signifies the modernity, the sexual freedom and the dissolving underpinnings of traditional domesticity. . . . Like the Nazi anti-Semites who found it much easier to attack a visible but relatively powerless symbol of modernity, heterosexists displace their fear and anger of modern society upon lesbians and gay men.[28]

In this way, Holocaust imagery allowed gay activists to clearly delineate victims and perpetrators and dramatize their plight. Lesbians and gay men were rhetorically absolved from responsibility for their stigma; heterosexists were implicated as enemies of sexual freedom.

During the early 1980s, as the AIDS epidemic unfolded in many urban gay communities, the Holocaust frame again appeared in gay activist literature, deflecting responsibility for the disease and assigning blame to conservative activists, government bureaucrats, and health professionals. Early in the trajectory of the disease, conservatives suggested that gays were carriers of AIDS, and that they should be quarantined, lest they contaminate the rest of the population.[29] Gay activists responded that they were being scapegoated for social anxieties surrounding the disease, and warned of a potential "gay Holocaust." Evoking the image of the epidemic as an act of extermination, in 1987, the direct action group ACT-UP (AIDS Coalition to Unleash Power) sponsored a float in the New York Gay Pride parade which depicted a concentration camp with people with AIDS (PWAs) trapped within its barbed-wire boundaries. The genocide frame challenged popular understandings of AIDS as a "gay plague," an understanding that rests upon a teleology in which diseases come to be seen as punishments visited upon individuals and groups from the "outside," often in retaliation for wrongdoings.[30] By substituting the metaphor of the Holocaust for a conception of AIDS as a "plague," AIDS activists challenged the blame-the-victim view that the disease was self-inflicted, the suffering deserved.

Larry Kramer, whose essays are collected in the 1989 book *Reports from the Holocaust: The Making of an AIDS Activist,* was largely responsible for popularizing the AIDS-as-Holocaust, or "genocide" frame. Kramer, one of the founders of ACT-UP, compared American gay communities to European Jewish communities on the brink of destruction some fifty years earlier. He likened government bureaucrats to Nazis, AIDS service organizations to Jewish councils, and imagined gay men as Jews herded off to gas chambers. He denounced the director of AIDS research at the National Institutes of Health as a "Nazi" and a "murderer," charging him with being more concerned with protecting scientific orthodoxy than with speeding the development of drugs. The slowness of government response at the federal and local levels of government, the paucity of funds for research and treatment, particularly during the early days of the epidemic, stemmed, Kramer argued, from deep-seated homophobic impulses and constituted "intentional genocide." But gay-run AIDS organizations were also at fault, he suggested, for making service provision for people with AIDS a priority over advocacy, and for failing to provide the united front that the gay community needed.

In many gay communities in the 1980s, the proliferation of AIDS cases was accompanied by a proliferation of texts—posters, fiction, and mass quilts—which aimed to "bear witness" to the horrors and to engage in political intervention. This collective mourning paralleled efforts on the part of Jewish Holocaust survivors to "bear witness" to the atrocities they experienced during World War II. Implicit in this "genocide frame" was the belief that gay men constitute an ethnic group roughly comparable to Jews, an idea that came into prominence among U.S. gays in many urban areas in the 1970s.[31] Since homosexuals represent a clearly defined interest group comparable to blacks or Jews, the argument goes, they should be able to make demands upon the state in order to take their rightful place in American society.

In the United States, the experience of the Holocaust has united Jews as much as any real or perceived connection to Israel, allowing them to make political claims which might not otherwise be possible in a

". . . And The Man Slept On," Photo Collage by S. Brett Kaufman, 1992.

country where anti-Semitism persists, though largely unacknowledged. Likewise, AIDS has provided a symbolic (and practical) focus for urban gay male communities in the 1980s and '90s. It is the experience of the AIDS epidemic perhaps more than anything else in recent memory that has constructed that sense of collective identity for gay men, and to a lesser extent lesbians.[32] The fear of gay people and the threat of AIDS have become indelibly linked in the popular imagination. Gay communities have taken the lead in the fight against the disease when the government response has faltered, and they have been transformed by that experience.

The Holocaust or genocide frame was thus very useful as a rhetorical tool, permitting people with AIDS to create an "antagonist frame," deflecting responsibility for the disease and assigning responsibility to others: conservative activists and inactive elites. It helped activists transform people with AIDS from a group deserving moral retribution to innocent casualties of state genocide. It was, however, less successful in specifying responses and remedies to the problem. Specifying a victim frequently calls forth a remedy. But as AIDS activists became "insiders," participating in the development of drug treatments with scientists and policy advocates, it became more and more difficult to sustain the "genocide frame."[33]

The Holocaust in Christian Right Rhetoric

In the 1990s, the Holocaust frame emerged once again, this time in relation to right-wing antigay campaigns. The Washington D.C.–based Christian Coalition initiated several ballot measures to amend state constitutions to define homosexuality and other so-called deviant sexual practices as "abnormal, wrong, unnatural and perverse" by law.[34] If passed, these measures would potentially have prevented lesbians, gays, and other sexual minorities from receiving public funds and civil rights protections. The use of state funds to teach positive views of homosexuality, for example, would be outlawed on the grounds that it would "promote" homosexuality. Describing the Oregon Citizens Alliance (OCA) antigay ballot measure, Gayle Rubin suggested that

> the initiative is reminiscent of several aspects of National Socialist legislation. . . . The OCA initiatives would, if passed, deprive sexual minorities of equal citizenship, make them "inferior" by law and public policy, mandate teaching such inferiority in all state-supported educational institutions, and suppress the promulgation of opinions or evidence that would contravene such legally dictated inferiority.[35]

In their campaign against Ballot Measure 9 in Oregon during 1991–92, lesbian/gay/bisexual/transgender activists frequently drew parallels to the Holocaust, stating that "this is how things began in Nazi Germany."[36] One group, calling itself "People of Faith Against Bigotry," in a paid statement in the State Voters pamphlet suggested: "The OCA is counting on people not to speak out to protect this minority, just as people were afraid to speak out to protest the persecution of minorities under the Nazi regime." In their campaign to defeat the measures, progay activists in many parts of the state sponsored a traveling exhibit detailing the life of Anne Frank, drawing parallels between the Holocaust and contemporary persecution of sexual and other minorities. In a small Oregon town, where the OCA sponsored a local antigay ordinance in 1993, a group of citizens organized a week-long showing of the Anne Frank traveling exhibit. "We wanted to do something positive," said one organizer. "This is a way of bringing the issue of discrimination to the community and saying, 'All discrimination is intolerable. We want to say it's not acceptable in our community; let's remember discrimination as it existed in the past and try to eradicate it.' "[37] These arguments were designed to generate a sense of responsibility among the general public to protect the rights of threatened minorities.

In summary, the specter of a Holocaust has been utilized by lesbians and gay men to dramatize their plight as an oppressed group in American society. Lesbians and gay men engaged in a form of revisionism, adjusting the historical record to reflect the historical oppression of homosexuals during the Nazi reign of terror. They also used the frame as metaphor, drawing parallels between contemporary homosexuals and the victims of Nazism fifty years earlier. In relation to the AIDS epidemic, lesbian and gay activists invoked the memory of the Holocaust to suggest that government inaction is tantamount to genocide. In response to the antigay campaigns of the Christian right, they suggested that homosexuals, a relatively powerless group, are being used as a convenient scapegoat for widespread social anxieties.

No, We're *the Real Victims*

Over the past twenty years, Holocaust denial has become "a tool" of the radical right. More recently, the Holocaust has also come to figure in the rhetoric of more respectable "mainstream" conservatism. Rather than denying the Holocaust, as does the racist and anti-Semitic far right, the Christian right has at times appropriated Holocaust memory, initiating a series of "frame disputes" that seek to counter gay victim claims. As Deborah Lipstadt suggests, "The general public tends to accord victims of genocide a certain moral authority. If you devictimize a people you strip them of their moral authority, and if you can in turn claim to be a victim . . . that moral authority is conferred on or restored to you."[38]

Since the early 1970s lesbian/gay activists, as I have suggested, sought to revise the historical record to reflect the extent of homosexual victimhood during the Holocaust and draw parallels between contemporary lesbian/gay oppression and the experience of the Holocaust. The Holocaust did not figure in Christian conservative rhetoric until the early 1990s, when Christian right activists entered into a "frame dispute" to counter these gay victim claims, denying any historical continuity between fascism and neoconservatism. Engaging in a much more egregious form of revisionism, some suggested that gays, far from being victims of the Nazis, were themselves instrumental in the Nazi Party, implying that Christians were among the "true victims" of the Holocaust.[39]

Historically, the right has drawn much of its strength, collective identity, and legitimacy from its ability to construct a coherent, visible enemy and to demonize the "enemies within."[40] Jews and homosexuals were frequently central to this demonology. In early twentieth century America, right-wing forces linked Judaism with communism, suggesting that Jews were at the forefront of a pervasive communist/liberal conspiracy bent on destroying Christian values. Such claims became central to the radical and moderate right-wing political movements, including religion-based parties such as the Christian Democrats and various prewar Catholic Action groups.[41] After World War Two, political anti-Semitism and the belief in a Jewish-communist conspiracy were publicly discredited; Joseph McCarthy, for example, went to some length to avoid association with anti-Semitism, and the homosexual came to replace the Jew as a central figure in right-wing demonology. McCarthy often used queer-baiting to attack his enemies, describing political opponents who could not be associated with communism as "lace pantied"—"not real men," in contrast to his own self-presentation as "tail gunner Joe."[42]

Lesbians and gay men provided a powerful focus for right-wing mobilization in the 1970s and '80s, externalizing the anxieties facing many people in this country. A defense of "the family" and of the "moral order" came to symbolize a series of social anxieties around social change and instability. Christian conservative activists positioned themselves as the moral guardians of the family against what they perceive as the excesses of homosexuality. At a time when African Americans, women, lesbians, and gays were using their status as victims to make political claims, antigay efforts sought to defend the "moral majority" against the so-called homosexual threat. By the 1980s, the Christian right had made antigay activity central to its political practice and social vision.

By the late 1980s and into the 1990s, a new Christian right cultural genre—books, videos, special reports—was specifically dedicated to identifying the gay threat and calling Christian believers to arms; dozens of conservative Christian organizations devoted themselves solely to antigay activities, and antigay discourse came to encompass an attack on the status of homosexuals as a "minority" group deserving equal rights under the law. This marked a shift on the right from a focus on the immorality of homosexuality to an attribution of superior power to gays. Gays were viewed as undeserving "special interest groups" which have won "special rights" by manipulating government corruption, gerrymandering elections, and appealing to a judicial system dominated by liberals, a powerful, morally corrupt school system, and a Congress that promotes the destruction of the family.[43]

At the same time, religious conservatives began to usurp the rhetoric of victimhood, redefining themselves in the language of interest group liberalism and identity politics.[44] Shifting from an earlier notion of Christians as guardians of the status quo who represent the "moral majority," the Christian right declared itself to be an oppressed minority comprised of social outcasts.[45] This new collective identity was accompanied by a more proactive political strategy, as Christian Right organizations began to sponsor ballot initiatives designed to deny civil rights to lesbians and gay men. In 1994, there were over twenty antigay measures on state and local ballots, many of which garnered considerable support.[46]

During these initiative campaigns, the Christian right at times deployed rhetoric and imagery that echoed European anti-Semitism. The Oregon Citizens Alliance film, *The Gay Agenda,* closely resembled the 1940 Nazi propaganda film, *The Eternal Jew.* Echoing traditional anti-Semitic propaganda that deliberately inflated the power of Jewish bankers, international Jewish conspiracies, and so forth, conservatives suggested that lesbians and gay men have higher incomes than others. A cartoon published by the Oregon Citizens Alliance showed a gay man manipulating the strings of the government and the economy. It was, one gay writer pointed out, "a virtual copy of a Nazi cartoon," one that replaced "the stooped, hook-nosed puppeteer with a fresh-faced gym boy."[47] At the same time, the OCA challenged the right of lesbians and gay men to align themselves with the victims of the Holocaust. In the 1994 campaign for Ballot Measure 13, which sought to deny civil rights to lesbians and gays, a right-wing group calling itself "Jews and Friends of Holocaust Victims" argued in favor of the ballot measure:

Who's a Nazi? Americans are watching history repeat as homosexuals promote the BIG LIE that everyone who opposes them is harmful to society. It's nothing new. They used this tactic in Germany against the Jews. . . . Don't buy the BIG LIE. Opponents of minority status for homosexuals are not "Nazis" or "bigots." And homosexuals aren't "victims" of your common sense morality. Protect our children![48]

Political commentator Patrick Buchanan, who has questioned whether six million Jews actually died in the gas chambers, railed against the "rhetorical hate crimes of the left" that have drawn links between conservative Christians and Nazis. Quite the contrary, Buchanan suggests, Christians were despised by Hitler, who tried to eradicate Christianity in Germany root and branch."[49] It is just a short leap from this notion of Christians-as-Holocaust-victims to televangelist Pat Robertson's suggestion that "many of those people involved with Adolf Hitler were homosexuals. The two things seem to go together. . . . It is a pathology, it is a sickness . . . God hates homosexuality."[50] Attempting to deflect accusations from the left that they are "Nazis," Christian conservatives argued the reverse: homosexuals are not victims; they are oppressors and the "real Nazis." The "true" victims are the guardians of "common sense morality," the Christian right. As a leader of the Oregon Citizens Alliance suggests, " 'gay rights' activists—not pro-family conservatives and OCA supporters—should be wearing the label of Nazi."

> Homosexuality was a CENTRAL element of the fascist system, the Nazi elite was rampant with homosexuality and pederasty, Adolph Hitler intentionally surrounded himself with homosexuals during his entire adult life, and the people most responsible for many Nazi atrocities were homosexual.[51]

This encapsulates the argument of *The Pink Swastika* (1995), authored by OCA activist Scott Lively, along with Kevin Abrams, who is identified as an Orthodox Jew residing in Israel. The book is a carefully constructed piece of political rhetoric, mixing serious scholarship with lies and outright distortions, truths with half-truths and falsehoods. The authors draw largely upon lesbian/gay scholarly sources to make the argument that many, if not all, of the major leaders of the Nazi movement in Germany were homosexuals—including Hitler, Goebbels, Goering, Himmler, and Hess. While they do admit that homosexuals were persecuted by the Nazis, they suggest that homosexuals comprised the core of the Nazi Party.

The *Pink Swastika* explains how homosexuals can be both Nazis and their victims. The authors contend that more masculine, "butch" homosexuals were responsible for building the Nazi Party and creating the SA, or Brownshirts. Male homosexual "femmes" were persecuted by the Nazis, but largely escaped death. "Regardless of Himmler's anti-homosexual rhetoric, homosexuals as a class were never targeted for extermination, as their continued role in the Third Reich demonstrates."[52] Lively and Abrams suggest that the Nazi-homosexual link is rooted in pre-Christian paganism, as in the Roman Empire. Pagans worshipped homosexuality and hated Christianity and Judaism. The Nazi persecution of Jews, following this logic, was a form of retaliation for Jewish suppression of homosexuality. The *Pink Swastika* concludes with the claim that the contemporary gay rights movement, far from sharing a historical lineage with Holocaust "victims," actually has historical links to the Nazi perpetrators of genocide.

Certainly there were homosexuals among the Nazis, as there are among all social movements, on the left and the right. SA leader Ernst Rohm, for example, is widely believed to have been openly homosexual.[53] Despite the claims of some on the gay/left, there is no "natural" link between homosexuality and liberal, progressive ideology. For example, for some members of the lesbian literary set in Paris between the wars, including Gertrude Stein and Natalie Barney, economic privileges and "separate status" made dominant rightist ideologies and repressive political regimes exceedingly attractive.[54] Affluent sexual minorities in the contemporary United States have supported elements of conservative ideology and been active in the conservative movement.[55]

The link between Nazism and homosexuality rests upon the belief that homosexuality is an essential component of aggressivity among male soldiers. They suggest that "latent" homosexuality creates enormous reserves of energy by suppressing drives, which in turn demand aggressive release.[56] Indeed, Nazi leaders incited homoeroticism through sports, physical culture, "strength through joy," and their estheticization of the male nude; they simultaneously brutally suppressed homosexual feelings, diverting them into various forms of militarism, brutality, and ideological fixations on powerful leadership figures. This does not prove that there were a disproportionate number of homosexuals within the fascist movement, however. As historian Erwin Haeberle notes:

> It is often assumed by casual students of Nazism that Hitler and many Nazi leaders were originally quite tolerant of homosexuality, that the entire SA leadership, for example, was homosexual, and that the intolerance set in only after the murder of Rohm and his friends in 1934. However, all these assumptions are false. While it is true that Rohm and some of his cronies were, in some situations, rather open about their homosexuality, the SA as such was by no means affected, even in most of its leadership. Moreover, although Hitler protected Rohm as long as he needed him, he never approved of his sexual orientation, which he considered a weakness. Most Nazi leaders themselves fought against "moral degeneracy," a concept which included homosexual conduct.[57]

Despite the claim of a direct link between Nazi ideology and homosexuality, historical evidence points to the opposite conclusion: that while the Nazis may have estheticized homoeroticism to a point, they identified homosexuality with the emasculation of men, which they saw as a threat to the traditional patriarchal, procreative family which they idealized.[58]

It would be easy to dismiss the claims of the *Pink Swastika* if the book were simply the work of a small right-wing fringe group, but during the last several years, the OCA, which is loosely affiliated with the Christian Coalition, has come close to winning electoral majorities on its antigay initiatives on several occasions. Framing gays-as-Nazis has aided their cause. In drawing parallels between gays and Nazis, the right is doing several things. It is attempting to dispel the notion that gay people are "victims" worthy of sympathy and support; pit two traditionally liberal constituencies, gays and Jews, against one another, thereby drawing parallels between Jews and Christians, and legitimating its own identity as an oppressed group.

Reversing the claims of the lesbian/gay movement, Lively and Abrams claim that while homosexuals were persecuted by Nazis, they were placed in work camps and therefore had a much better chance of survival than any other targeted group, particularly Jews. While such claims are true to some extent, the political uses to which they have been put deserve scrutiny. Through these claims, conservatives seek to strip gays of their moral authority. Once gays are stripped of their "victim" status, it becomes easier to paint them as the "oppressor," enemies not only of the religious right, but also of Jews, whom the Christian right is attempting to befriend. This logic is seen in a 1996 letter sent to OCA supporters, in which *Pink Swastika* author Scott Lively criticizes the inclusion of homosexuals in Holocaust memorials and educational campaigns, such as a traveling exhibit on Anne Frank.

> The "gay" Holocaust myth is [tremendously important] to the "gay rights" movement. All across the nation this arrogant revision of history is being used. . . . For example, the highly organized and well funded "Anne Frank" exhibit was most recently in New Mexico where it featured blatant pro-homosexual events and themes over an entire month. Thousands of New Mexicans were taught that opposition to "gay rights" is equivalent to supporting the Holocaust. Much more harmful are the permanent Holocaust memorials that present "gay" victim mythology in somber surroundings that lend it instant credibility. . . . I personally believe that all of these; the Anne Frank exhibit, the memorials, and similar "educational" and political projects promoting "diversity," are part of a single plan conceived and orchestrated by the national "gay rights" power structure. Once these institutions are in place and fully functional they will provide the homosexualists [*sic*] a nearly invulnerable position from which to denounce their adversaries. They will finally have the one thing they have lacked in their decades-long battle to defeat the Christian church—"moral" authority. The key to this strategy is the "gay" Holocaust myth.[59]

In sum, sectors of the Christian right have suggested that gays are revisionists who are trying to claim their piece of the Holocaust "memory pie." Suggesting that "a gay person seeking rights is like a Nazi seeking rights," they seek to prove that lesbians and gay men are undeserving of "special rights." With this role reversal, homosexual men, alleged perpetrators of genocide, become "illegitimate" minorities in the United States, where minority status is often tied to victimhood.[60]

Moreover, through its use of the Holocaust, the Christian right plays on the long-standing animosity between Orthodox Jews and homosexuals, a strategy designed to divide traditional liberal constituencies and court conservative Jews as allies.[61] While only a very few Jews are active in Christian right organizations, right-wing Jews have at times been supportive allies of the fundamentalist cause, in part because of its commitment to the state of Israel. Televangelist Pat Robertson is a staunch supporter of Israel who has courted Jewish support while promoting anti-Semitic beliefs in many of his writings. The Christian right supports the protection of Israel for biblical reasons: it suggests that the existence of a Jewish state is a necessary precondition for the second coming of Jesus Christ. Jewish neoconservatives, in turn, value fundamentalist support for U.S. military and economic subsidies to Israel.[62]

Ultimately, through its use of the Holocaust frame, the Christian right is attempting to consolidate its own legitimacy. Usurping the language and position of "minority" groups, conservative Christians argue that *they* are victims of discrimination. Religion, unlike sexuality, they claim, is an essential, core characteristic of the self; therefore Christians are the "true minorities." This has been a consistent theme on the far right, where the Christian Identity movement, among others, claims that white Christians are the "true chosen people" whose well-being is threatened by homosexuals, people of color, and immigrants.[63] Linking homosexuality and fascism, they suggest that Christianity alone is a force for social good. Through such claims, the right attempts to transform itself into a force worthy of wide public sympathy and support. Those who make such claims are using the memory of the Holocaust to vilify homosexuals, divide Jews and gays, two traditionally liberal constituencies, and garner public support for the Christian conservative movement. The claim that categorically Christians are among the "true" victims of Nazism, and that homosexuals perpetrated the Holocaust, has no basis in fact. In effect, it degrades the victims of the Holocaust and alleviates the guilt of the perpetrators.

Truth, Memory, and Politics of Appropriation

Historical memories are a potent symbolic resource for social movements, aiding the process of mobilization and the formation of collective identities. The Holocaust evokes a particularly powerful and disturbing set of images, associations, and emotions. It has therefore emerged as a common symbolic referent for contemporary social movements, particularly in the United States. I have shown how two opposing movements, the lesbian/gay movement and the Christian right, have utilized the Holocaust as a symbolic resource toward very different ends.

In appropriating these memories, social movement actors have attempted to define themselves as moral actors and, in the process, differentiate themselves from their enemies. Lesbians and gays position themselves as heirs to the homosexuals who perished through Nazi genocide, or as Jews on the brink of destruction. In response, sectors of the Christian right have attempted to deflect these victim claims, at times positioning themselves as Holocaust "victims." Using the Holocaust to construct a portrait of their opponents, lesbians and gays suggest that their enemies (negligent AIDS bureaucrats, Christian right antigay campaigners) are Nazis. Christian right activists attempt to reverse this claim, at times suggesting that the "real" Nazis are in fact gays, and Christians the "true" victims. Such rhetorical excesses are perhaps characteristic of the contemporary "culture wars," in which different groups utilize hyperbole to appeal to the "emotional predispositions" of the public.[64] As Patton has suggested, opposition between the gay and lesbian movement and the New Right has not only served to consolidate each group's identity but also encouraged each group to pursue the strategy of urging the broader public to "disidentify" with the other: "If neither group could reasonably hope to recruit many outsiders to its identity, promoting disidentification produced at least temporary allies."[65] As I have argued, the Holocaust frame was a rhetorical device utilized by both groups to further this goal.

To some, these "frame disputes" challenge Jewish "ownership" of the Holocaust frame. Survivors of the Holocaust, who are concerned with preserving their particular claims to memory, lament the trivialization of the Holocaust which is rife in the mass media and popular culture. As Irena Klepfisz suggests, "The Holocaust has [become] a fad, a rock group . . . it has been commercialized, metaphored out of reality, glamorized, been severed from the historical fact."[66] When the Holocaust becomes just another object of popular culture, they suggest, it loses its ability to shock. In this view, social movements that utilize Holocaust rhetoric are another instance of such trivialization. They suggest that efforts to associate contemporary social movements with Holocaust memory, or any attempt to compare the Holocaust to other events in human history, relativizes and thereby undercuts the specificity and uniqueness of that horrific and in many respects singular historical moment.[67]

Jewish Holocaust survivors understandably wish to preserve their version of the truth, or at least claim a special understanding based upon experience. From their standpoint, political actors on the right and the left may be equally guilty of appropriating the Holocaust. Some suggest that any effort to compare the Holocaust to other historical events constitutes, in effect, historical revisionism; it stands alone as the Ultimate Evil for which there is no comparison. By comparing the Holocaust to other instances of inhumanity, they de-Judaicize the Holocaust, transforming it into an instance of inhumanity bereft of special Jewish significance. For if everyone is a victim, then no one is.

Contemporary social movements which appropriate Holocaust memory are, in effect, universalizing such memories, questioning the authenticity of experience, and suggesting that historical memories are always contested. This poses a dilemma for social movements seeking to appropriate Holocaust memory for progressive ends. Such movements may appreciate the particularity of the Holocaust, its special significance to world Jewry, and its uniqueness. At the same time, by appropriating the Holocaust for their own political purposes, they are, in effect, challenging Jewish "ownership" of Holocaust memory.

Yet it seems inevitable that the historical memory of the Holocaust will be made and remade, appropriated and reappropriated. Particularly as we move farther and farther away from firsthand memory, and as subsequent generations are entrusted with keeping memory alive, the stories that will be told about the Holocaust will be second- and thirdhand ones. Moreover, the Holocaust is both unique *and* comparable. It belongs to Jewish history, but it also belongs to human history. The Nazis mobilized modern technology to destroy, for all intents and purposes, the unique cultures of European Jewry. But genocides occurred before and continue to occur after the Holocaust, albeit on a smaller scale. And even in this country, the genocidal mentality is present, in much milder form, in the effort to exclude whole populations from economic, political, and cultural resources.[68]

Perhaps Holocaust memory can be usefully employed, extending its meaning beyond firsthand survivors and their families without diminishing its significance for Jews, particularly for survivors and their families. As Robert Lifton suggests, the memory of the Holocaust, and of human trauma in general, may be utilized toward progressive ends, toward the development of a "species awareness" that can prevent future Holocausts from occurring. This is the philosophy behind such educational programs as "Facing History and Ourselves," which seek to draw connections between the anti-Semitism that precipitated the Holocaust, and contemporary strains of intolerance and bigotry that are directed toward Jews and other minority groups.[69]

But as efforts to universalize the Holocaust multiply, we must differentiate among competing stories, or memory claims. An ethical approach to the appropriation of historical memories, particularly atrocity memories such as the Holocaust, distinguishes among memory claims on the basis of the social contexts under which they are produced and deployed. Looking at the experiences of two social movements, I have differentiated between two types of Holocaust rhetoric: *revisionism,* which seeks to make claims about the Holocaust as a historical event, and *metaphor creation,* which seeks to make comparisons between the Holocaust and contemporary events.

The lesbian and gay movement has appropriated the Holocaust as metaphor, to dramatize its plight as a marginalized group in American society; it has also engaged in revisionism, attempting to correct the historical record to reflect the extent of gay victimhood. Despite some exaggerated claims, likening AIDS, for example, to state-sponsored genocide, they remind us that exclusion and extermination exist on a continuum. In terms of its psychic motivations as well as strategic uses, parallels can be drawn between the hate that is directed toward lesbians, gays, and other minorities in this country, and the historical scapegoating of Jews. Certainly, at different times, many lesbians and gay men have found themselves estranged from different aspects of American social life. They have not been targeted for destruction by state-sponsored genocide, but they have been excluded from jobs, housing, legal protections, and cultural affirmation.

In contrast, sectors of the Christian right, representing the dominant religious grouping in this country, have little claim to victim status, and even less claim to Holocaust memories. Christian conservatives have deliberately distorted Holocaust memories to deflect lesbian/gay victim claims, and to make moral claims of their own. In the process, they have degraded the memory of Holocaust victims and lessened the burden on the perpetrators. Though the memory of the Holocaust will inevitably be made and remade, all Holocaust stories are not equivalent.

8

Make Room for Daddy
Anxious Masculinity and Emergent Homophobias

Frankly, I don't think men know how to be men anymore. With
all these kids being raised by single parents, boys don't know the
first thing about how to be a man. You look at these women,
even wonderful women, trying very, very hard. But how do you
teach a boy to be a husband and a father if they aren't around
one, you know what I mean? They just don't know how to be a
father. How are they going to be a dad, a father, if they've never
had one?

— Woman activist against gay/lesbian rights[1]

While polls suggest that the vast majority of Americans are
wary of extreme efforts to legislate sexual morality, the popularity of
homophobic rhetoric among large sectors of the American public indi-
cates continuing ambivalence about the normalization of homosexuality. During the past three decades, the percentage of Americans who
think homosexuality is "wrong" declined significantly, and Americans
are much more willing to condone private homosexual behaviors, view
openly lesbian and gay characters in popular entertainment, and provide some limited benefits to the spouses and children of lesbians and
gay men.[2] Still, in terms of public discourse, as a nation we remain divided over whether or not lesbians and gay men are the moral equivalent of heterosexuals, and perhaps "no other issue taps into such potential conflict [between tolerance and need to adhere to common public
principles that can occasionally overrule tolerance] than the issue of
homosexuality," according to sociologist Alan Wolfe.[3]

To a great extent this ambivalence is gendered, with public opinion polls, data on hate crimes, and other indices revealing greater ambivalence toward homosexuality among heterosexual men than women.[4] Indeed, while much of the energy for antiabortion activism has come from women who wish to defend their special status as mothers, the issue of homosexuality has engaged the passions of men, particularly white working-class men, in unprecedented ways.[5] What are the sources of this continuing antipathy, and what might it tell us about changing forms of American masculinity?

One possible set of explanations comes from psychoanalytic theory, which suggests that homophobia serves a purpose: it allows men anxious about their masculinity to affirm themselves. As the story goes, masculinity is established through the repudiation of femaleness: heterosexual men are troubled by male homosexuality because it represents feminized masculinity.[6] Confronted with contradictions in their own masculinity, they project their insecurities onto others. Their audience is typically other men, often other heterosexual men. That's why boys police each other in playgrounds for signs of sissiness, why homosexuality has become a particularly fraught issue in traditionally all-male institutions such as the military and Boy Scouts, and why, in its most extreme form, homophobia has inspired such hateful acts as the brutal killing of Matthew Shepard in Wyoming.

This literature provides a compelling explanation for one type of male homophobia, but as a description of the variety of different homophobias now circulating, it is somewhat less useful. For example, in the early 1990s few of the activists I encountered in a conservative antigay campaign in a small Oregon town expressed homophobia that was directed primarily toward feminized men. Instead, their antigay rhetoric was directed against masculine homosexual men whom they imagined as culturally and economically privileged, and as sexually promiscuous. In opposition to this supposedly powerful group, male antigay rights activists positioned themselves as "strong but compassionate" committed fathers and faithful husbands, and suggested that if gay men (and lesbians) were offered civil rights their own sacrifices would be diminished.

Ten years later, in the course of a statewide campaign against gay marriage in Oregon sponsored by a similar grouping of religious conservatives, the target shifted from masculine men living outside the family, to same-sex couples in long-term committed relationships—particularly lesbian couples with children. Such families were criticized for their lack of differentiated gender roles, and for failing to provide their children with strong fathers. For social conservatives involved in the campaign, same-sex marriage called into question the father-headed household, placing children at risk.

The shifting symbolic targets of these two campaigns—the first directed against masculine gay men, the second against maternal lesbians —suggests that homophobia evokes multiple meanings and is capable of being deployed in varying ways depending upon the local context. In the following, I explore this shift in homophobic rhetoric as it has played out over the past fifteen years in two political campaigns in the state of Oregon: the first, an attempt to outlaw civil rights protections for lesbians and gay men; the second, a campaign to define marriage as the union between man and woman. What do these two rhetorical frames have in common? How do they differ? And what do they tell us about continuities and shifts in homophobic discourse?

Theorizing Homophobia

Psychologist George Weinberg, who coined the term "homophobia" to describe the "irrational fear or hatred of homosexuals," saw antigay prejudice as a pathology rooted in an individual's psychological make-up.[7] While his effort to label this widespread prejudice was exceedingly important, Weinberg's definition failed to account for why certain groups of individuals are more homophobic than others—and in particular why men, by most accounts, tend to be more homophobic than women. Missing, in part, was an analysis of the link between gender and sexual prejudice.

Taking this question up, theorists influenced by feminism argued that homophobia has something important in common with sexism: it affirms male identity by rejecting what is unmanly.[8] Homophobia directed toward lesbians may be somewhat more complex, rooted largely in men's antipathy toward women who choose to live without men, and to a lesser extent in heterosexual women's rejection of women who renounce "emphasized femininity."[9] But in general, feminists suggest that what is threatening about homosexuality is "men not being men and women not being women."[10] Gender theorist Bob Connell distinguished between "hegemonic" and "subordinate" masculinities and femininities, suggesting that hegemonic masculinity organizes itself around psychological, cultural, and social dominance over women, but it also organizes between masculinities, en-abling some men to dominate over other men culturally, psychologically, and even sexually.[11] Following from this, one might see homophobia as rooted largely in prejudice against gender nonconformity, with dominant men in particular subordinating less manly men in an effort to assert their power and dominance.

While it is certainly true that effeminate men (and to a lesser extent "masculine" women) tend to be the victims of the most violent forms of homophobia such as gay bashing, homophobia is directed toward gender-conforming homosexuals as well. We now know that homosexual men and women embody a range of different gender expressions, from hyperfemininity to hypermasculinity and all points in between.[12] Equating homosexuality with gender nonconformity glosses over the great variety of gender expressions among gay, lesbian, and queer-identified individuals, and the ways they elicit social stigma. Yet even masculine-appearing gay men and feminine-appearing lesbian women, though they are less visible, are victims of antihomosexual prejudice.[13]

What this suggests is that just as we should understand masculinities and femininities in plural rather than singular terms, so are there clearly homophobias in the plural. For example, psychoanalyst Elisabeth Young-Bruehl isolates at least eight different varieties of homophobia, with the classic Freudian example of "males prejudiced against males perceived as feminine" as just one of many possible variants:

> Males prejudiced against males perceived as feminine; males prejudiced against males perceived as masculine; males prejudiced against females perceived as masculine; males prejudiced against females perceived as feminine; females prejudiced against females perceived as masculine; females prejudiced against females perceived as feminine; females prejudiced against males perceived as feminine; females prejudiced against males perceived as masculine.[14]

This more complex understanding of homophobia helps us to understand emergent strains of "neopatriarchal" rhetoric on the right. Right-wing campaigns have long been organized around a patriarchal vision of family life, in which the strict father is moral authority and master of the household, dominating both the mother and children and imposing needed discipline.[15] Contemporary conservative politics turn these family "values" into political values: hierarchical authority, individual discipline, and military might. But as feminist critiques of traditional masculinity make their way into conservative rhetoric, and as men struggle to define a role that maintains male authority without sounding overly authoritarian, they have positioned themselves as "compassionate" protectors of the family—"responsible" fathers and husbands rather than old-style patriarchs.[16] Older notions of women's subservience to men and men's dominance over women have given way to "kinder, gentler" neopatriarchal understandings.

Because the old strategy of blaming women's growing independence for many of the social changes they see around them, including the decline of male authority in the family, is no longer politically tenable, neopatriarchal rhetoric does not attack women per se, does not call for the subordination of women, and does not explicitly support practices and arrangements that buttress gender inequality. Rather, it speaks of the importance of gender differentiation in the family, strong but compassionate fathers, and heterosexual-only marriage, and views the granting of legal rights to lesbian and gay men and their families as anathema to these values. And it does so by expressing "concern" for rather than overt antipathy toward groups and social practices it opposes. Illustrating this emergent neopatriarchal rhetoric and the multiple forms of homophobia it deploys are two campaigns in the state of Oregon; a ballot initiative against gay rights in the early 1990s, and a campaign against gay marriage ten years later.

The Politics of Anxious Masculinity

Men are anxious because the arena of masculinity is being rapidly reconstituted by a dazzling array of social changes which call patriarchal authority into question.[17] The rise of feminism, the economic restructuring of the labor force, and the decline of cultural hierarchies in general are calling into question the naturalness of male dominance. Consequently, many men, white working-class men in particular, are experiencing an erosion of their power at home, in the workplace, and in the community.

Oregon is an ideal place for examining how "anxious masculinity" has fueled resentments that find their expression in campaigns against gay rights. For the past two decades, national social conservative organizations have used Oregon as a testing ground for a number of antigay initiatives. Because it has a very open state referendum system and is highly polarized politically, divided between progressive urban areas and highly conservative rural and suburban areas, it has been fertile ground for "culture wars" battles. During the past few decades, Oregon, like the rest of the Pacific Northwest, has undergone massive economic restructuring, from a timber-based economy to a service-based one, diminishing the power of many blue-collar men in the workforce and at home, and making them more receptive to right-wing appeals.

In the rural Pacific Northwest, the masculine culture of lumbering, based upon the image of men taming the wilds, was for generations a source of masculine pride and economic wealth.[18] During the immediate post–World War II period, when the logging industry was in its heyday, most of the mills were unionized, and workers earned salaries that pushed them and their families into the middle class. In the mid-1980s, as hundreds of mills closed down, many small timber-based communities throughout the Pacific Northwest lost their traditional economic base. Kids in the local schools used to have jobs waiting for them in the mills when they graduated from high school. But fewer and fewer stayed in town after graduation. Thousands of retired southern Californians cashed in their home equity and moved north, and small timber towns were increasingly absorbed into the larger culture and economy of the state and region.

Middle-aged men who had worked at the local mills had to settle for low-paid service-sector jobs that paid far less than a family wage. More women worked for pay outside of the home. There was a growing sense of displacement, particularly among men whose identity had been founded upon being the family breadwinner. If men do not share a distinctive identity based on their economic role as family providers, then what is a man? As Kathleen Gerson asks: "If men can no longer claim special rights and privileges based on their unique responsibilities and contributions, then how can they justify their power?"[19]

In the early 1990s, the arrival of politicized Christian conservatism fused the discontent and resentments that had been brewing among the white working classes into a political force. It permitted white working men to imagine themselves and their families as strong and independent. They could become the stewards of their families and their communities by standing up to "the homosexual threat."

In 1992, a grassroots Christian conservative organization, the Oregon Citizens Alliance, sponsored a highly controversial statewide ballot measure that sought to amend the state constitution to prevent antidiscrimination protections for gays and lesbians and prohibit government spending to promote homosexuality. These ballot measures would prevent the state and its jurisdictions from "mak[ing], pass[ing], adopt-[ing], or enforc[ing] any ordinance, rule, regulation, policy or resolution that extends minority status, affirmative action, quotas, special class status, or any similar concepts, based on homosexuality or which establishes any categorical provision such as 'sexual orientation,' 'sexual preference,' or any similar provision which includes homosexuality."[20] The initiatives lost by a fairly large margin in the state's two most populous metropolitan areas but won across rural Oregon. Ultimately, though these efforts were unsuccessful, they managed to place the issue of homosexuality, and the Christian right, on the political map, paving the way for future efforts.

In 1993, in an effort to build upon its success in rural areas, the Oregon Citizens Alliance targeted eight counties and three dozen small communities where the statewide initiative (Ballot Measure 9) had passed the year before. These measures sought to amend local bylaws to prevent antidiscrimination protections for gays and lesbians and prohibit government spending to promote homosexuality. For nearly a year, small towns throughout Oregon were deeply polarized around the issue of homosexuality. During 1997–99, a few years after these ballot measures deeply divided the state, I conducted fieldwork in a small town in central Oregon in order to paint a portrait of one fairly typical small town, which I call "Timbertown," as it became embroiled in this conflict.

The battles waged in the culture wars are typically fought by a small number of highly motivated activists who exploit potentially polarizing issues such as gay/lesbian rights. In contrast, I wanted to go beyond the relatively small number of people who took public roles in the campaign. I began with these activists, whom I located fairly easily through newspaper accounts and prior contacts, asking each one to refer me to two other people in the community: one who shared his/her opinion on the issue of gay rights and who may or may not have been active in the campaign, and one who probably did not share his/her opinion. From this list, I selected a larger sample of interview subjects, including a number of "opinion leaders," elected officials, business people, and longtime residents who were well known in the town. In all, I interviewed fifty residents of this community. I also analyzed campaign literature and tracked the campaign in newspaper accounts.

The interviews were loosely structured, to permit my subjects to focus on those aspects of the campaign, their involvement in it, and any feelings about the issue of homosexuality that seemed salient to them. I also gathered biographical material about each person, trying to understand who they were as individuals, as political actors, and as residents of Timbertown. What was their relationship to the town? How did they feel about how the town was changing? What were their hopes and dreams for the future? The interviews, which lasted anywhere from an hour to three hours, were tape recorded, and the tapes were later transcribed. My book, *The Stranger Next Door,* documents this fieldwork, some of which I draw upon in this essay.[21]

The issue of gay rights resurfaced again ten years later when an initiative to outlaw gay marriage appeared on the state ballot, one of eleven state initiatives designed to bring socially conservative voters to the ballot box during the 2004 presidential election. The measure sought to amend the Oregon constitution to declare "only marriage between one man and one woman is valid or legally recognized as marriage."[22] By that time, gay rights, and indeed the issue of gay marriage, had become highly politicized at the national level, and a conservative Christian occupied the White House, giving his blessing to the fight to outlaw gay marriage. The nation was embroiled in a full-blown "culture war" over same-sex marriage, and Oregon was once again deeply divided.

This time, I followed the conflict from afar, tracking campaign literature, newspaper reports, and local and national Web sites linked to the campaign, and conducting a content analysis of material distributed by the Defense of Marriage Coalition, the religious conservative organization that sponsored the ballot measure. How did the campaign literature frame its appeals? How did it speak of heterosexual marriage, same-sex marriage, and the roles of men and women in families? What themes came up most frequently? I would not suggest that a content analysis of campaign literature is comparable to the ethnographic data I collected in the earlier study, which allowed me to look at the ways different individuals in one community interpreted the activist frames constructed by national and local conservative organizations. Nonetheless, in focusing upon the rhetoric of activist elites who took public positions in both campaigns, as I do in this article, one can see some striking similarities and differences in the kinds of homophobic appeals made by antigay rights forces from 1993 to 2004. In the following, I discuss the themes invoked by these campaigns, beginning with the earlier one.

Father Knows Best

By the early 1990s, in many parts of the nation, homosexuality was becoming more normalized. In an earlier study, I found that as lesbians of the baby boom moved into middle age and into motherhood, families, and the labor force, their subcultural identities became less salient, and individuals came to view their sexual identities as only one of many identities they possessed. Similarly, interviewing gay men and lesbians in the mid-1990s, a group of researchers found that "many Americans have normalized and routinized their homosexuality to a degree that the concept of the closet is less descriptive of their lives." In other words, their lives were less systematically shaped by the need to conceal and manage their homosexuality.[23]

These cultural shifts, though centered in urban, middle-class milieus, reverberated even in small-town Oregon. In Timbertown, the assistant school superintendent was a highly respected woman whose lesbianism was known to many in the community, and several small businesses were owned and operated by lesbians who were out in varying degrees. Once viewed as a shameful secret, homosexuality was becoming a plausible lifestyle—which displeased a small but vocal minority of social conservatives, mainly evangelical Christians, in town. The campaign against gay rights promised to give them a public voice and a sense of unity. Joining the campaign meant that the evangelical community could assert moral leadership and bring religious values to the secular public sphere. Individual church leaders could become more visible in the community, unifying their congregations and disavowing Christians who they felt did not possess the necessary degree of religious commitment. Activists could take a stand against the secular world and its disappointments and in favor of what is right and true, inviting secular conservatives to join them and boldly articulate their vision of the community.

Religious people did not universally support the antigay campaign, and there were those who actively opposed it, but many came to be persuaded that gay men, in particular, posed a threat to hegemonic forms of masculinity. These individuals were troubled by what they perceived as a decline of male authority in the family, and by the increasing ambiguity of gender roles, and they struggled to maintain masculine authority against threats from homosexuality and feminism, and also from "welfare cheats" and others seen as lacking in self-restraint and work ethics. But rather than imagine the "homosexual threat" in the body of a feminine gay man, the stereotypical image of homosexual gender non-conformity, they exhibited antipathy toward more masculine homosexual males, who they believed called into question the belief in natural gender differences and promoted nonprocreative sexuality without apologies.

This image was promoted by Christian conservative organizations, which circulated "The Gay Agenda," a 1992 video produced by a charismatic church in California, featuring images of gay men at gay pride parades sporting sadomasochistic paraphernalia. Campaign literature and videos such as "The Gay Agenda" constructed "the homosexual" as male—not the limp-wristed, feminized men who were synonymous with homosexuality in the popular imagination, but the hypermasculine gay man, the leather-clad sadomasochist who flaunts his aggressive sexuality in public, refusing to feel shame for his desires. In the film, homosexuals represent undisciplined male sexuality, freed of the "civilizing" influence of women.

In contrast, the campaign put forth a vision of heterosexual masculinity that stressed the important role of fathers as providers who are committed to the well-being of their families and "tamed" by the women in their lives. Barney Wooten, a big burly fellow in his forties, who was a leader of the local campaign against gay rights, exemplified this image. Wooten works as a scientist for the state and drives a maroon Cadillac. On the back is a bumper sticker depicting a Jesus fish eating a Darwin fish. A caption reads: "Survival of the fittest." The first thing one sees as you enter his house is his wedding photo, next to a framed marriage certificate. Scattered throughout the living room are religious prints depicting images of submission before God.

Barney met his wife Annie after having gone through a painful divorce, after which he became born-again, dedicating his life to Christ. Annie quit her job as a scientist working for the state when she and Barney married. Together, they are raising Annie's three children from a previous marriage. While his wife quietly worked in the kitchen, Barney went to great lengths to tell me how he actively participates in the life of his family. He travels hundreds of miles on a weekly basis to pick up his stepchildren, who live in another part of the state. He has long been active in school politics. He helps his stepkids with their homework. He is, as he describes himself, living the life of a Christian parent who is deeply committed to his family's well-being.

Indeed, Barney has been involved in the Promise Keepers, a national Christian men's group founded in 1990, a "Christ-centered ministry dedicated to uniting men through vital relationships to become godly influences in their world."[24] The Promise Keepers seeks to restore fathers to their rightful place at the head of the patriarchal family, calling upon them to be better fathers, more responsive to their families, and more active in their communities.[25] Similarly, Barney has repudiated a past in which he readily admits he did not give as much to his family as he should have. Today, as he describes it, he leads a life based upon submission to the needs of his family. Christianity gives these sacrifices meaning. It also informs his activism against gay rights and for parental rights in the public school system.

What bothers him most about gay people—whom he describes exclusively as men—is that they refuse to make sacrifices. They refuse to submit themselves to wives and children. They flaunt excess. They fail to tame their sexual impulses. Their relationships have no strings attached and no guarantee of duration. It's striking that Barney describes male homosexuality in terms that closely resemble stereotypes of hegemonic male heterosexuality. Left to its own devices, some suggest, male sexuality is aggressive, individualistic, impulsive. For Barney, homosexuals represent untamed, undisciplined male sexuality, unrestrained by women.[26]

A central claim here is that families need fathers in order to function effectively—a position promoted by the "fatherhood movement"—but if left to their own devices, men will not necessarily choose to join families. By withholding sex until marriage and then consenting to traditional gender role differentiation in marriage, women coerce men into being responsible fathers and family men. Without the institution of heterosexual marriage and the obligation of biological paternity, men are unattached and dangerous. Therefore, to control the naturally aggressive tendencies of men, who would otherwise be left unsupervised and unconstrained, they must become fathers.[27]

Such arguments harken back to a 1950s functionalist view of the family that sees the structure of the nuclear family as ideally suited to keeping the wayward desires of individuals (particularly men) in check. The problem with homosexuality for Parsons (and Barney Wooten) is that it is a "mode of structuring of human relationships which is radically in conflict with the place of the nuclear family in the social structure and in the socialization of the child." As Parsons explains,

"[Homosexuality's] nearly universal prohibition is a direct consequence of the 'geometry' of family structure."[28] In other words, only a sex-differentiated, heterosexual nuclear family can restrain the desires of men.

"Good Christian" men like Barney have turned away from the excesses of their past and the demands of their desires; they channel their energies for the good of the family unit. But gay men are undisciplined, selfish children who refuse to grow up. They need to be led back on track, punished for their excesses, and not rewarded for their bad behavior. Here, using Young-Breuhl's schema, we see homophobia as expressed by males prejudiced against males perceived as masculine. Perhaps because effeminate homosexuals can easily be mocked and marginalized, masculine homosexuals pose a greater challenge. Male homosexuality is threatening because it represents a model of masculinity that heterosexual men have been forced by feminists, and by economic shifts, to abandon.

Indeed, antigay activist Paul Cameron suggests that many men may find homosexuality more satisfying than heterosexuality, planting the fear among women that their husbands might leave them for men: "The evidence is that men do a better job on men. . . . If you want the most satisfying orgasm you can get, then homosexuality is too powerful to resist. . . . It's pure sexuality."[29] Heterosexual marriage tames male desire; unmarried gay men are "naughty boys" run amok whose desires need to be disciplined, not rewarded. Recognizing that passing a ballot measure to prevent homosexual "special rights" might not change very much, Barney nonetheless believes it represents a first step. As the strict parent disciplining "the naughty boy," he is affirming a sense of himself as a moral leader in his family and in the larger society.

Ironically, most gay people in Timbertown were in fact women, and mothers to boot, and very far from the (distorted) image of egocentric, predatory gay men. Perhaps the appearance of normalized lesbians in town was all the more disturbing to religious conservatives, for they challenged the stereotyped ways that they conceived of homosexuality, and by implication heterosexuality, and revealed that the heterosexual-homosexual dichotomy was far less rigid and enduring than many Christian right spokespersons suggested. But during a subsequent campaign, a decade later, the lesbian mother would become the focus of righteous indignation.

Father Still Knows Best

First Comes Love, Then Comes Marriage, Then Comes Mommy and
Daddy Pushing a Baby Carriage.

—Sign at rally against same-sex marriage,
Washington D.C., October 2004

In November 2003, the Massachusetts Supreme Court ruled that both
same-sex and opposite-sex couples are entitled to equal marriage rights
under the Massachusetts state constitution. In February 2004, the same
court clarified its ruling, stating that only access to civil marriage (not
civil unions) would provide equal protection to same-sex couples under the state constitution. The following month, Multnomah County,
Oregon's most populous county, granted marriage licenses to gay and
lesbian couples, following similar actions in San Francisco. The San
Francisco licenses were later nullified by the California Supreme Court,
which ruled they had been issued without legal authority. Several states
quickly began to amend their state constitutions to ban same-sex marriages, and in November 2004 initiatives designed to ban same-sex marriage appeared on eleven state ballots throughout the nation, including
Oregon.

Ballot Measure 36 in Oregon sought to amend the Oregon constitution to declare that "only marriage between one man and one woman is
valid or legally recognized as marriage," thereby nullifying earlier marriages granted by Multnomah County and circumventing future efforts
to open marriage to same-sex couples, locally or nationally.[30] A coalition of local religious conservative groups, the Defense of Marriage
Coalition, based in evangelical churches and linked to national organizations such as Focus on the Family, Concerned Women for America,
and the Family Research Council, sponsored the initiative.

In mobilizing support for the measure, some spokespeople invoked
religious arguments. "The question is, should the State of Oregon put
its stamp of approval on what God has clearly said is wrong?" asked
one. "Marriage is the work of heaven and every major religion and culture throughout world history," another declared, echoing the belief
that marriage is "a covenant established by God wherein one man and
one woman, united for life, are licensed by the state for the purpose of
founding and maintaining a family."[31]

However, the vast majority of arguments against same-sex marriage in Oregon utilized secular understandings, arguing for the supposed naturalness of heterosexuality, the nuclear family, and distinct gender roles. Proponents of the ballot measure warned against diminished sex role differentiation in the family. Earlier campaigns against gay/lesbian rights in the state suggested that homosexual men posed a challenge to the family because they flaunt the uncivilized desires of men unchained by wives, and pose a threat to children and young adults. In the campaign against same-sex marriage, we see a variation on this theme: marriage is good for men because it tames them. "Men who are married earn more, work harder, drink less, live longer, spend more time attending religious services, and are more sexually faithful. They also see their testosterone levels drop, especially when they have children in the home."[32] But while marrying is beneficial to heterosexual men, conservative activists suggested, it does not have the same effect on gay men because of the absence of the "civilizing" influence of a wife.

> If the distinctive sexual patterns of "committed" gay couples are any indication, it is unlikely that homosexual marriage would domesticate men in the way that heterosexual marriage does. It is also extremely unlikely that the biological effects of heterosexual marriage on men would also be found in homosexual marriage. Thus, gay activists who argue that same-sex civil marriage will domesticate gay men are, in all likelihood, clinging to a foolish hope. This foolish hope does not justify yet another effort to meddle with marriage.[33]

To make the case for same-sex marriage, some gay activists have suggested that same-sex marriage, like heterosexual marriage, will restrain unwieldy desires and domesticate gay men.[34] As conservative opponents tried to refute this view one man made the (tautological) argument that homosexual relationships did not deserve to be sanctioned legally because "research shows that homosexuals are less likely to enter into long-term relationships, be sexually faithful to a partner, and have relationships last a lifetime."[35] Homosexuals, if granted the right to marry, would diminish the institution of marriage by their very presence, he and others claimed.

The Family Research Council, a Washington, D.C.–based group that was linked to the Oregon campaign, proclaimed that "same-sex 'marriage' would undercut the norm of sexual fidelity within marriage," on the grounds that "more than 79 percent of heterosexual married men and women, along with lesbians in civil unions, reported that they strongly valued sexual fidelity. Only about 50 percent of gay men in civil unions valued sexual fidelity."[36] Of course, if homosexual relationships are in fact less stable, it is probably precisely because gay men and lesbians have been denied social supports, such as legal and symbolic affirmation through marriage, which might provide economic and cultural incentives for relationship stability.

Not only would same-sex marriage fail to integrate gay men and lesbians into marital norms, they suggested, it would also prove harmful to families in general and contribute to the breakdown of marriage. A man identified as a retired deputy superintendent of the Oregon Department of Education suggested: "The breakdown of marriage hurts kids. It has contributed to increased emotional, behavioral, and health problems that have resulted in lower academic achievement." Some predicted mayhem and mass confusion should marriage between members of the same sex be sanctioned. "If measure 36 fails, there will be mass confusion over the definition of marriage in Oregon. . . . Teachers will be forced to teach sex education to middle school children based on the new interpretation of marriage in Oregon."[37]

The campaign emphasized the importance of fathers and the dangers posed by father-absence in lesbian-headed families. An Oregon politician, arguing in favor of the ballot measure, said that "children do better with a mother and father," citing the research of a Yale professor of psychology. "Infants, by 8 weeks, can tell the difference between a male and female interacting with them. This diversity in itself provides children with broader, richer, experience of various relational interactions— more so than for children who are raised by only one gender."[38]

Focus on the Family, one of the organizations spearheading the marriage ban nationally, reserved particular wrath for celebrity Rosie O'Donnell, whom they accused of selfishly wanting children. A spokesperson for the organization recounted a television interview in which O'Donnell's son asked her why he can't have a father, to which she replied: "Because I'm the kind of mommy who wants another mommy." For the Focus on the Family spokesperson, this represents the ultimate in selfishness: "Her son doesn't get a daddy because Rosie has certain emotional and sexual desires."[39] One of the chief petitioners for the ballot measure personalized this theme:

I know the immeasurable importance of their mother in the lives of my three kids. I now understand from experience the importance a father can make in the lives of his children. A father-child relationship more than any other defines a child's entire life. It affects their dating and marriage relationships, their identity, their sexuality, their work performance, how they express emotion, and how they become independent. A child's relationship with dad shapes their view of God, their significant life decisions, and ultimately who they turn out to be as individuals.[40]

"Children Need Fathers," warned the Family Research Council,

If same-sex civil marriage becomes common, most same-sex couples with children would be lesbian couples. This would mean that we would have yet more children being raised apart from fathers. Among other things, we know that fathers excel in reducing antisocial behavior and delinquency in boys and sexual activity in girls. What is fascinating is that fathers exercise a unique social and biological influence on their children. For instance, a recent study of father absence on girls found that girls who grew up apart from their biological father were much more likely to experience early puberty and a teen pregnancy than girls who spent their entire childhood in an intact family . . . a father's pheromones influence the biological development of his daughter, and a strong marriage provides a model for girls of what to look for in a man, and gives them the confidence to resist the sexual entreaties of their boyfriends.[41]

In summary, same-sex parent households pose a threat to heterosexual families for two main reasons: they fail to domesticate men and they remove women from the marriage pool, increasing the chance that men will remain single and undomesticated, and they raise children without fathers, thereby threatening their children's normal gender development. It is not simply a father's presence or absence that is important, as we can see in the preceding quotation: his ongoing biological linkage to his progeny is key, as the statement about the beneficial impact of a father's pheromones on his daughter suggests. Without this biological and social influence, conservatives claim, daughters are placed at "risk" for early puberty, premarital sexuality, teen pregnancy, and a host of social problems.

As we saw, arguments for the civilizing influence of marriage on men circulated in an earlier campaign against gay rights, echoing functional-ist accounts of the nuclear family. In the context of the fight against gay marriage, however, they focus on the destructive impact of father-absence, which implicitly and explicitly targets lesbian mothers. As a "fatherhood movement" came to blame feminism, gay/lesbian families and single mothers for the social problems caused by men and teenage boys, the Christian right variant of this argument is that traditional gen-der roles are natural, unchangeable, and God-given.

In his book *Bringing Up Boys,* James Dobson criticized efforts to call into question the naturalness of gender roles, linking this "unisex" idea to a "powerful gay and lesbian agenda" whose propagandists are teach-ing a revolutionary view of sexuality called 'gender feminism.' " Femi-nist critiques of gender, he believes, are dangerous for both sexes, but particularly for boys: "Protect the masculinity of your boys," he warns, "who will be under increasing political pressure in years to come," an argument echoed by the Christian women's organization Concerned Women for America, which blames feminism—in particular its support for legal equality, reproductive freedom, female sexual pleasure, and no-fault divorce—for eroding the "protections" that traditional mar-riage and family law provide women. Feminist assaults on the tradi-tional family, they suggest, have made it easier for men to renounce their familial responsibilities.[42]

If father-absence is the linchpin of what is wrong with gay marriage, and lesbians are much more likely to have children than gay men, such arguments explicitly and implicitly single out lesbians for special blame. While growing numbers of gay male couples are choosing to have chil-dren through adoption or surrogacy, nationally lesbians are much more likely to be parents than gay men.[43] Moreover, the majority of same-sex couples seeking to marry are women—57 percent of same-sex couples who wed in San Francisco between February 12 and March 11, 2004, and 66 percent of first-day applicants in Massachusetts were women, as are two-thirds of Vermont civil unions.[44] Clearly, if an earlier campaign against gay marriage focused its attack upon the unattached, promiscu-ous gay man, the campaign against gay marriage saw the "domesti-cated" lesbian as the principal threat.

Indeed, the vast majority of arguments for the maintenance of het-erosexual-only marriage rested upon the argument that it was in the "best interests of the children" to be raised by a man and a woman. Mobilizing decontextualized social science research (and to a lesser

Theresa Hammond and Cal Bouchard, Cambridge, Massachusetts, July 2004, photograph by Octavio Tivoli.

extent religious arguments), such rhetoric, in other words, "accepts heterosexual parenting as the gold standard and investigates whether lesbigay parents and their children are inferior," implying that differences indicate deficits.[45] The campaign against same-sex marriage conceived of the ideal family as the father-headed, father-dominant household that socializes children to be highly gendered and most certainly heterosexual, and saw family diversity as something to be feared.

Joshua Gamson and Richard James Knight, Chilmark, Massachusetts, August 2004, photograph by Nicole Friedler.

Multiple Homophobias

These two campaigns are interesting for their similarities: both directed their wrath against gender-conforming homosexuals, masculine gay men and feminine lesbians, diverging from common understandings of homosexuality as gender nonconformity. At the same time, these campaigns also show a shift in homophobic frames: from an earlier targeting of masculine homosexual men, to a focus upon the dangers of domesticated lesbian couples who raise children. This shift, from a focus on promiscuity to domesticity, was hastened by the convergence of several developments: the legalization of sodomy, the growing visibility of "normalized" lesbian and gay families, and the increasing symbolic importance of heterosexual marriage promotion in conservative discourse.

In 2003, the Supreme Court, in *Lawrence v. Texas,* legalized sodomy, and thereby weakened the equation of homosexual behavior and perversion that had been the basis of earlier conservative campaigns. At the same time, as more gay and lesbian baby boomers moved into middle age, many formed families of their own and sought legal protections and symbolic recognition for them, or at least these demands were becoming more visible. The dominant, sexualized image of the lone gay individual who stood apart from family life, was giving way to the image of "virtually normal" domesticated gay men and lesbians, dedicated to consumerism and child rearing.[46] It is striking, too, that ontological claims about the origins of homosexuality, in which religious conservatives claimed that homosexuality was a moral choice, and liberals often responded by claiming that sexuality was innate, marked the earlier campaign against gay rights. By 2004, however, such arguments were barely visible, indicating, perhaps, how far homosexual normalization had progressed during the intervening decade.

During this period, we also see the growing importance of heterosexual marriage in conservative discourse, as marriage promotion became the core of a conservative agenda to transfer many previously state-financed activities to families and religious institutions. For religious conservatives, marriage is the signal event in the life course, representing a covenant between the individual and God. For secular conservatives, marriage is the nexus between the individual and the community, and a check against selfish impulses. Old-fashioned family-values warriors, mainly right-wing Republicans and religious conservatives who had previously dominated discussions of divorce, homosexuality, and teen pregnancy, were joined by an interlocking network of scholarly and policy institutes, think tanks, and commissions—the "neo-family values" movement—to forge a national consensus on family values that shaped the family ideology and politics of the Clinton administration.[47]

During the presidency of George W. Bush, these institutions, such as the Institute for American Values and the Council of Families in America, circulated policy statements on marriage that bore close similarity

Advertisement for Human Rights Campaign Foundation, working
for lesbian, gay, bisexual, and transgender equal rights, from their
website www.hrc.org.

to the emerging right-wing consensus on the family, calling for the reduction of unmarried pregnancy, the promotion of heterosexual marriage, the reduction of divorce, and the encouragement of childbearing
among heterosexually married couples. As part of their promotion of
marriage, the Institute for American Values called for government policies that would "protect the boundaries of marriage":

For marriage to function as a social institution, the community must know who is married. To support marriage, laws and policies must distinguish married couples from other family and friendship units so that people and communities can tell who is married and who is not. Treating cohabiting couples as if they were married is one example of such a legal change that tends to blur the distinction between marriage and non-marriage.[48]

Though same-sex partnerships were rarely if ever explicitly targeted by the "neo-family values" campaigners (as opposed to religious conservatives), their efforts to promote marriage clearly omitted any provision for expanding the marriage pool to include same-sex partners. One can imagine, in view of the preceding comments, that they would seek to draw firm boundaries between the married and the unmarried.

What I am describing is the emergence of homophobic forms that may be roughly analogous to what some have called "symbolic racism." Symbolic racism expresses racist attitudes indirectly, opposing government programs designed to erase racial inequality on the grounds that they violate the popular belief that progress should be based on merit, for example. Such racism expresses feelings that are based less in hate or raw hostility than in discomfort, uneasiness, and fear. Often the racism is thought to be self-protective (as in anti-affirmative-action rhetoric), when it is no more than an effort to retain privilege and discriminate against others' opportunity to acquire privilege and power.[49]

Similarly, the two campaigns I have described seek to draw boundaries to keep heterosexual and homosexual worlds separate and stave off the growing normalization of homosexuality. Though these campaigns pursued different strategies and foregrounded different abject figures, or symbolic targets, both targeted gender-conforming homosexuals and affirmed the importance of the heterosexual couple to the preservation of the family. Perhaps feminine gay men and masculine lesbians were somehow less threatening because they were visibly Other. But if homosexuality is compatible with gender conformity, and lesbian mothers and masculine gay men are more visible, integrated members of society, the boundaries between gays and straights, and men and women, become exceedingly blurry. They challenge the notions that firm boundaries separate the homosexual and heterosexual worlds, and that homosexuals occupy a discrete and identifiable homosexual "role."[50]

The existence of homosexual men who are aggressively masculine

and lesbian women who are mothers and who exhibit other traditionally feminine traits represent the normalization and integration of homosexuality into the conventional social world, threaten the conservative belief in absolute gender differences, and reveal a fundamental inco-
herence in its discourse. The existence of such figures also challenges the
privileged roles that fathers play in the family: masculine gay men do so
by suggesting that heterosexual males do not have a monopoly on masculinity; lesbian mothers, by suggesting that fathers may be dispensable
altogether.

To fully understand the reasons for homophobia's continuing appeal,
then, we must theorize it in multiple rather than singular ways. Homophobia takes multiple forms, varying in different contexts. The dominant image of homophobia, male anger toward feminized men, is overly
generalized. Homophobia is a malleable cultural frame that can be deployed in different ways, and at the current moment, conservative social
movements, such as those documented in Oregon, have focused upon
more gender-normative lesbians and gay men. In striking contrast to prohibitions against homosexuality that emerged most visibly in the 1950s,
when the "male provider" role was at its peak, these newer forms of homophobia emerge at a time of increasing homosexual normalization and
gender equality. I would not go as far as to suggest that such variants
of homophobia are supplanting earlier forms that focused upon homosexual gender-nonconformity.[51] Rather, they may coexist alongside them,
becoming more or less salient depending upon the local context.

At a time of economic decline, participation in antigay campaigns
offered men, and their women allies, the momentary promise of restora-
tion: of manhood and identity. Addressing anxieties about shifts in masculinity and the decline of male authority, activists against gay rights
imagined homosexuals as a threat to men's authority in the family, and
declared that marriage must be heterosexual, and fathers manly, strong,
and decisive, but not wholly dominating. Their neopatriarchal politics
tried to make room for daddy, restoring faith in patriarchal masculinity
while incorporating some feminist critiques of its worst excesses.

Epilogue

In the introduction, I described a recurring dream in which I have forgotten to get dressed and my body, unclothed, is revealed for all to see. Nakedness suggests feelings of vulnerability, of being physically as well as emotionally exposed, and of being shamed. Shame, in turn, leads us to hide the vulnerable parts of who we are and reveal to others only those aspects of ourselves that make us seem powerful and in control. As philosopher Martha Nussbaum suggests, we all carry around a good deal of "primitive shame": we are shaped by a sense of neediness and the shame that arises out of it.[1] Consequently, we try to hide from shame and are prone to shaming others in order to displace our own shameful feelings onto them.

In an ironic commentary on the pervasiveness of shame and Americans' fascination with biological fixes, Jonathan Franzen's 2001 novel *The Corrections* describes a pharmaceutical company's attempt to develop a miracle drug that blocks "deep" or "morbid" shame. A handsome doctor encourages an aging housewife to expunge the "the vicious bipolarity of shame, that rapid cycling between confession and concealment" by taking a designer drug that will remake her personality.[2] Though we might welcome such quick-fix solutions, our actions in the world are what really make the difference, alleviating shameful feelings or exacerbating them. Activists have tried to remove the stigma and shame associated with sexuality, a primary arena in which we play out our shameful feelings. By speaking openly about our desires and the social forces that hold them at bay, they believe, we release our feelings of shame, ridding ourselves of the false selves that mask who we "really" are.

Those who wish to alleviate shame do so because they believe that liberal societies should acknowledge our inherent neediness and do its utmost to protect each individual from it through social welfare provisions, educational opportunities, and the creation of a culture of empathy. Linguist George Lakoff suggests that liberals tend to see government in the role of nurturing parents whose job is to nurture their children and teach them to nurture others. Nurturance has two dimensions: empathy and responsibility, for oneself and others. Responsibility requires strength and competence. The strong nurturing parent is protective and caring, builds trust and connection, promotes family happiness and fulfillment, fairness, freedom, openness, cooperation, community development. She or he would see the development of shame as a barrier to the development of such progressive ideals.[3]

On first glance, one might think that we live in a world without shame. Today, sexual imagery is everywhere: in advertising, where sex sells all manner of products; in television programs that feature openly gay characters and no longer blink at allusions to premarital sex; in news reports of controversies surrounding condom provision in developing countries. This proliferation of sexual speech has been partially successful in normalizing homosexuality and (to a lesser extent) in decentering traditional gender and family norms. Yet during the past two decades, those who speak about sexuality in public, thanks to the vast amounts of money that have been pouring into right-wing think tanks and advocacy groups, are more likely to argue for a highly traditionalist, shame-based conception of sexual morality.[4]

If liberals, with few exceptions, have been dedicated to alleviating shame, conservatives have done quite the opposite: they seek to alleviate their own shame by amplifying the shame of others. For example, going back to my example of being unclothed and shamed in front of my students, those who are fearful of public speaking are often urged to play a trick in their minds and imagine their audience is undressed. The logic here is that in order for the speaker to assume a position of power in relation to her audience, she must picture them as naked, vulnerable, ashamed. There's but a short leap from this strategy to the efforts of the conservative activists I described in the second half of this book, who displace their own feelings of shame onto those who are less powerful.

In contrast to liberals' "nurturant parent," conservatives embrace the "strict father" as the model of family and political life, according to Lakoff. The strict father is moral authority and master of the household, dominating both the mother and children and imposing needed discipline. Contemporary conservative politics turns these family values into political values: hierarchical authority, individual discipline, military might. To counter the supposed cultural anarchy wrought by feminism, sexual liberation, and the rise of the welfare state, the "strict father" says we must substitute punitive measures, including shaming. Young drug dealers caught in their first offense, they say, should be sent home with their heads shaved and without their pants.[5] Welfare recipients should be thrown off the dole. Gays and lesbians should be denied the right to protection against job and housing discrimination, and legal validation through the right to marry.[6] The strict father wants to defend a model of marriage that installs him as king, and where his authority, and often even physical and emotional coercion, holds the family structure intact. The nurturant parent, in contrast, has a more democratic understanding of family life, and a more gender-neutral understanding of the marital bond. While the conservative tends to oppose efforts to offer same-sex partners full legal status, the liberal is more likely to welcome it.

The battle for marriage rights has captivated the imagination and energy of many gay/lesbian Americans—proof, to many, of just how conventional we have become. At the same time, because our society values marriage so highly, it is understandable that many would seek to validate themselves through association with it. Heterosexual marriage in this country (as opposed to many European nations, where rates of marriage are much lower and religious belief is much weaker) preserves the marital couple's central place in the social structure. It installs heterosexuality, in philosopher Cheshire Calhoun's words, "as the foundation of civilization," while "displac[ing] gays and lesbians . . . by refusing to recognize that [they] belong in either the public or the private sphere."[7] If the state were forced to recognize plural forms of intimacy, then the political dimensions of marriage would become transparent. This may explain why a growing number of Americans seem willing to extend legal rights (including domestic partnerships and civil union protections) to gays and lesbians, while stopping short of full marriage rights.

The idea that gays and lesbians inhabit a space "outside" the family is no longer really true, if it ever was. We certainly have families, if we define family as a circle of intimates who care for one another. And as the "typical" family structure has become less standardized, queer families look more and more typical. (That's certainly true of my partner and me, who have among us one brother who is single and childless; another brother, who never married, who has joint custody of a daughter born out of wedlock; and a sister who married a man with children from a previous marriage.) The normalization of homosexual relationships through marriage poses a threat to those who want to maintain hierarchical distinctions in the family and clear gender roles. It threatens those who see heterosexual marriage as the signal passageway into adulthood, and as the primary institution binding the individual to his or her faith. Conservatives fear that same-sex marriage would de-center heterosexuality by making heterosexual marriage one option among many morally equivalent ones—and little more than a "life-style" choice. Choices such as these tyrannize us, they suggest, because they depart from tradition, unmoor the individual from social re-straints, and fail to offer clear distinctions between what is good and true and what is not.

Yet this is more than simply a cultural war over religious faith, as market fundamentalism joins religious fundamentalism as the order of the day. The widespread refusal to empathize with the weakest among us, and to acknowledge our common weaknesses, comes at a time when fewer and fewer Americans enjoy job security and the economic and psychological benefits that such security provides, and is rooted at least partly in changes in American corporate culture. Increasingly, CEOs make decisions on the basis of what will boost dividends in the short term rather than retain employees in the long term. Manufacturing jobs that once lifted the economic fortunes of many working Ameri-cans have migrated to low-wage countries in Asia and Latin America. Such market fundamentalism means that American workers have little redress.

It is no longer simply those at the bottom of the economic ladder who contend with instability and low pay, according to Barbara Ehren-reich in a recent book about her experience hunting for a white-collar job. More and more, she says, middle class people occupy a "transi-tion zone," searching endlessly for good-paying, secure jobs with bene-fits, but finding little more than temporary employment. This newer, harsher, dog-eat-dog corporate culture has propelled many of us into a Darwinian struggle for survival.[8] Insecure people who refuse to ac-knowledge their insecurity and the shame associated with it tend to support public policies that appear to them to champion a strict and punitive rather than caring, compassionate role for government, and they want to enshrine these punitive measures, including shaming, into law.[9] "Compassionate conservatives," it turns out, are not very compas-sionate at all.

"Human beings are deeply troubled about being human—about being highly intelligent and resourceful, on the one hand, but weak and vulnerable, helpless against death, on the other," writes Martha Nussbaum, suggesting that human frailty is what is really at the root of shame.[10] This sense of frailty is exacerbated in periods of rapid social change. Today we live in a world in which global, faceless corporations have more and more power to make decisions about what we will eat, how we will work, and where we will live. Many of us feel that we have little control over the course of our lives. Some try to compensate for their own sense of weakness by weakening others, or keeping them in a weak state. How much better off we would all be, though, if we acknowledged our common frailty. Addressing our differences and our vulnerabilities should be, in the end, what morality is all about.

Notes

NOTES TO THE INTRODUCTION

1. Bill Carter, "Many Who Voted for 'Values' Still Like Their Television Sin," *New York Times*, November 22, 2004, www.nytimes.com.

2. Janet Jacobsen and Ann Pellegrini, *Love the Sin: Sexual Regulation and the Limits of Religious Tolerance* (Boston: Beacon, 2004), 6

3. Jonathan Alter and Pat Wingert, "The Return of Shame," *Newsweek*, February 6, 1995, 20.

4. Karin Martin, "I Couldn't Even Picture Myself Having Sex . . .": Gender Differences in Sex and Sexual Subjectivity," in Christine L. Williams and Arlene Stein, eds., *Sexuality and Gender* (Malden , MA, and Oxford: Blackwell, 2002), 156.

5. As feminists expressed skepticism toward visions of sexual revolution, the rise of French thought in the academy, in particular the writings of philosopher Michel Foucault, led many intellectuals to discard linear understandings of history and the view of sexual history as a forward march toward progress. The belief that one can "liberate" sexuality by simply speaking it freely and openly, these critics suggest, obscures the ways that even the language of liberation, upon which many of the social movements of the 1960s and '70s had staked their claims, is implicated in the workings of power. This understanding of sexuality freed scholars to see sexuality as constituted in society and history, and not as biologically ordained. At the same time, poststructuralist thought has inspired skepticism toward "progress narratives" of all kinds, and in the process sensitized us to the fact that sexual liberalization has not been simply a matter of freeing the individual from social constraints. As old rules fall by the wayside, new rules and norms typically crop up. For example, as queer theorists suggest, the decline of stigma toward homosexuality has been accompanied by new normative expectations about how lesbian/gay/bisexual/transgender people should be in the world. See, for example, Michael Warner, *The Trouble with Normal* (New York: Free Press, 1999).

6. A more positive understanding of shame, which draws upon the work of American psychologist Silvan Tomkins, has recently become the focus of a number of works of cultural criticism. See, for example, Eve Kosofsky Sedgwick and

Adam Frank, *Shame and Its Sisters: A Silvan Tomkins Reader* (Durham, NC: Duke University Press, 1995), and Elspeth Probyn, *Blush: Faces of Shame* (Minneapolis: University of Minnesota Press, 2005). In this understanding, shame, signaling attunement to others, is constitutive of the self rather than something that can be eradicated by political or other action (such as movements for "gay pride"). I share these authors' interest in the affective power of shame, agree that shameful feelings are not easily erased, and recognize along with them that members of relatively powerless groups (such as gays and lesbians) also wield shame as a weapon. Still, I remain less convinced of shame's positive contributions to individual or group identities.

7. Gail Hawkes, *Sex and Pleasure in Western Culture* (Cambridge UK: Polity, 2004), 43.

8. Norbert Elias, *The Civilizing Process*, vols. 1–3 (New York: Pantheon, 1994), quoted in Thomas J. Scheff, "Shame and the Social Bond: A Sociological Theory," at http://www.soc.ucsb.edu/faculty/scheff/2.html.

9. Leonard Kass, "The End of Courtship," *The Public Interest*, April 5, 2004, 26.

10. Wendy Shalit, *A Return to Modesty: Discovering the Lost Virtue* (New York: Free Press, 1999).

11. Dr. James Dobson, "In Defending Marriage—Take the Offensive," Focus on the Family Web site, April 2004.

12. Stephanie Coontz, "The Heterosexual Revolution," *New York Times*, op-ed, July 7, 2005, http://www.nytimes.com.

13. Gayle Rubin, "Thinking Sex: Notes for a Radical Theory of the Politics of Sexuality," in C. Vance, ed., *Pleasure and Danger* (New York: Routledge, 1984), 267.

NOTES TO CHAPTER 1

An earlier version of "Shapes of Desire" was published as "Difference, Desire, and the Self: Three Stories," in Carol Franz and Abigail Stewart, *Women Creating Lives: Identities, Resilience, and Resistance* (Boulder, CO: Westview, 1994). Reprinted by permission of Westview Press, a member of Perseus Books, L.L.C.

1. Susan Krieger, "Lesbian Identity and Community: Recent Social Science Literature," *Signs* (1982): 557–575. Ken Plummer called the first account the "orientation" model and the second the "identity construct" model; they are also referred to, respectively, as essentialist and constructionist conceptions of homosexuality. See his "Homosexual Categories," in Ken Plummer, ed., *The Making of the Modern Homosexual* (Totowa, NJ: Barnes and Noble, 1981). Lillian Faderman wrote that lesbians of this generation were divided between the "essential" and "existential" varieties, glossing over the complex ways in which individuals utilize elements of both accounts, as I show. See her *Odd*

Girls and Twilight Lovers: A History of Lesbian Life in Twentieth-Century America (New York: Columbia University Press, 1991).

2. In 1991, when most of the interviews were conducted, the women ranged in age from thirty-three to forty-seven. Two-thirds were white.

3. On the confessional mode of sexual narratives, see Ken Plummer, *Telling Sexual Stories in a Late Modern World* (London: Routledge, 1995); Bonnie Zimmerman, *The Safe Sea of Women* (Boston: Beacon, 1990).

4. I have adapted the concepts of "surface" and "deep" identities from Arlie Hochschild's work on emotional labor, *The Managed Heart: Commercialization of Human Feeling* (Berkeley: University of California Press, 1983).

5. Beth Zemsky cited studies that indicate that the mean age for women to recognize and pronounce (at least to themselves) that this sense of difference and disquiet has something to do with lesbianism is approximately fourteen. See her "Coming Out Against All Odds: Resistance of a Young Lesbian," *Women and Therapy*, vol. 11, nos. 3/4: 185–200. There may be some correlation between lesbian identity and gender identity insofar as "butch" or more masculine-identified lesbians were less likely to see their sexual identities as being elective than feminine-identified women. But the reasons for this are unclear. Is it because "mannish" lesbians were more "essentially" lesbian in orientation? Or is it because butches were the most identifiable lesbian figure since they stood out, often from an early age, and were more apt to be labeled lesbian by family members and other authority figures? For whichever reason, or combination of reasons, gender inversion is a symbolic marker of lesbianism and a warning to women who step out of their prescribed roles that the taint of lesbianism will follow them. See Esther Newton, "The Mythic Mannish Lesbian: Radclyffe Hall and the New Woman," *Signs* 9 (1984): 557–575.

6. Deborah L. Tolman, "Adolescent Girls, Women and Sexuality: Discerning Dilemmas of Desire," in Carol Gilligan, Annie Rogers, and Deborah L. Tolman, eds., *Women and Therapy*, vol. 11, nos. 3/4 (1991): 55–70.

7. For a sense of how dominant cultural norms shaped the lives of teenage girls in the 1950s and how girls resisted these norms, see Wini Breines, *Young, White and Miserable: Growing Up Female in the 1950s* (Boston: Beacon, 1992).

8. Faye Ginsburg, "Dissonance and Harmony: The Symbolic Function of Abortion in Activists' Life Stories," in Personal Narratives Group, ed., *Interpreting Women's Lives* (Bloomington: Indiana University Press, 1989), 59–84.

9. See also Beverly Burch, *On Intimate Terms* (Urbana: University of Illinois Press, 1993). This would seem to imply the necessity of "bringing the body back in," acknowledging that bodily sensation and function play a role, albeit one that is always mediated by culture and subjectivity. Also see Carole Vance, "Social Construction Theory: Problems in the History of Sexuality," in Helen Crowley and Susan Himmelweit, eds., *Knowing Women: Feminism and Knowledge* (London: Polity, 1992). In this sense, I depart from the tradition of inter-

actionist studies in which the importance of physical experience is downplayed, such as Barbara Ponse, *Identities in the Lesbian World: The Social Construction of Self* (Westport, CT: Greenwood, 1978). On the history of sexual theorizing in relation to this question, see my "Three Models of Sexuality: Drives, Identities and Practices," *Sociological Theory,* 7 (Spring 1989): 1–13.

10. Peter Davies, "The Rule of Disclosure in Coming Out among Gay Men," in Ken Plummer, ed., *Modern Homosexualities: Fragments of Lesbian and Gay Experience* (London and New York: Routledge, 1992), 75–83.

11. Karla Jay and Joanne Glasgow, *Lesbian Texts and Contexts: Radical Revisions* (New York: New York University Press, 1990), 6.

NOTES TO CHAPTER 2

An earlier version of "The Year of the Lustful Lesbian" was published in *Sisters, Sexperts, Queers: Beyond the Lesbian Nation,* ed. Arlene Stein (New York: Plume, 1993). © 1993 by Arlene Stein. Used by permission of Dutton Signet, a division of Penguin Group (USA) Inc.

1. The term "false consciousness" derives from Marxist theory, signifying a failure to recognize the instruments of one's oppression or exploitation as one's own creation, as when members of an oppressed class, such as women, unwittingly adopt views of the oppressor class, such as men.

2. See Carole Vance, ed., *Pleasure and Danger: Exploring Female Sexuality* (Boston: Routledge, 1984).

3. Judy Grahn, "Lesbians as Bogeywoman," *Women: A Journal of Liberation* 1, no. 4 (Summer 1970): 36.

4. Interview with author, January 1990.

5. Susie Bright left *On Our Backs* in 1990. In 2004, the magazine celebrated its twentieth anniversary,

6. JoAnn Loulan, *Lesbian Sex* (Minneapolis: Spinsters, 1984).

7. Janice Irvine, *Disorders of Desire* (Philadelphia: Temple University Press, 1990).

8. Interview with author, June 1990.

9. JoAnn Loulan, *Lesbian Passion* (Minneapolis: Spinsters,1987).

10. JoAnn Loulan, *The Lesbian Erotic Dance* (Minneapolis: Spinsters, 1990).

11. Cindy Patton, "Brave New Lesbians," *Village Voice,* July 2, 1985.

12. Joan Nestle, "Butch-Fem Relationships: Sexual Courage in the 1950s," *Heresies* 12 (1981).

13. Samois, *Coming to Power: Writings and Graphics on Lesbian S/M* (Boston: Alyson, 1982).

NOTES TO CHAPTER 3

From Karen Kelly and Evelyn McDonnell, eds., *Stars Don't Stand Still in the Sky: Music and Myth*, (New York: Dia Arts Foundation/New York University Press, 1999). Reprinted with permission.

1. Robin Morgan, quoted in Karen Durbin, "Can a Feminist Love the World's Greatest Rock and Roll Band?" *Ms.*, October 1974, 24–27. See also Simon Frith and Angela McRobbie, "Rock and Sexuality," in Simon Frith and Andrew Goodwin eds. *On the Record: Rock, Pop, and the Written Word* (New York: Pantheon, 1990).

2. Ethel Spector Person, *Dreams of Love and Fateful Encounters* (New York: Penguin, 1988), 267.

3. Shulamith Firestone, *The Dialectic of Sex* (New York: Morrow, 1970), 147, 150.

4. See, for example, Janice Radway, *Reading the Romance: Women, Patriarchy, and Popular Literature* (Chapel Hill: University of North Carolina Press, 1984); Tania Modleski, *Loving with a Vengeance: Mass Produced Fantasies for Women* (New York: Methuen, 1982); Barbara Bradby, "Do-Talk and Don't-Talk: The Division of the Subject in Girl-Group Music," in Frith and Goodwin, *On the Decord*.

5. Ellen Willis, "Beginning to See the Light," in *Beginning to See the Light* (New York: Knopf, 1981), 99. For more recent contributions to the feminist conversation about rock, see Gillian Gaar, *She's a Rebel* (Seattle: Seal Press, 1992), and the essays collected by Evelyn McDonnell and Ann Powers in *Rock She Wrote* (New York: Delta, 1995).

6. Alice Echols, "We Gotta Get Outta This Place: The Sixties," in Marcy Darnovsky, Barbara Epstein, et. al. eds., *Cultural Politics and Social Movements* (Philadelphia: Temple University Press, 1995), 123.

7. Simon Frith, "Music and Identity," in S. Hall and Paul du Gay, eds., *Questions of Cultural Identity* (London: Sage, 1996), 109, 123.

8. Angela McRobbie, "Romantic Individualism and the Teenage Girl," in *Feminism and Youth Culture* (London: Macmillan, 1991), 131.

9. Ibid., 101.

10. Simon Reynolds and Joy Press, *The Sex Revolts* (Cambridge, MA: Harvard University Press, 1995), xv.

11. Jane Flax, "Mother-Daughter Relationships," in H. Eisenstein and A. Jardine eds., *The Future of Difference* (New Brunswick: Rutgers University Press, 1985), 37.

12. Rockin Rina's Women of 1970s Punk Web site at http://www.comnet.ca/~rina/index.html.

13. "Typical Girls" by the Slits (Ari Up/Tessa Pollitt/Viv Albertine/Palmolive), Island Records, September 1979.

14. http://www.salon.com/weekly/phair960617.html. I should note, however, that Fair has altered her image of late, becoming the sexy vixen, a ploy, some suggest, to boost her record sales.

15. Gina Arnold, "Fools Rush In," *East Bay Express,* December 27, 1996.

16. It is notable that Ani diFranco controls her own music through Righteous Babe Records, her own independent label.

17. Angela McRobbie, "Shut Up and Dance: Youth Culture and Changing Modes of Femininity," in *Postmodernism and Popular Culture* (London: Routledge, 1994), 164.

18. Arlene Stein, *Sex and Sensibility: Stories of a Lesbian Generation* (Berkeley: University of California Press, 1997).

NOTES TO CHAPTER 4

An earlier version of "Crossover Dreams" was published in *The Good, The Bad, and the Gorgeous: Popular Culture and Sexuality,* eds. Diane Hamer and Belinda Budge (London: Pandora, 1994). Reprinted with permission.

1. Herbert Gans, *Popular Culture and High Culture* (New York: Basic Books, 1974). See also Angela McRobbie's comments on the importance of looking at "identity-in-culture," in "Post-Marxism and Cultural Studies: A Post-script," in Lawrence Grossberg, Cary Nelson, and Paula Treichler, eds., *Cultural Studies* (London: Routledge, 1992).

2. Gans, *Popular Culture,* 95. Stuart Hall's "Cultural Identity and Cinematic Representation," *Framework,* no. 36, is also relevant to this discussion.

3. Jon Savage, "Tainted Love: The Influence of Male Homosexuality and Sexual Divergence on Pop Music and Culture since the War," in Alan Tomlinson ed., *Consumption, Identity and Style* (London: Routledge, 1990).

4. Michel Foucault, *The History of Sexuality,* vol. I (New York: Random House, 1978).

5. See also Bonnie Zimmerman's study of lesbian-feminist fiction, *The Safe Sea of Women: Lesbian Fiction 1969–1989* (Boston: Beacon, 1990).

6. On the "massification" of culture, see Walter Benjamin, *Illuminations* (New York: Harcourt, 1968).

7. On the history of women's music and its relationship to American radical feminism, see Alice Echols, *Daring to Be Bad: Radical Feminism in America* (Minneapolis: University of Minnesota Press, 1989). For a history of women in music that places women's music in a larger historical perspective, see Gillian Gaar, *She's a Rebel: The History of Women in Rock and Roll* (Seattle: Seal, 1992).

8. Holly Near, interviewed by Gillian Gaar in *She's a Rebel,* 154.

9. Simon Frith, *Music for Pleasure* (London: Routledge, 1988).

10. Arlene Stein, "Androgyny Goes Pop," in Arlene Stein ed., *Sisters, Sexperts, Queers: Beyond the Lesbian Nation* (New York: Plume, 1993), 101.

11. Arlene Stein, "Sisters and Queers: The Decentering of Lesbian Feminism," *Socialist Review,* January–March, 1992.

12. Olivia Records turned down overtures from Melissa Etheridge before she was signed to a major label. Redwood Records, the label that Holly Near founded, tried to sign Tracy Chapman when she was still in school in Boston, but could not compete with Elektra.

13. Susan Wilson, "Talkin' 'bout a Revolution for Women in Pop?" *Boston Sunday Globe,* November 20, 1988.

14. Lisa Lewis, *Gender Politics and MTV: Voicing the Difference* (Philadelphia: Temple University Press, 1990).

15. On the Madonna phenomenon and her relationship to lesbian/gay subcultures, see *The Madonna Connection: Representational Politics, Subcultural Identities and Cultural Theory,* ed. Cathy Schwichtenberg (Boulder, CO: Westview, 1993).

16. Stein, "Androgyny Goes Pop," 103.

17. k.d. lang openly declared her lesbianism only after achieving considerable commercial success.

18. "Folksinger," by Phranc, from *I Enjoy Being a Girl,* Island Records, 1989.

19. Ginny Z. Berson, "Who Owes What to Whom? Building and Maintaining Lesbian Culture," *Windy City Times,* June 22, 1989.

20. Interview with author, 1991.

21. "Age, Race, Class and Sex: Women Redefining Difference," in Audre Lorde, *Sister Outsider* (New York: Crossing, 1984).

22. Lawrence Grossberg, "MTV: Swinging on the (Postmodern) Star," in Ian Angus and Sut Jhally, eds., *Cultural Politics in Contemporary America* (London: Routledge, 1989).

23. Stein, "Androgyny Goes Pop," 108.

24. Barbara Bradby, "Lesbians and Popular Music: Does It Matter Who Is Singing?" in Gabriele Griffin, ed., *Outwrite: Lesbianism and Popular Culture* (London: Pluto, 1993); Holly Kruse, "Subcultural Identity in Alternative Music Culture," *Popular Music* 12 (January 1993).

25. Biddy Martin, "Sexual Practice and Changing Lesbian Identities," in *Destabilizing Theory: Contemporary Feminist Debates* (Stanford, CA: Stanford University Press, 1992).

NOTES TO CHAPTER 5

An earlier version of "Sisters and Queers" by Arlene Stein was published in the now defunct *Socialist Review,* January–March 1992.

1. Janice Raymond, "Putting the Politics Back into Lesbianism," *Women's Studies International Forum* 12, no. 2 (1989).

2. *San Francisco Examiner,* November 12, 1991, 3.

3. Howard Winant makes a similar argument about the politics of race in "Post-modern Racial Politics: Difference and Inequality," *Socialist Review* 20, no. 1 (January–March 1990).

4. These ideas are based on archival research and interviews conducted primarily in the San Francisco Bay Area. Parts of the analysis may not hold true for other parts of the country, particularly nonurban areas, where the pace of change may be slower.

5. Alain Touraine, *Return of the Actor* (Minneapolis: University of Minnesota Press, 1988); Alberto Melucci, *Nomads of the Present: Social Movements and Individual Needs in Contemporary Society* (London: Century Hutchinson, 1989); Ernesto Laclau and Chantal Mouffe, *Hegemony and Socialist Strategy: Towards a Radical Democratic Politics,* trans. Winston Moore and Paul Cammack (London: Verso, 1985).

6. Pierre Bourdieu, "What Makes a Social Class? On the Theoretical and Practical Existence of Groups," *Berkeley Journal of Sociology* 32 (1987): 13. Also see Scott Lash, *Sociology of Postmodernism* (New York: Routledge, 1990); Sandra Harding's discussion of epistemologies as "justificatory strategies," in "Feminism, Science and the Anti-Enlightenment Critiques," in Linda Nicholson, ed., *Feminism/Postmodernism* (New York: Routledge, 1990), 87.

7. Looking at the construction of collective identity in social movements provides a link between the symbolic interactionist tradition and more recent theories of social movements. See Herbert Blumer, "Collective Behavior," in A. M. Lee, ed., *New Outline of the Principles of Sociology* (New York: Barnes and Noble, 1946).

8. Jonathan Katz, *Gay American History* (New York: Harper and Row, 1976), 7. See also Jeffrey Weeks, "The Development of Sexual Theory and Sexual Politics," in Mike Brake, ed., *Human Sexual Relations* (New York: Pantheon, 1982).

9. See Rose Weitz, "From Accommodation to Rebellion: The Politicization of Lesbianism," in Trudy Darty and Sandee Potter, eds., *Women-Identified Women* (Palo Alto, CA: Mayfield, 1984); Barry Adam, *The Rise of a Gay and Lesbian Movement* (Boston: Twayne, 1987).

10. Radicalesbians, "The Woman-Identified Woman," reprinted in Sarah Hoagland and Julia Penelope, eds., *For Lesbians Only* (London: Onlywoman Press, 1988); Adrienne Rich, "Compulsory Heterosexuality and Lesbian Existence," *Signs,* Summer 1980.

11. Eve Sedgwick, *Epistemology of the Closet* (Berkeley: University of California Press, 1990), 36.

12. Gayle Rubin, "The Traffic in Women," in Rayna Reiter, ed., *Toward an Anthropology of Women* (New York: Monthly Review, 1975).

13. Jill Johnston, *Lesbian Nation: The Feminist Solution* (New York: Simon and Schuster, 1973), 58.

14. See Carole Smith-Rosenberg, *Disorderly Conduct* (New York: Knopf, 1985); "The Female World of Love and Ritual," in Nancy F. Cott and Elizabeth Pleck, eds., *Heritage of Her Own* (New York: Simon and Schuster, 1979).

15. Judy Grahn, "Lesbians as Bogeywoman," *Women: A Journal of Liberation* 1, no. 4 (Summer 1970): 36.

16. Vivienne C. Cass, "Homosexual Identity Formation: A Theoretical Model," *Journal of Homosexuality* 4, no. 3 (1979).

17. Barbara Ponse, *Identities in the Lesbian World: The Social Construction of Self* (Westport, CT: Greenwood, 1978), 160.

18. Ibid., 162.

19. *Lesbian Tide*, May–June 1978, 19.

20. Beverly Burch, "Unconscious Bonding in Lesbian Relationships: The Road Not Taken," unpublished dissertation, Institute for Clinical Social Work, Berkeley, Calif. 1989, 91.

21. Jeane Cordova, *Lesbian Tide*, May–June 1973.

22. Alice Echols, *Daring to Be Bad: Radical Feminism in America 1967–75* (Minneapolis: University of Minnesota Press, 1989); Bonnie Zimmerman, *The Safe Sea of Women: Lesbian Fiction 1969–1989* (Boston: Beacon, 1990).

23. Ponse, *Identities in the Lesbian World*, 139.

24. Alberto Melucci, *Nomads of the Present: Social Movements and Individual Needs in Contemporary Society* (London: Century Hutchinson, 1989), 209.

25. Iris Marion Young, "The Ideal of Community and the Politics of Difference," in Linda J. Nicholson, ed., *Feminism/Postmodernism* (New York: Routledge, 1990); Shane Phelan, *Identity Politics: Lesbian Feminism and the Limits of Community* (Philadelphia: Temple University Press, 1989); Cheryl Cole, "Ethnographic Sub/versions," unpublished dissertation, University of Iowa, 1991.

26. Susan Krieger, *The Mirror Dance: Identity in a Woman's Community* (Philadelphia: Temple University Press, 1983), xv.

27. Carole Vance, ed., *Pleasure and Danger: Exploring Women's Sexuality* (Boston: Routledge, 1984); B. Ruby Rich, "Feminism and Sexuality in the 1980s," *Feminist Studies* 12, no. 3 (Fall 1986).

28. Joan Nestle, "Butch-Fem Relationships," *Heresies* 12 (Summer 1981).

29. Julia Creet, "Lesbian Sex/Gay Sex: What's the Difference?" *OUT/LOOK: National Lesbian and Gay Quarterly*, no. 11 (Winter 1991); Gayle Rubin, "Thinking Sex: Notes for a Radical Theory of the Politics of Sexuality," in Vance, *Pleasure and Danger*. The autonomous bisexual movement suggested a politics along much the same lines, but tended to privilege self-identified bisexuals. See, for example, *Bi Any Other Name: Bisexual People Speak Out*, eds., Loraine Hutchins and Lani Kaahumanu (Boston: Alyson, 1990).

30. Michael Warner, "Fear of a Queer Planet," *Social Text* 29 (1991); Allan Bérubé and Jeffrey Escoffier, "Queer/Nation," *OUT/LOOK: National Lesbian and Gay Quarterly*, no. 11 (Winter 1991); Dan Levy, "Queer Nation in

S.F. Suspends Activities," *San Francisco Chronicle*, December 27, 1991; Michele DeRanleau, "How the Conscience of an Epidemic Unraveled," *San Francisco Examiner*, October 1, 1990.

31. These included *This Bridge Called My Back: Writings by Radical Women of Color*, eds. Cherrie Moraga and Gloria Anzaldua, eds. (Watertown, MA: Persephone Press, 1981); *All the Women Are White, All the Blacks Are Men, but Some of Us Are Brave*, eds. Gloria Hull, Patricia Bell Scott, and Barbara Smith (New York: Feminist Press, 1982); *Home Girls: A Black Feminist Anthology*, ed. Barbara Smith (New York: Kitchen Table/Women of Color Press, 1983).

32. Stuart Hall, "Cultural Identity and Cinematic Representation," *Framework*, no. 36 (1989).

NOTES TO PART II

1. Jeffrey Weeks, *Invented Moralities: Sexual Values in an Age of Uncertainty* (New York: Columbia University Press, 1995).

2. Gayle Rubin, "Thinking Sex: Notes for a Radical Theory of the Politics of Sexuality," in C. Vance, ed. *Pleasure and Danger* (New York: Routledge, 1984).

3. Andrew Sullivan, *Virtually Normal* (New York: Knopf, 1995), 12–13, 92.

4. Michael Warner, *The Trouble with Normal* (New York: Free Press, 1999), 88.

5. Zygmunt Bauman, *Postmodern Ethics* (Oxford: Blackwell,1993).

NOTES TO CHAPTER 6

An earlier version of "Revenge of the Shamed" was published in *Passionate Politics: Emotions and Social Movements,* eds., J. Goodwin, J. Jasper, and F. Polletta (Chicago: University of Chicago Press, 2001). © 2001 by The University of Chicago. All rights reserved. Reprinted with permission.

1. George Lakoff, *Moral Politics* (Chicago: University of Chicago Press, 1996).

2. James Davison Hunter, *Culture Wars: The Struggle to Define America* (New York: Basic Books, 1991).

3. Craig Calhoun, "Introduction," *Social Theory and the Politics of Identity,* ed. Craig Calhoun (New York: Blackwell, 1994); Marcy Darnovsky, Barbara Epstein, and Richard Flacks, eds., *Cultural Politics and Social Movements* (Philadelphia: Temple University Press, 1995).

4. In January 1993, the OCA selected eight counties and thirty-five cities for initiatives that would prevent antidiscrimination protections for gays and lesbians and prohibit government spending to promote homosexuality.

5. I conducted eight semistructured in-depth interviews, averaging ninety minutes in length with these individuals.

6. James Jasper, *The Art of Moral Protest: Culture, Biography and Creativity in Social Movements* (Chicago: University of Chicago Press, 1998), 215.

7. Sandra Morgen, in Myra Marx Feree and P. Yancey, eds., *Feminist Organizations: Harvest of the New Women's Movement* (Philadelphia: Temple University Press, 1995). Also see Alberto Melucci, *Nomads of the Present: Social Movements and Individual Needs in Contemporary Society* (London: Century Hutchinson, 1989); Verta Taylor and Nancy Whittier, "Collective Identity in Social Movement Communities: Lesbian Feminist Mobilization," in Aldon Morris and Carol Mueller, eds., *Frontiers of Social Movement Theory* (New Haven: Yale University Press, 1995).

8. On the first, see Richard Hofstadter, *The Paranoid Style in American Politics and Other Essays* (New York: Vintage, 1967); on the second, see Erich Goode and Nachman BenYehuda, *Moral Panics: The Social Construction of Deviance* (Cambridge and Oxford: Blackwell, 1994).

9. Linda Kintz, *Between Jesus and the Market: The Emotions That Matter in Right-Wing America* (Durham, NC: Duke University Press, 1997), 67.

10. Thomas J. Scheff, "Socialization of Emotions: Pride and Shame as Causal Agents," in Theodore D. Kemper, ed., *Research Agendas in the Sociology of Emotions* (Albany: State University of New York Press, 1990), 281–304.

11. Erving Goffman, *Interaction Ritual* (New York: Anchor, 1967); Arlie Hochschild, *The Managed Heart* (Berkeley: University of California Press, 1983).

12. Thomas Scheff and Suzanne M. Retzinger, *Emotions and Violence: Shame and Rage in Destructive Conflicts* (Lexington, MA: Lexington Books); Helen B. Lewis, *Shame and Guilt in Neurosis* (New York: International Universities Press, 1971), 251.

13. Scheff, "Socialization of Emotions," 281

14. Lewis, *Shame and Guilt*, 41.

15. Ibid., 197; Scheff, "Socialization of Emotions," 298.

16. All individuals except for Lon Mabon, head of the OCA, are given pseudonyms, as is the town where most of this research was conducted.

17. I have conducted numerous other interviews on different topics and in different regions of the country, and I have never before encountered these patterns.

18. Lewis, *Shame and Guilt*, 186–189.

19. Although I was "out" to them as a Jew, I did not reveal my lesbianism for fear that it would cut off the conversation.

20. Lewis, *Shame and Guilt*, 41.

21. Ibid., 218.

22. Joshua Gamson, *Freaks Talk Back: Tabloid Television and Sexual Nonconformity* (Chicago: University of Chicago Press, 1998).

23. Loretta Neet, Letter to Editor, *Eugene Register-Guard*, June 6, 1993.

24. Susan Johnston, "On the Fire Brigade: Why Liberalism Can't Stop the Anti-Gay Campaigns of the Right," *Critical Sociology* 20 (4) (1994):3–19.

25. Kai Erikson, *Wayward Puritans: A Study in the Sociology of Deviance* (New York: John Wiley and Sons, 1966).

26. Alan Wolfe, *One Nation, After All* (New York: Viking, 1998).

27. Katherine Newman, *Declining Fortunes* (New York: Basic Books, 1993).

28. Goffman, *Interaction Ritual*; Lewis, *Shame and Guilt*, 26.

29. Lewis, *Shame and Guilt*, 407.

30. Hunter, *Culture Wars*; Jeffrey Alexander, "Citizen and Enemy as Symbolic Classification: On the Polarizing Discourse of Civil Society," in Michele Lamont and Marcel Fournier, eds., *Cultivating Differences: Symbolic Boundaries and the Making of Inequality* (Chicago: University of Chicago Press, 1992).

31. Harry Esteve, "OCA Fund-Raising Dinner Draws Political Protests," *Eugene Register-Guard*, January 15, 1994, B1.

32. Richard Slotkin, *Regeneration through Violence* (Middletown, CT: Wesleyan University Press, 1973); Charles Strozier, "Christian Fundamentalism and the Apocalyptic in the 1990s," Chi Rho Lectures, Central Lutheran Church, Eugene, Oregon, November 6–8, 1998.

33. Kintz, *Between Jesus and the Market*, 67.

34. Lisa Duggan, "Queering the State," *Socialtext* 39 (1994): 1–14; Didi Herman, *The Antigay Agenda: Orthodox Vision and the Christian Right* (Chicago: University of Chicago Press, 1997).

35. *Timbertown Gazette*, January 20, 1993, 2A.

36. Letter to the Editor, *Timbertown Gazette*, July 28, 1993.

37. Zygmunt Bauman, *Postmodern Ethics* (Oxford: Blackwell, 1993), 155.

38. Ibid., 156.

39. Nancy Chodorow, "The Enemy Outside: Thoughts on the Psychodynamics of Extreme Violence with Special Attention to Men and Masculinity," *Journal for the Psychoanalysis of Culture and Society* 3, no. 1 (1998).

40. Lewis, *Shame and Guilt*, 411.

41. Paul Neevel, "Wake Up Call," *Eugene Weekly*, March 17, 1997, 7.

42. Strozier, "Christian Fundamentalism."

NOTES TO CHAPTER 7

An earlier version of "Whose Memories? Whose Victimhood?" by Arlene Stein was published in *Sociological Perspectives* 41, no. 3 (1998). © 1998 by the Pacific Sociological Association.

1. Lawrence Langer, *Holocaust Testimony: The Ruins of Memory* (New Haven: Yale University Press, 1991); R. Ruth Linden, *Making Stories, Making Selves: Feminist Reflections on the Holocaust* (Columbus: Ohio State University Press, 1993); Ken Plummer, *Telling Sexual Stories* (New York: Routledge, 1995).

2. Judith Miller, *One by One by One* (New York: Touchstone/Simon & Schuster, 1990); Charles Maier, *The Unmasterable Past: History, Holocaust,*

German National Identity (Cambridge, MA: Harvard University Press, 1988); David Biale, "Power, Passivity and the Legacy of the Holocaust," in *Tikkun* 2 (1) (1987): 68–73; Yael Zerubavel, *Recovered Roots: Collective Memory and the Making of Israeli National Tradition* (Chicago: University of Chicago Press, 1995).

3. Lin Collette, "Encountering Holocaust Denial," in Chip Berlet, ed., *Eyes Right! Challenging the Right Wing Backlash* (Boston: South End Press, 1995); Deborah Lipstadt, *Denying the Holocaust: The Growing Assault on Truth and Memory* (New York: Free Press, 1993).

4. Michael Cooper, "Debate on Role Played by Anti-Abortion Talk," *New York Times,* January 15, 1992; Wendy Steiner, "Declaring War on Men," *New York Times Book Review,* September 15, 1992, 11; Charisse Jones, "Bringing Slavery's Long Shadow to the Light," *New York Times,* April 2, 1995, 1; Larry Kramer, *Reports from the Holocaust: The Making of an AIDS Activist* (New York: St. Martin's, 1989).

5. Michele Lamont, "Colliding Moralities between Black and White Workers," in Elizabeth Long, ed., *From Sociology to Cultural Studies* (Malden/ Oxford: Blackwell, 1997).

6. Marcy Darnovsky, Barbara Epstein, and Richard Flacks, eds., *Cultural Politics and Social Movements* (Philadelphia: Temple University Press, 1995).

7. William Gamson, *Talking Politics* (Cambridge, UK: Cambridge University Press, 1992).

8. Scott Hunt and Robert D. Benford, "Identity Talk in the Peace and Justice Movement." *Journal of Contemporary Ethnography* 22 (4) (1994): 488–517; David Snow and Robert Benford, "Ideology, Frame Resonance and Participant Mobilization," *International Social Movement Research* 1 (1998): 197–217; David Snow and Robert Benford, "Master Frames and Cycles of Protest," in Aldon Morris and Carol Mueller, eds., *Frontiers in Social Movement Theory* (New Haven: Yale University Press, 1992); Scott Hunt, Robert Benford, and David Snow, "Identity Fields: Framing Processes and the Social Construction of Movement Identities," in Enrique Larana, Hank Johnston, and Joseph Gusfield, eds., *New Social Movements, from Ideology to Identity* (Philadelphia: Temple University Press, 1994); Hank Johnston and Bert Klandermans, eds., *Social Movements and Culture* (Minneapolis: University of Minnesota Press, 1995).

9. Doug McAdam, "Culture and Social Movements," in Enrique Larana, Hank Johnston and Joseph Gusfield, eds., *New Social Movements, from Ideology to Identity* (Philadelphia: Temple University Press, 1994).

10. Steven Epstein, "Gay Politics, Ethnic Identity: The Limits of Social Constructionism," in *Socialist Review* 17 (3–4) (1987): 9–50; also see my *Sex and Sensibility: Stories of a Lesbian Generation* (Berkeley: University of California Press, 1997).

11. Michael Berenbaum, "The Nativization of the Holocaust," *Judaism* 35 (4) (1986): 447–457.

12. Hunt, et al., "Identity Fields," 193.

13. Jeffrey Alexander, "Citizen and Enemy as Symbolic Classification: On the Polarizing Discourse of Civil Society," in Michele Lamont and Marcel Fournier, eds., *Cultivating Differences: Symbolic Boundaries and the Making of Inequality* (Chicago: University of Chicago Press, 1992), 292.

14. Joseph Gusfield, "The Reflexivity of Social Movements: Collective Behavior and Mass Society Theory Revisited," in Enrique Larana, Hank Johnston and Joseph Gusfield, eds., *New Social Movements, from Ideology to Identity* (Philadelphia: Temple University Press, 1994).

15. Todd Gitlin, *The Whole World Is Watching: The Mass Media in the Making and Unmaking of the New Left* (Berkeley: University of California Press, 1980); Joshua Gamson, "Silence, Death and the Invisible Enemy: AIDS Activism and Social Movement 'Newness,'" *Social Problems* 36 (4) (1989): 351–366; James Davison Hunter, *Culture Wars: The Struggle to Define America* (New York: Basic Books, 1991).

16. Robert Lifton and Greg Mitchell, *Hiroshima in America: Fifty Years of Denial* (New York: Grossett/Putnam), 352.

17. Sara Diamond, *Spiritual Warfare: The Politics of the Christian Right* (Boston: South End Press, 1989); Dinitia Smith, "With the Apocalypse Almost Now, It Becomes a New Field of Study," *New York Times,* November 8, 1997, A15; John Fiske, *Media Matters* (Minneapolis: University of Minnesota Press, 1994); Ann Marie Smith, "A Symptomology of an Authoritarian Discourse," in Erica Carter et al. eds., *Cultural Remix: Theories of Politics and the Popular* (London: Lawrence and Wishart, 1995).

18. Conservative evangelical Protestants constitute a movement that can be distinguished from the Far Right, which is overtly racist and violent, and the new right, which is much more concerned with economic issues than with issues of morality. See Didi Herman, *The Antigay Agenda: Orthodox Vision and the Christian Right* (Chicago: University of Chicago Press, 1997).

19. Cindy Patton, "Tremble, Hetero Swine!" in Michael Warner, ed., *Fear of a Queer Planet* (Minneapolis: University of Minnesota Press, 1993), 145.

20. Soon thereafter, the Institute of Sexology, administered by Magnus Hirschfeld, a Jew, a leftist, and advocate of homosexual rights, was closed and vandalized and homosexual contact was outlawed in German society. See Erwin Haeberle, "Swastika, Pink Triangle, and Yellow Star: The Destruction of Sexology and the Persecution of Homosexuals in Nazi Germany," in Martin Duberman, Martha Vicinus, and George Chauncey, eds., *Hidden From History: Reclaiming the Gay & Lesbian Past* (New York: Plume, 1989).

21. Estimates of the exact number of homosexuals who were imprisoned in concentration camps vary widely. Haeberle (1989) suggests that the "most de-

fensible guess" is approximately ten thousand (375). Goldhagen estimates "tens of thousands" (Daniel Jonah Goldhagen, "There is No Hierarchy among Victims," *New York Times,* January 18, 1997, 23). On Nazi doctrine and treatment of homosexuals, also see Richard Plant, *The Pink Triangle* (New York: Owl Books 1988) and Richard Plant, "The Swastika and the Pink Triangle: Nazis and Gay Men," in Lawrence D. Mass, ed., *Dialogues of the Sexual Revolution,* vol. 1 (New York: Harrington Park, 1990); Heinz Heger, *The Men with the Pink Triangle* (Boston: Alyson, 1980). Relatively few women were persecuted by the secret police and in the camps for being lesbians. Nazi leader Heinrich Himmler excluded women from antihomosexual laws because they were not soldiers, and because "they could always be forced to carry pregnancies" (Plant, "The Swastika and the Pink Triangle," 191).

22. Heger, *The Men with the Pink Triangle.*

23. Randy Shilts, *The Mayor of Castro Street: The Life and Times of Harvey Milk* (New York: St. Martin's, 1982), 10.

24. Mary McIntosh, "The Homosexual Role," *Social Problems* 16 (2) (1968): 182–192; Jonathan Katz, "The Invention of Heterosexuality," *Socialist Review* 20 (1) (1990): 7–34; Michel Foucault, *The History of Sexuality,* vol. 1 (New York: Random House, 1978).

25. James Holstein and Gayle Miller, "Rethinking Victimization: An Interactional Approach to Victimology," *Symbolic Interactionism* 1 (1990): 109.

26. This is not to suggest that the Holocaust frame is embraced universally by lesbian/gay and feminist activists. For dissenting views, primarily by feminists, see R. Amy Elman, "Triangles and Tribulations: The Politics of Nazi Symbols," *Journal of Homosexuality* 30 (3) (1996): 1–11; Nancy Ordover, "Visibility, Alliance, and the Practice of Memory," *Socialist Review* 25(1) (1996): 119–134; Suzanne Pharr, *In the Time of the Right* (Berkeley: Chardon Press, 1996).

27. Barry Dank, "Bryant's Brigade Uses Hitler's Tactics," *Los Angeles Times,* October 23, 1977, 61.

28. Barry Adam, *The Rise of a Gay and Lesbian Movement* (Boston: Twayne, 1987), 111.

29. Diamond, *Spiritual Warfare,* 101–102; Mab Segrest and Leonard Zeskind, *Quarantines and Death: The Far Right's Homophobic Agenda* (Center for Democratic Renewal, 1991).

30. Susan Sontag, "AIDS and Its Metaphors," *New York Review of Books,* October 27, 1988, 23.

31. Simon Watney, "Acts of Memory," in *OUT,* September 1994; Geoffrey Hartman, *Holocaust Remembrance: The Shapes of Memory* (Oxford: Blackwell, 1994).

32. Dennis Altman, *AIDS in the Mind of America* (Garden City, NY: Anchor, 1986).

33. James Holstein and Gayle Miller, "Rethinking Victimization"; Steven Epstein, "Gay Politics, Ethnic Identity."

34. Lisa Duggan, "Queering the State," *Socialtext* 39 (1994): 1–14; Susan Johnston, "Paradoxes of Identity: Liberalism, Bio-Power and 'Homosexual' Politics in Oregon," Ph.D. dissertation, Department of Sociology, University of Oregon, 1996; Susan Johnston, "On the Fire Brigade: Why Liberalism Can't Stop the Anti-Gay Campaigns of the Right," *Critical Sociology*, 20 (4) (1994): 3–19.

35. Gayle Rubin, "Thinking Sex," in Henry Abelove, Michele Ann Barale and David Halperin, eds., *The Lesbian and Gay Studies Reader* (New York: Routledge, 1993), 43.

36. Johnston, "On the Fire Brigade," 134.

37. Eric Mortenson, "Anne Frank, Cottage Grove Cross Paths," *Cottage Grove Sentinel*, March 14, 1993, 5.

38. Lipstadt, *Denying the Holocaust*, 7.

39. Herman, *The Anti-Gay Agenda*, 90.

40. Smith, "A Symptomology," 224.

41. James Ridgeway, *Blood in the Face* (New York: Thunder's Mouth Press, 1995).

42. Chris Simpson, American University, Washington, DC, personal communication.

43. Herman, *The Anti-Gay Agenda*.

44. This is overlooked by conservative critic Charles Sykes in *A Nation of Victims: The Decay of the American Character* (New York: St. Martin's, 1992).

45. Gillian Liechtling, Jonathon Mazzochi, and Steve Gardiner, "The Covert Crusade," Western Progressive Leadership Network1993; Peter, Steinfels,. "Evangelicals Lobby for Oppressed Christians," *New York Times*, September 15, 1996, 26.

46. Duggan, "Queering the State."

47. Alisa Solomon, "Notes on Klez/Camp," *Davka* (Winter 1997): 7.

48. Official State of Oregon Voters Pamphlet 1994, 79.

49. Patrick Buchanan, "Christians, Nazis and Jesse," *The Conservatives*, January 1, 1995, 6.

50. David Dunlap, "Gay Advertising Campaign on TV Draws Wrath of Conservatives," in *New York Times*, November 12, 1995, 16. Moreover, right-wing ideologies do not exist in isolation; there is a continuum of right-wing thought and activity. See Raphael Ezekiel, *The Racist Mind: Portraits of American Neo-Nazis and Klansmen* (New York: Viking, 1995).

51. Scott Lively, February. 7, 1996, Lively Communications, Inc., Salem, OR.

52. Scott Lively and Kenneth Abrams, *The Pink Swastika* (Keizer, OR: Founders Publishing, 1995), 123.

53. Haeberle, "Swastika, Pink Triangle."

54. Shari Benstock, "Paris Lesbianism and the Politics of Reaction, 1900–1940," 332–346 in Martin Duberman, Martha Vicinus, and George Chauncey, eds., *Hidden from History: Reclaiming the Gay and Lesbian Past* (New York: Plume, 1989).

55. For examples of recent gay conservative writing in the United States, see Bruce Bawer, *A Place at the Table: The Gay Individual in American Society* (New York: Simon and Schuster 1994); Andrew Sullivan, *Virtually Normal: An Argument about Homosexuality* (New York: Knopf, 1995).

56. Klaus Theweleit, *Male Fantasies,* vol. 1 (Minneapolis: University of Minnesota Press, 1987). It is noteworthy that discussion of the 9/11 hijackers, particularly their leader Mohammed Atta, has at times involved accusations of possible homosexuality.

57. Haeberle, "Swastika, Pink Triangle," 374.

58. Hitler's cultural rhetoric concerning "degenerate art" and the supposed corrupting effects of "Jewish" movies and literature frequently linked homosexuality and enlightened attitudes about human sexuality in general to a puported Jewish-communist conspiracy. The Nazis attempted to draw a distinction between "Jewish" (i.e., sexual) science and culture and "Aryan" (heroic, clean, strong) science and culture (Chris Simpson, American University, Washington, DC, personal communication). Within these cultural scripts, women were frequently demonized, associated with sexually degenerate behavior, held responsible for social chaos and male impotence. On the vilification of female sexuality and estheticization of sexual crimes against women in the Weimar period, see Maria Tatar, *Lustmord: Sexual Murder in Weimar Germany* (Princeton, NJ: Princeton University Press, 1995).

59. Scott Lively, "Letter to OCA supporters," Salem, Oregon, 1996. Such claims are particularly ironic after the recent release of the "fully restored" Anne Frank diary, which suggests that Anne had homoerotic fantasies and even experiences. Thanks to Ilene Kalish for this insight.

60. This can be seen as part of an effort on the Christian right to deconstruct the notion that lesbians and gay men constitute a cohesive "ethnic minority." On the origins and development of the "ethnic" model, see Epstein, "Gay Politics, Ethnic Identity."

61. The Christian right has also sought to divide blacks and gays. On the right's "divide and conquer" strategy, see Urvashi Vaid, *Virtual Equality* (New York: Anchor, 1995).

62. Philip Zuckerman, "Jews and the Christian Right," *Journal of Jewish Communal Service* 73 (1) (1996): 21–31.

63. Ezekiel, *The Racist Mind*; Ridgeway, *Blood in the Face.*

64. James Davison Hunter, *Before the Shooting Begins: Searching for Democracy in America's Culture War* (New York: Free Press, 1994), 46.

65. Cindy Patton, "Tremble, Hetero Swine!" 145

66. Irena Klepfisz, *Dreams of an Insomniac: Jewish Feminist Essays, Speeches and Diatribes* (Portland, OR: Eighth Mountain Press, 1990), 64.

67. As Elie Wiesel has written, "The Event remains unique, unlike any other product of history, it transcends history." (Quoted by Christopher Shea in "Debating the Uniqueness of the Holocaust," *Chronicle of Higher Education*, May 31, 1996, A7.) On Holocaust "uniqueness," see Alan S. Rosenbaum, *Is the Holocaust Unique? Perspectives in Comparative Genocide* (Boulder, CO: Westview, 1996).

68. William Gamson, "Hiroshima, the Holocaust, and the Politics of Exclusion," *American Sociological Review* 60 (1) (1995): 1–20.

69. Robert Jay Lifton, *The Protean Self* (New York: Basic Books), 217. Facing History and Ourselves is a nonprofit foundation that trains teachers to incorporate the Holocaust into a curriculum that looks at the relationship between history and individual moral choices.

NOTES TO CHAPTER 8

"Make Room for Daddy" by Arlene Stein also appears in *Gender & Society*, vol. 19, no. 5 (2005): 601–620. © 2005 Sociologists for Women in Society.

1. A fifty-six-year-old woman activist in the Oregon Citizens Alliance interviewed by the author in 1997.

2. Alan Wolfe, *One Nation, After All* (New York: Viking Press, 1998); Steven Seidman, Chet Meeks, and Francine Traschen, "Beyond the Closet? The Changing Social Meaning of Homosexuality in the United States," in C. Williams and A. Stein, eds., *Sexuality and Gender* (Malden, MA, and Oxford: Blackwell, 2002); Joshua Gamson, *Freaks Talk Back: Tabloid Talk Shows and Sexual Nonconformity* (Chicago: University of Chicago Press, 1998); Suzanna Danuta Walters, *All the Rage: The Story of Gay Visibility in America* (Chicago: University of Chicago Press, 2003); M. V. Lee Badgett, *Money, Myths, and Change: The Economic Lives of Lesbians and Gay Men* (Chicago: University of Chicago Press, 2001).

3. Thomas Linneman, "Homophobia and Hostility: Christian Conservative Reactions to the Political and Cultural Progress of Lesbians and Gay Men," *Sexuality Research and Social Policy* 1, no. 2 (April 2004): 56–76; James Davison Hunter, *Before the Shooting Begins: Searching for Democracy in America's Culture War* (New York: Free Press, 1994); James Davison Hunter, *Culture Wars: The Struggle to Define America* (New York: Basic Books, 1991); Alan Wolfe, "One Nation, After All," 72.

4. K. Franklin, "Unassuming Motivations: Contextualizing the Narratives of Antigay Assailants," in Gregory Herek, ed. *Psychological Perspectives on Lesbian and Gay Issues*, vol. 4 (Thousand Oaks, CA: Sage, 1998): 1–23; Gregory Herek, "On Heterosexual Masculinity: Some Psychical Consequences of the

Social Construction of Gender and Sexuality," *American Behavioral Scientist* 29 (1986): 563–577.

5. Faye Ginsburg, *Contested Lives: The Abortion Debate in an American Community* (Berkeley: University of California Press, 1989); Kristin Luker, *Abortion and the Politics of Motherhood* (Berkeley: University of California Press, 1984); Stephen J. Ducat, *The Wimp Factor: Gender Gaps, Holy Wars, and the Politics of Anxious Masculinity* (Boston: Beacon, 2004); Arlene Stein, *Sex and Sensibility: Stories of a Lesbian Generation* (Berkeley: University of California Press, 1997).

6. Richard Goldstein, "The Hate That Makes Men Straight," *Village Voice* December 16, 1998, 32; Richard Isay, "On the Analytic Therapy of Gay Men," in T. S. Stein and C. J. Cohen, eds., *Contemporary Perspectives on Psychotherapy with Lesbians and Gay Men* (New York: Plenum, 1986).

7. George Weinberg, *Society and the Healthy Homosexual* (Boston: Alyson, 1972 [1992]).

8. Gregory Herek, "Beyond Homophobia: Thinking about Sexual Prejudice and Stigma in the Twenty-First Century," *Sexuality Research and Social Policy* 1, no. 2, (2004): 6–24; Michael Kimmel, "Masculinity as Homophobia," in M. Gergen and S. Davis, eds., *Toward a New Psychology of Gender* (New York: Routledge, 1997); Suzanne Pharr, *Homophobia: A Weapon of Sexism* (Inverness, CA: Chardon Press, 1988).

9. Herek, "Beyond Homophobia"; Adrienne Rich, "Compulsory Heterosexuality and Lesbian Existence," *SIGNS* 5, (1980): 631–660; R. W. Connell, *Masculinities* (Berkeley: University of California Press, 1995).

10. Nancy Chodorow, "Homophobia: Analysis of a Permissible Prejudice," American Psychoanalytic Association Public Forum, New York, December, 1998.

11. Connell, *Masculinities*.

12. George Chauncey, "From Sexual Inversion to Homosexuality: Medicine and the Changing Conceptualization of Female Deviance," *Salmagundi* no. 58.59 (1982): 114–146; Judith Halberstam, *Female Masculinity* (Durham, NC: Duke University Press, 1998); Martin Levine, *Gay Macho: The Life and Death of the Homosexual Clone* (New York: New York University Press, 1998); Joan Nestle, ed., *The Persistent Desire: A Femme-Butch Reader* (Boston: Alyson, 1992).

13. Ellen Lewin, *Lesbian Mothers: Accounts of Gender in American Culture* (Ithaca, NY: Cornell University Press, 1993); Stein, *Sex and Sensibility*.

14. Elisabeth Young-Bruehl, *The Anatomy of Prejudices* (Cambridge, MA: Harvard University Press, 1997), 150.

15. George Lakoff, *Moral Politics* (Chicago: University of Chicago Press, 1996).

16. Judith Stacey and Susan Gerard, "We Are Not Doormats," in M. Baca-Zinn, P. Hondagneu-Sotelo, and M. Messner, eds., *Through the Prism of Difference* (Boston: Allyn and Bacon, 1997).

17. Connell, *Masculinities*; Michelle Fine, L. Weis, J. Addelston, and J. Marusza, "(In)secure Times: Constructing White Working-Class Masculinities in the Late 20th Century," *Gender & Society*, 11, no. 1 (February 1997): 52–68.

18. Beverly Brown, *In Timber Country: Working People's Stories of Environmental Conflict and Urban Flight* (Philadelphia: Temple University Press, 1995); Michael Hibbard and James Elias, "The Failure of Sustained-Yield Forestry and the Decline of the Flannel-Shirt Frontier," in Thomas A. Lyson and William W. Falk, eds., *Forgotten Places: Uneven Development in Rural America* (Lawrence, KS: University Press of America, 1993).

19. Kathleen Gerson, *No Man's Land: Men's Changing Commitment to Family and Work* (New York: Basic Books, 1993).

20. Oregon Official 2004 General Election Voters Pamphlet (Salem, OR), 77.

21. Arlene Stein, *The Stranger Next Door: The Story of a Small Community's Battle over Sex, Faith, and Civil Rights* (Boston: Beacon, 2001).

22. Oregon 2004 General Election Voters Pamphlet, 77.

23. Stein, *Sex and Sensibility*; Seidman, Meeks, and Traschen, "Beyond the Closet?" 434.

24. R. Claire Snyder, "Neopatriarchy and the Antihomosexual Agenda," in Cynthia Burack and J. Josephson, *Fundamental Differences: Feminists Talk Back to Social Conservatives* (Lanham, MD: Rowman and Littlefield, 2003), 165.

25. John P. Bartkowski, "Breaking Walls, Raising Fences: Masculinity, Intimacy and Accountability among the Promise Keepers," in Christine L. Williams and Arlene Stein, eds., *Sexuality and Gender* (Malden, MA, and Oxford: Blackwell, 2002).

26. R. W. Connell, *Masculinities*.

27. Cynthia Burack, "Defense Mechanisms: Using Psychoanalysis Conservatively," in Cynthia Burack and J. Josephson, eds., *Fundamental Differences: Feminists Talk Back to Social Conservatives* (Lanham, MD: Rowman and Littlefield, 2003).

28. Talcott Parsons and Robert F. Bales, *Family, Socialization and Interaction Process* (Glencoe, IL: Free Press, 1955), 103–104.

29. Quoted in Snyder, "Neopatriarchy," 162.

30. Oregon 2004 General Election Voters Pamphlet, 77.

31. R. Claire Snyder, "The Federal Marriage Amendment and the Attack on American Democracy," *Logos* 3.4 (Fall 2004), 4.

32. Defense of Marriage Coalition Web site, http://www.defenseofmarriage coalition.org/.

33. Ibid.

34. Gabriel Rotello, "Creating a New Gay Culture," *The Nation* 4/21 (1997): 11–16.

35. Oregon 2004 General Election Voters Pamphlet, 85.

36. "Ten Arguments from Social Science against Same-Sex 'Marriage,'" Family Research Council Web site, http://www.frc.org/get.cfm?i=IF04G01&f=LH04G03.

37. Oregon 2004 General Election Voters Pamphlet, 81, 82.

38. Ibid, 80.

39. Ibid, 80.

40. Ibid, 86.

41. Family Research Council Web site.

42. Snyder, "The Federal Marriage Amendment," 9–10.

43. Given the impossibility of finding "representative samples" of gays and lesbians, or gay and lesbian parents, it is impossible to compile accurate population estimates. The 2000 census grossly undercounted the number of same-sex partner households and failed to provide estimates of how many of those households contained children; see David M. Smith and G. Gates, "Gay and Lesbian Families in the United States: A Preliminary Analysis of 2000 Census Data," Human Rights Campaign, Washington, DC, 2001. Some studies are instructive, to a point. E. Dilapi ("Lesbian Mothers and the Motherhood Hierarchy," *Journal of Homosexuality* 18, nos. 1–2 [1989]:101–121) estimates there are two million lesbian mothers in the United States; Frederick W. Bozett (*Gay and Lesbian Parents* [New York: Praeger, 1987]) says there are 1.1 to 2.3 million gay fathers. Even if such numbers are somewhat accurate, they have undoubtedly changed over the past decade and a half. There are few comparative estimates of the percentage of gay men and lesbians who are parents. A national organization of lesbian/gay parents reports that 60 percent of their members are female and 40 percent are male (Family Pride Coalition, Washington, DC), though this too is hardly a representative sample of same-sex families.

44. Snyder, "The Federal Marriage Amendment," 11.

45. Judith Stacey and Timothy J. Biblarz, "(How) Does the Sexual Orientation of Parents Matter?" in Cynthia Burack and J. Josephson, eds., *Fundamental Differences: Feminists Talk Back to Social Conservatives* (Lanham, MD: Rowman and Littlefield, 2003), 31.

46. Steven Seidman, C. Meeks, and F. Traschen, "Beyond the Closet?" Michael Warner, *The Trouble with Normal* (New York: Free Press, 1999).

47. Judith Stacey, *In the Name of the Family* (Boston: Beacon, 1996).

48. "Can Government Strengthen Marriage?" Institute for American Values, Washington, DC, 2002.

49. J. R. Feagin and H. Vera, *White Racism: The Basics* (New York: Routledge, 1995); R. H. Weigel and P. Howes, "Conceptions of Racial Prejudice: Symbolic Racism Reconsidered," *Journal of Social Issues* 41(3) (1985): 117–138.

50. Mary McIntosh, "The Homosexual Role," *Social Problems* 16 (1968): 262–270.

51. Parsons and Bales, *Family, Socialization and Interaction Process*.

NOTES TO THE EPILOGUE

1. Martha C. Nussbaum, *Hiding from Humanity: Disgust, Shame, and the Law* (Princeton, NJ: Princeton University Press, 2004), 15.

2. Jonathan Franzen, *The Corrections* (New York: Farrar, Strauss and Giroux, 2001), 323.

3. George Lakoff, *Moral Politics* (Chicago: University of Chicago Press, 2002).

4. Janice Irvine, *Talk about Sex* (Berkeley: University of California Press, 2002).

5. This is a suggestion made by communitarian theorist and sociologist Amitai Etzioni, cited in Nussbaum, *Hiding from Humanity*, 4.

6. Lakoff, *Moral Politics*.

7. Cheshire Calhoun, *Feminism, the Family, and the Politics of the Closet* (New York: Oxford, 2001), 123. Thanks to Chet Meeks for this reference.

8. Barbara Ehrenreich, *Bait and Switch: The (Futile) Pursuit of the American Dream* (New York: Public Affairs, 2005).

9. Lakoff, *Moral Politics*.

10. Nussbaum, *Hiding from Humanity*, 336.

Index

". . . And The Man Slept On" (Kaufman),
133
2 Nice Girls (band), 78

Abortion, 3, 11, 152
Abrams, Kevin, 143–146
Abstinence movement, 3, 4, 5, 15
ACT UP (AIDS Coalition to Unleash
Power), 99, 136
Adam, Barry, 136
Adorno, Theodor, 126
AIDS: coalition building, 97–99; gay/les-
bian activism/activists, 136–139; govern-
ment response, 137, 138; Holocaust
memories, 136–139; "just say no" pol-
icy, 15; lesbianism/lesbians, 55, 138
Alexander, Jeffrey, 132
Ambient fears, 110
Ambient/techno music, 63
American Express advertisement, 86
Anderson, Kirk, 125
Anderson, Pamela, 1
Androgyny, 66, 75, 77–80
Anti-Semitism, 142
Antiabortion activism, 152
Antigay activists: Christian right,
141–142; feminists' influence on, 173;
gender, 153; homosexuality/homosexu-
als, 126; masculine homosexual men,
152, 162, 169, 172–173; neopatriarchal
politics, 173; Oregon, 152–153. See also
Oregon Citizens Alliance (OCA)
Arnold, Gina, 68
Autonomy: rock 'n' roll, 63, 65, 67, 70;
shame, 119

Bad Attitude (magazine), 46
Badu, Erykah, 69

Bakker, Jim, 126
Barnard College conference (1982), 97
Barney, Natalie, 144
Bauman, Zygmunt, 110, 125–126
Beatles (band), 65
Bechdel, Alison, 46
Behind the Green Door II (film), 45
Bent (Sherman), 134
Berg, Margaret (a pseudonym), 30–34, 36,
37, 38
Bernhard, Sandra, 81
Bikini Kill (band), 68
Bisexuality, 54
Bitch (newsletter), 76
Bouchard, Cal, 168
Bound and Determined, 56
Bowie, David, 66, 75, 77
Boys: early sexual experiences, 5; father-
absence, 165–167; masculinity, 167;
popular culture, 63
Bright, Susie (Susie Sexpert), 39–48; advice
to lesbians, 41; bisexuality, 54; celebrity-
hood, 44–45; lesbian separatism, 53; life
with men, 23; on Loulan, 49; Loulan
on, 52; On Our Backs, 39, 46, 55, 58;
pornography, 45, 46–48; pregnancy of,
54–55; road show, 44; San Francisco
Lesbian and Gay Film Festival (1989),
39–42; "sex debates" among lesbians,
19–20; sexism, 48; sexual libertarianism, 43–44; sexual violence, 48; Sontag
and, 45
Bringing Up Boys (Dobson), 167
Brugmann, Natalie (a pseudonym), 21, 71
Bryant, Anita, 135–136
Buchanan, Patrick, 143
Burch, Beverly, 92
Bush, George W., 170

Calhoun, Cheshire, 176
Califia, Pat, 49, 56
Cameron, Paul, 118, 162
Captain Swing (record album), 78
Chapman, Tracy: femininity in popular
music, 77; identity, 80; lesbian culture,
83; lesbian subcultures, 78; New Music
Awards (1989), 79; Olivia Records,
185n12
Christian Coalition, 112, 139, 145
Christian right, 111–128; activists, case
studies of, 115–122, 128; antigay
activists, 141–142; apocalyptic rhetoric,
133; appeal of, 115; ballot measures,
142–143; base of, 124; collective identity, 124, 131; conservative evangelical
Protestants, 192n18; culture wars, 123,
128; desire, 126–127; education, 122;
Gay Agenda (film), 142, 160; gay/les-
bian activism/activists, 133, 134, 135,
148; gender, 167; good families, 111,
128; Holocaust memories, 106, 130,
133, 140–148, 150, 195n60; homophobia, 127; homosexuality/homosexuals,
124–127, 141–142, 159; ideal family,
168; identity politics, 119, 124; inde-
pendence/individualism, 122, 127, 128,
156; individualistic ethos, 122; Jews,
145–146; left's rhetoric, 119; lesbian
mothers, 162; middle-class morality,
120; as a moral movement, 114; Others,
124–127; personal strength, 122, 123,
127, 128, 156; personality type, 115;
role of fathers, 160–162; self-realization,
112; shame, 115, 119, 123, 124, 128;
social change, 141; speech patterns,
116–117; strategy, 115, 146–147,
195n61; strict father morality, 111; support for Israel, 147; value system, 122,
123; victimhood/victimization feelings/
rhetoric, 116, 118–119, 121–122,
142–143; vilification of, 118–119; white
working classes, 156; worldview,
111–112, 128. *See also* Homophobia
Christianity: nonprocreative sex, 7, 14;
pleasure, 7; premarital sex, 9; sexuality,
127; shame, 7
Civil rights movement, 131
Clash (band), 63
Class. *See* Social class

Clausen, Jan, 53
Clips (film), 42
Colette (Sidonie-Gabrielle Colette), 39
Collective identity: Christian right, 124,
131; formation of, 87, 101; gay/lesbian
activism/activists, 138; homosexuality/
homosexuals, 19; lesbianism/lesbians,
131; shame's contribution to, 179n6;
social movements, 131
Coming out: Etheridge and, 82; gay/les-
bian activism/activists, 115; homosexu-
ality/homosexuals, 17, 108; lang and,
82; lesbianism/lesbians, 17, 27–38, 69,
82; same-sex marriage, 108; shame, 115
Communism, 132, 133, 141
Compassionate conservatives, 177
Concerned Women for America, 163
Connell, Bob, 153–154
Conservative Christians. *See* Christian
right
Conservative movement, 11–15; abortion,
3, 11; compassionate conservatives, 177;
constituency, 105–106; contraception,
11; contradictions embedded in, 110;
conversion to heterosexuality, 13; death
of the family, 14; democratization of
personal life, 11; "don't ask don't tell"
policy, 12; family values, 170, 175; fascism, 135–136, 141; feminism's influence on, 4; gay/lesbian activism/activists,
136; gay/lesbian civil rights, 3; gender,
173; Holocaust memories, 140; homophobia, 105; homosexuality, 3, 11,
13–14; "just say no" policy, 15; marriage, 12, 14–15; nineteen sixties, 12;
nonprocreative sex, 11, 14; opposition
to sexual revolution/liberalization, 2–3;
Oregon, 155–156; permissiveness,
11–12; political values, 175; pornography, 11; remoralization of society, 12;
representativeness of, 110; same-sex
marriage, 152–153, 176–177; sex education, 3, 12; sexual expression, 3; sexual moralizing, 3; sexual repression, 12;
sexualization of culture, 14; shame, 175;
shame as a weapon against sexual liberalization, 3, 4, 12; solutions proposed
by, 13; strict father morality, 175–176;
teen sexuality, 3, 13; Victorians, 12. *See
also* Christian right; Right, the

Contingent lives, 10–11
Contraception, 10, 11
Cooksson, Jack (a pseudonym), 120–121
Cooksson, Jeri (a pseudonym), 115–116,
    120–122, 124–125
Coontz, Stephanie, 14
Corinne, Tee, 26, 49
Corrections, The (Franzen), 174
Council of Families in America, 170–171
"Courtship" culture, 12–13
Crossover artists, 73, 82–83
Cultural values and television choices, 2
Culture wars, 123, 128, 156–157

Daltrey, Roger, 65
Dank, Barry, 135
Dating, 51
Daughters of Bilitis, 46
Defense of Marriage Coalition, 158, 163
Democratization of personal life, 10, 11
Desert Hearts (film), 41
Desire: Christian right, 126–127;
    lesbianism/lesbians, 33, 90; as a moral
    problem, 7; restraints on men's sexual
    desires, 161–162, 164, 166–167;
    same-sex desires, 13; shame,
    126–127
DiFranco, Ani, 68, 83, 184n16
Disclosure, 38
Disco music, 77
Disorders of Desire (Irvine), 49
Dobson, James, 14, 167
Domino system of sexual peril, 14
"Don't ask don't tell" policy, 12
Doors (band), 63
Double standard, 2, 4, 5
Dransfield, John, 98
Dykes: butch-femme relationships, 56, 97;
    Loulan's readership, 48–49; masculine
    lesbians (butches), 154, 172, 181n5; old
    dykes, 32, 38; sadomasochism, 56

Echol, Alice, 61
Ehrenreich, Barbara, 177
Elias, Norbert, 7
Ellen (TV show), 69
Eno, Brian, 63
Eternal Jew (film), 142
Etheridge, Melissa: coming out, 82; cover
    girl, 68; femininity in popular music, 77;

lesbian subcultures, 78; mainstream
    popularity, 82; Olivia Records,
    185n12
Europe, 13, 142
Exile in Guyville (record album), 68
Exile on Main Street (record album), 68

Facing History and Ourselves, 149–150,
    196n69
Faderman, Lillian, 180n1
Falwell, Jerry, 1
Family life: Christian right's ideal family,
    168; death of the family, 14; father-
    absence, 165–167; feminism/feminists,
    167; homosexuality/homosexuals,
    176–177; role of fathers, 160–162; sex-
    ual behavior, 2; strict father morality,
    176. *See also* Marriage
Family Research Council, 163, 164–165,
    166
Family Research Institute, 118
Family values: conservatives, 170, 175;
    "neo-family values" movement, 170,
    172; neopatriarchal rhetoric, 154–155;
    political values, 175; the right, 4
Far right, 192n18
Fascism: conservatives, 135–136, 141;
    homosexuality/homosexuals, 147; sex-
    ual repression, 136
Fatherhood movement, 161, 167
Femininity in popular music, 68–69, 77
Feminism/feminists: Barnard College con-
    ference (1982), 97; conflation with les-
    bianism, 32; critiques of gender, 167;
    divisions among, 4–5, 19; double stan-
    dard, 2, 4; family life, 167; female per-
    formers, 69, 70; female rock fans, 59;
    homophobia among, 89; influence on
    antigay activists, 173; influence on the
    right, 4; lesbianism/lesbians, 43, 84, 85,
    88–89, 100; music industry, 20–21;
    nineteen eighties, 97; nineteen seventies,
    97; orgasms, 49; pornography, 4–5,
    41–43, 97; post-feminism, 100–101;
    prostitution, 4–5; the right, 4; rock 'n'
    roll, 61, 66, 70; romance, 60–61; sado-
    masochism (s/m), 4–5, 51–52; "sex
    debates"/"porn wars" (1980s), 4–5, 19,
    41, 97; sexual expression, 2; sexual
    repression, 9–10; sexual violence, 97;

Feminism/feminists (*continued*)
  as theory, 88. *See also* Lesbian feminism/
  feminists
Feminist music, 66
Firestone, Shulamith, 60
Flax, Jane, 66
Focus on the Family, 163, 165
Foucault, Michel, 73, 179n5
Frank, Anne, 106, 139–140, 146, 195n59
Franzen, Jonathan, 174
Freud, Sigmund, 8
Frith, Simon, 62
Frye, Marilyn, 58

Gabriel, Peter, 81
Gamson, Joshua, 118, *169*
Gamson, William, 131–132
Gans, Herbert, 71
Gay Agenda (film), 142, 160
Gay/lesbian activism/activists: AIDS,
  136–139; Anne Frank exhibit, 139, 146;
  anxiety about masculinity, 155; apocalyptic rhetoric, 133; assimilation into the
  dominant culture, 108; Christian right,
  133, 134, 135, 148; coalition building,
  97–99; collective identity, 138; coming
  out, 115; conservatives, 136; culture
  wars, 157; desire for citizenship, 107;
  destigmatizing homosexuality, 135–136,
  179n5; double standard, 2; Holocaust
  memories, 106, 129, 130, 133–140,
  150; identity politics, 22, 101; impulses
  of, 107; pink triangle, 134; political
  fragmentation, 107; reverse affirmation,
  135; same-sex marriage, 176; sexual
  expression, 2; sexual repression, 9–10;
  sexual transgression, 107; successes,
  21–22; vision of gay liberation, 19
Gay/lesbian civil rights: antigay ballot
  measures, 139, 142–143, 156–157,
  163–164; civil unions, 176; conservatives, 3; desire for citizenship, 107;
  grassroots opposition, 103–105; Oregon, 3, 124–125, 155, 159–162; same-
  sex marriage, 176. *See also* Antigay
  activists
Gender: antigay activists, 153; bedrock of,
  89; Christian right, 167; compulsory
  heterosexuality, 89; conservatives, 173;
  feminist critiques of, 167; gender development, 166; gender nonconformity,
  154, 160, 169; gender rebellion, 70;
  gender transgression, 63; homophobia,
  154; neopatriarchal rhetoric, 155; passionate quests, 60; rock 'n' roll, 65–66;
  sexuality, 10, 99; Smith on, 59; traditional role, 167
Gerson, Kathleen, 156
Giddens, Anthony, 10–11
Gilligan's Island (TV show), 81
Girls: abstinence movement, 5; early sex-
  ual experiences, 5; popular culture, 63;
  rock 'n' roll and, 65; self-valuation, 6;
  virginity pledges, 5
Girls' fiction, 62–63, 69
"Girls Just Want to Have Fun" (song), 77
Gitlin, Todd, 132–133
Glasgow, Joanne, 38
Goebbels, Joseph, 143
Goering, Hermann Wilhelm, 143
Goffman, Erving, 122
Goldstein, Al, 39
Government response: AIDS, 138
Grahn, Judy, 43, 89
Grossberg, Larry, 80–81
Guilt, shame compared to, 6, 114

Haeberle, Erwin, 145
Hall, Marny, 57–58
Hall, Stuart, 101–102
Hammond, Theresa, *168*
Harvey, Polly, 68, 69
"Hasbians," 54
Hawkes, Gail, 7
Helms, Jesse, 48
Heritage Foundation, 105
Hess, Rudolph, 143
Heterosexuality: boundary between it and
  homosexuality, 17, 24, 25; compulsory
  heterosexuality, 2, 89, 101; conversion
  to, 13; heterosexual marriage promo-
  tion, 170; romance, 62–63; as a social
  construction, 91
Himmelfarb, Gertrude, 11
Himmler, Heinrich, 143, 144
Hirschfeld, Magnus, 8–9, 192n20
Historical memories, 131–132, 150
History of Rock and Roll (TV series), 59
Hitler, Adolph, 135, 143, 145, 195n58
Hole (band), 68

Holocaust memories, 129–150; AIDS, 136–139; appropriation of, 129–130, 147–150; Christian right, 106, 130, 133, 140–148, 150, 195n60; collapse of communism, 132, 133; conservatives, 140; denial of Holocaust, 140; gay/lesbian activism/activists, 106, 129, 130, 133–140, 150; Holocaust survivors, 148–149; homosexuality/homosexuals, 134; Jewish ownership of, 149; metaphor creation, 130, 150; moral authority, 132; pink triangle, 134; revisionism, 130, 150; social movements, 129–133; as symbol of injustice, 132

Homophobia, 151–173; among feminism/feminists, 89; anxiety about masculinity, 152; appeal of, 173; Christian right, 127; conservatives, 105; effeminate men, 154, 160, 162, 172; feminine lesbians, 169; gay/lesbian civil rights, 159–162; gender, 154; gender-conforming homosexuals, 169, 172; gender nonconformity, 154, 160; lesbian mothers, 162; masculine homosexual men, 152, 162, 169, 172–173; masculine lesbians, 154, 172; meanings of, 153; Oregon, 155–159; popularity, 173; popularity of, 151; purpose, 152; same-sex marriage, 163–168; sexism, 153; shift of focus from promiscuity to domesticity, 170; symbolic racism, 172; varieties, 173; varieties of, 154; Weinberg on, 153. *See also* Antigay activists

Homosexuality/homosexuals: antigay activists, 126; boundary between homosexuality and heterosexuality, 17, 24, 25; categorization, 21–22; Christian right, 124–126, 141–142, 159; collective identity, 19; coming out, 17, 108; conservatives, 3, 11, 13–14; destigmatization of, 135–136; domestication of gay men, 164; effeminate men, 154, 160, 162, 172; family life, 176–177; fascism, 147; gender-conforming homosexuals, 169, 172; gender nonconformity, 160; Hitler and, 143, 195n58; Holocaust memories, 134; households, 199n43; legitimate sexuality, 107–108; masculine homosexual men, 152, 162, 169,

172–173; masculinity, 126; medical conception, 24–25, 55, 88, 89–91; Nazism, 129, 134, 141, 143–145, 147, 192n21; normalization of, 151, 159, 170, 172–173, 175, 177; Oregon, 112–113; Oregon Citizens Alliance, 124–127; Orthodox Jews, 146; as Others, 124–127; parenthood, 167, 199n43; as a potential in everyone, 17, 19, 75; the right, 141; sadomasochism, 160; same-sex desires, 13; sexual fidelity, 165; as a social construction, 87; stereotypes of, 127, 160, 161, 162; threats posed by, 162; victimhood/victimization feelings/rhetoric, 135, 145–146; visibility of, 21–22, 172. *See also* Gay/lesbian activism/activists; Gay/lesbian civil rights; Lesbianism/lesbians; Same-sex marriage

House music, 77

Human Rights Campaign, 108

Human Rights Campaign Foundation, *171*

Humphries, Sally (a pseudonym), 116, 117, 127

I Enjoy Being a Girl (record album), 78

Identity. *See* Collective identity; Personal identity

Identity politics: Christian right, 119, 124; gay/lesbian activism/activists, 22, 101; integralism, 95; lesbian feminism/feminists, 93–96; lesbianism/lesbians, 83; sexuality, 19

Indigo Girls (band), 21, 69, 77, 79

Individuation, 38

Insemination, 54

Institute for American Values, 170–171

Integralism, 95

Irigaray, Luce, 39

Irvine, Janice, 49

Island Records, 80

Israel, 147

Jacobsen, Janet, 2

Jagger, Mick, 61, 65–66

Jasper, James, 113

Jay, Karla, 38

Jews: Christian right, 145–146; communism, 141; homosexuality/homosexuals, 146; Nazi persecution, 144, 195n58;

Jews (*continued*)
  ownership of Holocaust memories, 149;
  right-wing, 146–147; scapegoating of,
  150
Jews and Friends of Holocaust Victims,
  142–143
Johnston, Jill, 89
Joplin, Janice, 77–78
Joyce, Cynthia, 68
"Just say no" policy, 15
"Justify My Love" (video), 77

Kass, Leonard, 12–13
Kaufman, S. Brett, *138*
King, Martin Luther, Jr., 131–132
Kinks (band), 64
Kinney, Nan, 44
Kinsey, Alfred, 9
Kintz, Linda, 114
Klepfisz, Irena, 148
Knight, Richard James, *169*
Kovick, Kris, 49
Kramer, Larry, *137*
Krieger, Susan, 95–96

"Ladder, The" (newsletter), 46
Lakoff, George, 175
lang, k.d.: album cover, 72; appearance,
  71, 72; coming out, 82; cover girl,
  68; femininity in popular music, 77;
  lesbian culture, 83; lesbian subcultures,
  78; mainstream popularity, 21, 73, 82
Larson, Elizabeth Rae, 57
Lauper, Cyndi, 77
Lawrence v. Texas, 170
LBD (Lesbian Bed Death), 50, 56
Left, rhetoric of the, 119
Left, the, 9–10, 119
"Legal Matter, A" (song), 63
Lennox, Annie, 78
Lesbian artists, 73, 79
Lesbian Bed Death (LBD), 50, 56
Lesbian culture: bar culture, 97; come-out
  groups, 33; dating, 51; feminist culture,
  32–33; lesbian artists, 73, 79; lesbian
  bars, 85; lesbian communities, 95–96;
  lesbian feminism, 22, 73 (*see also* Les-
  bian feminism/feminists); Lesbian Moth-
  ers' Group, 33; lesbian music, 79–80;
  old dykes, 32, 38; production of, 24;

pulp novels, 28, 34–35; visions of,
  32–33; women's dances, 33
Lesbian Erotic Dance (Loulan), 49, 52–53
Lesbian feminism/feminists, 84–102; affirmation of the erotic, 43; conflation of
  feminism and lesbianism, 32; constructionist critique of sexual behavior, 87;
  contributions of, 22; decentering of, 22,
  80, 83, 84–102; democratic potential,
  101; emergence, 83; goals, 86–87, 88;
  identity politics, 93–96; lesbian communities, 95–96; lesbian culture, 22, 73
  (*see also* Lesbian culture); possibility of
  lesbian experience, 75; post-feminism,
  100–101; racial/ethnic identifications,
  99–100; social class, 96; as a totalizing
  identity, 100; two projects of, 100; West
  Coast Lesbian-Feminist Conference
  (1973), 93; women of color, 94, 96;
  women's community, 94
Lesbian Insanity Phase (LIP), 50
Lesbian music, 79–80
Lesbian Nation, 84, 85
Lesbian Passion (Loulan), 49, 51, 53
Lesbian separatism, 53
Lesbian Sex (Loulan), 49, 50–51
Lesbianism/lesbians, 24–38, 71–83; AIDS,
  55, 138; archetypal lesbian relationship,
  50; baby boomers, 27; bisexuality, 54;
  butch-femme relationships, 56, 97; central characteristic, 24; coalition building
  with gay men, 97–99; collective identity,
  131; coming out, 17, 27–38, 69, 82;
  conflation with feminism, 32; constructionist conception, 180n1; cover girls,
  68; definition, 17, 18–19, 84, 93–94;
  desexualization of, 43; desire, 33, 90;
  difference/similarity in relation to heterosexual culture, 38, 92; disclosure, 38;
  discovery of, personal, 28, 31–32, 92;
  divisions among, 18–20; dominant
  accounts of, 29; dykes, 32, 38, 48–49,
  56; "elective" lesbians, 34, 91–93;
  essentialist conception, 180n1; feminine
  lesbians, 169; feminism/feminists, 43,
  84, 85, 88–89, 100; as a form of female
  bonding, 20, 89; "hasbians," 54; hetero-
  geneity, 90; identity construct model of,
  180n1; identity politics, 83; ideological
  proclivities, 90; individuation, 38;

insemination, 54; interacting with self-identified lesbians, 37, 181n9; lesbian consciousness, 33; lesbian mothers, 162; liberationist impulse, 19; as a lifestyle choice, 25, 90; markers of, 181n5; masculine lesbians (butches), 154, 172, 181n5; medical conception, 89–91; nineteen eighties, 42–43, 85; nineteen nineties, 85; nineteen seventies, 25, 88, 92; "old gay" *vs.* "new gay," 25–27, 33, 88; orientation model of, 180n1; parenthood, 167; as a personal identity, 20, 24, 25, 33–34, 37, 55, 80, 101; "politically correct" and, 18; popular music, 71–83; popular understandings of, 90; pornography, 58; post-Stonewall, 98; as practices, 55, 88, 90; pre-Stonewall, 97; "primary" lesbians, 91–92, 94; "representation" of, 20; sadomasochism, 56–57; same-sex marriage, 167; self-esteem, 51; sense of male threat, 99; "sex debates," 19–20; sexperts, 41; sexual dissidence, 23; sexual fidelity, 165; sexual role playing, 56–57; sexuality, 19; shame as a weapon against "politically incorrect" desires/practices, 18; sleeping with men, 53; social class, 92–93, 96; as socio-sexual category, 27; as a taste public, 71, 82; "through feminism," 18, 73, 84; "true" lesbians, 18; visibility, 57, 99, 172; as a way for women to gain strength, 32; woman identification, 33, 88. *See also* Homosexuality/homosexuals; Lesbian culture; Lesbian feminism/feminists
Letterman, David, 81
Lewis, Helen, 115, 117
Lewis, Lisa, 77
Liberals, 175, 176
Lifton, Robert, 133, 149
Lilith Fair (music festival), 69
LIP (Lesbian Insanity Phase), 50
Lipstadt, Deborah, 140
Lively, Scott, 143–146
Lorde, Audre, 43, 80
Loulan, JoAnn, 48–55; advice to lesbians, 41; books by, 49; on Bright, 52; Bright on, 49; on dating, 51; Frye on, 58; lesbians sleeping with men, 54; life with men, 23; on orgasms, 52–53; *Out/Look*

magazine, 49; readership, 48–49; road show, 50; on self-esteem, 51; "sex debates" among lesbians, 20; on sexual reticence, 51; teaching career, 49
Love comics, 60
Luscious Jackson (band), 68

Mabon, Lon, 123
Madonna (Madonna Louise Veronica Ciccone), 77, 83
Marcuse, Herbert, 136
Market fundamentalism, 177
Marriage: conservatives, 12, 14–15; definition, 14; premarital sex, 9; removal of women from the marriage pool, 166; restraints on men's sexual desires, 161–162, 164, 166–167; tenuousness of, 11; as a voluntary relationship, 14–15. *See also* Family life; Same-sex marriage
Martin, Biddy, 83
Martin, Karin, 5
Masculinity: anxiety about, 152, 155; boys, 167; fragility, 126; hegemonic masculinity, 153–154; homophobia, 152; homosexuality/homosexuals, 126; masculine homosexual men, 152, 162, 169, 172–173; in Pacific Northwest, 156; patriarchal authority, 155
McAdam, Doug, 131
McCarthy, Joseph, 141
McIntosh, Mary, 19
McLachlan, Sarah, 69
McRobbie, Angela, 63, 69
Melucci, Alberto, 95
Men of the Pink Triangle (Heger and Muller), 134–135
Milk, Harvey, 135
Miller, Craig (a pseudonym), 118, 119–120
MIP (Moving In Phase), 50
Mitchell, Greg, 133
Mitchell Brothers (Jim and Artie), 45
Monkees (band), 64
Morality, 111, 120, 175–176
Morgan, Robin, 59, 74
Moving In Phase (MIP), 50
Ms. (magazine), 59, 74
Music industry: ambient/techno music, 63; crossover artists, 73, 82–83; disco music, 77; female performers, 69, 70,

Music industry (*continued*)
73, 77; feminism/feminists, 20–21; feminist music, 66; house music, 77; lesbian artists, 73, 79; lesbian music, 79–80; punk music, 75; women's music, 66, 73–76, 79. *See also* Popular music; Rock 'n' roll

Nakedness, 1, 6, 174, 175
Nazism: homosexuality/homosexuals, 129, 134, 141, 143–145, 147, 192n21; persecution of Jews, 144; sexual dissidence, 9
Near, Holly, 74–75, 80, 185n12
"Neo-family values" movement, 172
Neopatriarchal rhetoric, 154–155, 173
Nestle, Joan, 56
New left, 9–10
New right, 136, 192n18
Nonprocreative sex, 7, 11, 14
Nurturance, 175
Nussbaum, Martha, 174, 178

O'Connor, Sinead, 69
Odd Girl Out (Bannon), 28
O'Donnell, Rosie, 165
off our backs (journal), 44, 46, 54
Olivia Records, 74–75, 76, 185n12
On Our Backs (magazine): Bright and, 39, 46, 55, 58; cartoons in, 46; cover, 40, 45; editors, 39, 46; politics, 47; pornography, 46; publisher, 42; sexual behavior, 57; sexual libertarianism, 44; state of lesbian life, 46
Oregon, 152–168; antigay activists, 152–153; antigay ballot measures, 139, 142–143, 156–157, 163–164, 188n4 (ch. 6); anxiety about masculinity, 152; conservatives, 155–156; culture wars, 156–157; Defense of Marriage Coalition, 158, 163; economic changes, 156; gay/lesbian civil rights, 3, 103–105, 124–125, 155, 159–162; homosexuality/homosexuals, 112–113; Jews and Friends of Holocaust Victims, 142–143; same-sex marriage, 3, 155, 158, 163–168; schools, 125; vilification/mockery of Christian right, 118–119
Oregon Citizens Alliance (OCA): antigay ballot measures, 139, 156–157, 188n4 (ch. 6); Christian Coalition, 112, 145;

European anti-Semitism, 142; *Gay Agenda* (film), 142; homosexuality/homosexuals, 124–127; leaders, 123; love-the-sinner-hate-the-sin rhetoric, 127; members, 113
Orgasms, 49, 52–53
Out/Look (magazine), 49, 53
Outcasts, 56
Outrageous Women (magazine), 46

Parsons, Talcott, 161–162
Partridge Family (band), 64
Patton, Cindy, 55, 148
Pellegrini, Ann, 2
Permissiveness, 4, 11–12
Person, Ethel, 60
Personal identity: lesbianism/lesbians, 20, 24, 25, 33–34, 37, 55, 80, 101; shame, 179n6; social movements, 132
Personal life, democratization of, 10, 11
Personal relationships, political nature of, 2
Phair, Liz, 68
Phranc (folksinger), 79, 80
Pink Floyd (band), 63
Pink Swastika (Lively and Abrams), 143–146
Pleasure: Christianity, 7; nonprocreative sex, 7, 11; power, 62–63; sexual revolution/liberalization, 10
Plummer, Ken, 180n1
"Politically correct," 18
Ponse, Barbara, 91–92, 94
Popular culture, 2, 63
Popular music: androgynous women in, 77–80; femininity, 68–69, 77; lesbianism/lesbians, 71–83; niche audiences, 80; sexual ambiguity, 81
Pornography: Bright and, 45, 46–48; conservatives, 11; feminism/feminists, 4–5, 41–43, 97; lesbianism/lesbians, 58; *On Our Backs*, 46; sexual violence, 41, 48; Women Against Pornography, 41
Post-feminism, 100–101
Poststructuralism, 179n5
Power and Trust, 56
Power Exchange (magazine), 46
Premarital sex, 9
Press, Joy, 63, 66
Price of Salt (Highsmith), 28

Promise Keepers, 161
Prostitution, 4–5
Punk music, 75
Pure and the Impure, The (Colette), 39

Quadrophenia (record album), 64
"Queer," 99
Queer communities, 22
Queer Eye for the Straight Guy (TV show), 21
Queer Nation, 99
Queerness, 99

Raincoats (band), 67
Raymond, Janice, 84–85
Reclines (band), 72
Redwood Records, 185n12
Religious fundamentalism, 177
Reports from the Holocaust (Kramer), 137
Return to Modesty (Shalit), 13
Reverse affirmation, 73, 135
Reynolds, Simon, 63, 66
Right, the: family values, 4; far right, 192n18; feminism's influence on, 4; homosexuality/homosexuals, 141; neopatriarchal rhetoric, 154–155; new right, 136, 192n18; permissiveness, 4; right-wing Jews, 146–147; sexual restriction, 4; sexual revolution/liberalization, 4; victimhood/victimization feelings/rhetoric, 106. *See also* Christian right; Conservative movement
Righteous Babe Records, 184n16
Robertson, Pat, 143, 147
Rock Against Sexism, 75
Rock 'n' roll, 59–70; androgyny, 66, 75, 77–80; autonomy, 63, 65, 67, 70; dominant trope, 63; female bands, 67–68; female fans, 59, 61–62, 65, 66, 70, 74; female rock stars, 68; feminism/feminists, 61, 66, 70; gender, 65–66; gender transgression, 63; girls and, 65; male style, 59, 74; masculinity, 65; power, 63, 64, 65; psychedelic tradition, 63; romance *vs.*, 63; separation, 63, 70
Rohm, Ernst, 144
Rolling Stones (band), 59, 61, 63, 65
Romance, 60–61, 62–63
Ross, Geoffrey, 98
Royalle, Candida, 47

Rubin, Gayle: on compulsory heterosexuality, 89; domino system of sexual peril, 14; legitimate sexuality, 107–108; on OCA antigay ballot measure, 139; sadomasochism, 56; on times of uncertainty, 15

Sadomasochism (s/m): dykes, 56; feminism/feminists, 4–5, 51–52; homosexuality/homosexuals, 160; lesbianism/lesbians, 56–57; Rubin and, 56; violence against women, 51
Salton, Joan (a pseudonym), 34–37
Same-sex marriage: civil unions, 176; coming out, 108; conservatives, 152–153, 176–177; conventional marriage, 14; domestication of gay men, 164; Family Research Council on, 164–165, 166; father-absence, 165–167; gay/lesbian activism/activists, 176; gender development, 166; households, 199n43; legitimacy of, 107; lesbianism/lesbians, 167; liberals, 176; Massachusetts, 163, 167; "neo-family values" movement, 172; normalization of homosexuality/homosexuals, 177; Oregon, 3, 155, 158, 163–168; removal of women from the marriage pool, 166; restraints on men's sexual desires, 161–162, 164, 166–167; San Francisco, 163, 167; sexual fidelity, 165; shame, 109; stability of, 165; state ballots opposing, 163; Vermont, 167
San Francisco: lesbian bars, 85; same-sex marriage, 163, 167; sexology, 49; sexual nonconformity, 49
San Francisco Lesbian and Gay Film Festival (1989), 39–42
Sane, Aladdin. *See* Bowie, David
Savage, Jon, 72
Scheff, Thomas, 7, 114
Scrawl (band), 68
Sedgwick, Eve, 88–89
Self as a reflexive project, 10–11
Self-esteem, 51
Self expression, 2
Self-realization, 60, 112
Seventeen (magazine), 64
Sex education: abstinence-only programs, 3, 4, 15; conservatives, 3, 12; Kass's view, 12–13

Sex organs, 39
Sexism, 48, 153
Sexology, 49
Sexpert, Susie. *See* Bright, Susie (Susie Sexpert)
Sexperts, 41
Sexual behavior: American norms, 9; constructionist critique of, 87; family life, 2; as a moral problem, 7; nationhood, 2; nonprocreative sex, 7, 11, 14; *On Our Backs*, 57; premarital sex, 9; sexual expression, 2, 3, 13; sexual revolution, 57; social anxieties, 15
Sexual dissidence, 9, 23
Sexual expression, 2, 3, 13
Sexual liberalization: moral crisis, 2; *On Our Backs*, 44; poststructuralism, 179n5; women's liberation, 43
Sexual repression/restriction: conservatives, 12; dangers of, 5–6; fascism, 136; feminism/feminists, 9–10; gay/lesbian activism/activists, 9–10; marriage, 161–162, 164, 166–167; mockery of, 23; new left, 9–10; nineteen sixties, 12; repressiveness of, 4; the right, 4; shame, 8–9; times of uncertainty, 15
Sexual reticence, 51
Sexual revolution/liberalization: battle cry, 10; conservative opposition, 2–3; dangers of, 5–6; feminism/feminists, 9–10; gay/lesbian activism/activists, 9–10; legacy of, 5; new left, 9–10; pleasure, 10; representations of sexuality, 57; the right, 4; sexual behavior, 57
Sexual role playing, 56–57
Sexual transgression, 107
Sexual violence, 41, 48, 97
Sexuality: bisexuality, 54; Christianity, 127; gender, 99; gender definitions, 10; "good" *vs.* "bad" sex, 7; identity politics, 19; legitimate sexuality, 107–108; lesbianism/lesbians, 19; liberation of, 179n5; as male, 43; representations of, 57; self expression, 2; shame, 7, 23, 174; similarity of male and female, 49; social class, 92–93; Victorians, 7–8
Sexualization of culture, 5–6, 14, 175
Shalit, Wendy, 13
Shame, 6–11; autonomy, 119; being ashamed, 7; bypassed shame, 114–115, 123; Christian right, 115, 119, 123, 124, 128; Christianity, 7; coming out, 115; conservatives, 175; desire, 126–127; displacement of shameful feeling onto others, 174; effects on persons, 1; fear of bodily exposure, 6; guilt compared to, 6, 114; healthy forms, 6, 179n6; identity, 179n6; imagery and, 117; individuals most prone to, 114; insecurity, 177; internal ideal image, 6; Kinsey reports, 9; liberals, 175; loss of self-esteem, 122; markers of, 117; nakedness, 6, 174; neediness, 174; overt shame, 114–115; positive contributions to identity, 179n6; progressive ideals, 175; promulgation of, 6–7; psychoanalytic accounts, 117; rage, 122–123; same-sex marriage, 109; self-transformation, 17; sexual failure, 126; sexual repression, 8–9; sexuality, 7, 23, 174; sexualization of culture, 175; social interactions, 114; sources of, 106; speech patterns, 115; types, 114–115; victimhood/victimization feelings/rhetoric, 123; Victorians, 8; vulnerability, 174, 178; as a weapon against sexual liberalization, 3, 4, 12, 18; women, 117
Shepard, Matthew, 152
Sherman, Bobby, 65
Shocked, Michelle, 77, 78, 79, 80
Simon, Paul, 81
Sinister Wisdom (journal), 58
Sleater-Kinney (band), 83
Slits (band), 67–68
Slotkin, Richard, 123
Smith, Patti, 59, 67, 77–78
Smiths (band), 78
Social anxieties, 15
Social class: lesbian feminism/feminists, 96; lesbianism/lesbians, 92–93, 96; middle-class morality, 120; middle-class women, 96; sexual choices, 92–93; sexuality, 92–93; white working classes, 156
Social movements: agency, 131, 132; collective identity, 131; emotion in, 113–114; historical memories, 131–132, 150; Holocaust memories, 129–133; injustice, 132; media, 132–133; moral

movements, 114; personal identity, 132; primary target and audience, 132
Social welfare, 13
Sontag, Susan, 45
Southern Kink, 56
Spears, Britney, 68–69
Speech patterns, 115, 116–117
Stardust, Ziggy. *See* Bowie, David
Stein, Gertrude, 144
Strange Sisters (novels), 28
Strict father morality, 111, 175–176
Sullivan, Andrew, 108–109
Sundahl, Debi, 44
Swaggart, Jimmy, 126
Symbolic racism, 172

Tanzer, Jessica, 67
Taste publics, 71, 82
Team Dresch (band), 68
Teen crooners, 60
Teen sexuality: conservatives, 3, 13; "courtship" culture, 12–13; early experiences, 5; visibility, 5
Television choices and cultural values, 2
Tomkins, Silvan, 179n6
Touraine, Alain, 87
Townsend, Pete, 65, 66
Transgender activists, 23
"Travel On Ride" (song), 68
Treut, Monika, 45
Trouble with Normal, The (Warner), 109

Urania, 56

Victimhood/victimization feelings/rhetoric: Christian right, 116, 118–119, 121–122, 142–143; homosexuality/homosexuals, 135, 145–146; the right, 106; shame, 123
Victorians, 7–8, 12
Virgin Machine, The (film), 45

Virginity pledges, 5
Visibility: homosexuality/homosexuals, 21–22, 172; lesbianism/lesbians, 57, 99, 172; teen sexuality, 5
Vulnerability, 174, 178

Warner, Michael, 109
Weeks, Jeffrey, 107
Weinberg, George, 153
West Coast Lesbian-Feminist Conference (1973), 93
Westheimer, Ruth (Dr. Ruth), 39
Who (band), 64, 65
Wilde, Oscar, 8
Will and Grace (TV show), 21
Williams, Erica (a pseudonym), 116–118
Willis, Ellen, 61, 66
Wolfe, Alan, 120, 151
Women: antiabortion activism, 152; of color, 94, 96; feminine lesbians, 169; middle-class, 96; removal from the marriage pool, 166; sense of entitlement, 69–70; sexual violence, 41, 48, 97; shame, 117; violence against, 51; working-class, 96
Women Against Pornography, 41
Women's community, 94
Women's liberation, 43, 131
Women's music, 66, 73–76, 79
Wooten, Barney (a pseudonym), 118, 127, 160–162
Wuerker, Matt, 112

X-Ray Specs (band), 67

"Yantra #22" (Corinne), 26
Yerba, Barb (a pseudonym), 27–30, 36, 37, 38
Young-Bruehl, Elisabeth, 154, 162

Zemsky, Beth, 181n5

About the Author

Arlene Stein is Associate Professor of Sociology and Women's and Gender Studies at Rutgers University. She is the author of *The Stranger Next Door: The Story of a Small Community's Battle over Sex, Faith, and Civil Rights.*